Building DIY Websites

by Jennifer DeRosa

Building DIY Websites For Dummies®

Published by: **John Wiley & Sons, Inc.,** 111 River Street, Hoboken, NJ 07030-5774, www.wiley.com

Copyright © 2024 by John Wiley & Sons, Inc., Hoboken, New Jersey

Published simultaneously in Canada

For general information on our other products and services, please contact our Customer Care Department within the U.S. at 877-762-2974, outside the U.S. at 317-572-3993, or fax 317-572-4002. For technical support, please visit https://hub.wiley.com/community/support/dummies

Wiley publishes in a variety of print and electronic formats and by print-on-demand. Some material included with standard print versions of this book may not be included in e-books or in print-on-demand. If this book refers to media such as a CD or DVD that is not included in the version you purchased, you may download this material at http://booksupport.wiley.com. For more information about Wiley products, visit www.wiley.com.

Library of Congress Control Number: 2024932051

ISBN 978-1-394-23298-7 (pbk); ISBN 978-1-394-23300-7 (ebk); ISBN 978-1-394-23299-4 (ebk)

SKY10073597_042424

Contents at a Glance

Table of Contents

Introduction

Welcome to *Building DIY Websites For Dummies*, a book that focuses on building your own website from start to finish. It includes many secrets and best practices that web developers know and implement when building any quality website.

Throughout this book, I walk you through the steps of building a website in a way that streamlines the process and gives you the best result.

About This Book

Building a quality website is not about learning how to use software. Anyone can learn to use software. Building a quality website is not about choosing a theme and uploading text and images. Anyone can take or find photos and write some text.

Building a quality website is about getting people to a thank you page, getting a phone call, an email, or a walk-in because they found your amazing website online, and they think you can solve their problem and want to engage with you. Building a quality website is also about building a website that search engines understand and want to match with Internet searchers when the search intent matches the offer of a website.

There is a lot that goes into building a website. This book teaches you how to think about your new marketing tool and take the most effective building steps in the best order possible. You discover how you can supercharge the tools and the platforms available today to build a website for your endeavor using sound best practices.

This book does not explain how to use software; anyone can learn to use software. Each web building platform also has support and documentation to help you.

This book teaches you all of the other "stuff" that web developers know about building great websites. It teaches you concepts that permanently empower you. You learn about tasks that you need to perform and learn *why* you are performing them. These concepts will make your digital marketing efforts better.

This book covers the thought process that goes into each step of building a website with the end in mind: more customers/visitors. Whether you end up building the site yourself or handing over the assets to a professional web developer, the skills you learn in this book will help you create websites that work!

Conventions Used in This Book

I've established the following conventions to make it easier for you to navigate this book:

>> New terms are in *italics,* and I define them for you.

>> Website URLs are shown in this special font: https://wpengine.com/.

>> **Bold** text highlights key words in bulleted lists and action parts in numbered lists.

Foolish Assumptions

In writing this book, I've made some assumptions about you:

>> You want to enhance your organization's online presence.

>> You want to build a website that attracts visitors and converts leads.

>> You are not technical or might be semi-technical, but need guidance about how websites function.

>> You like being empowered.

I've used these assumptions to help explain how to build a tool that will work for you by preselling your products or services. My philosophy is that anyone can learn to use website-building tools to get their message out and resonate with visitors This book empowers you with the knowledge to help you market your business overall, not just teach you to click here or there.

How This Book Is Organized

This book begins by helping you get set up. It then moves into thinking about the end users of your website: visitors and search engines. After you are in the right mindset, you will be well prepared (and hopefully excited) to get your content ready and display it with amazing results.

To make the content more accessible, I divided it into six parts:

>> Part 1, "Getting Started with DIY Websites," includes lots of ideas about getting your domain name and web building space set up. One of the most frequent questions I see online and hear from soon-to-be DIY website builders is "Which platform is the best?" This part will help you determine the answer to that question.

>> Part 2, "Creating a Site That People Will Visit," will get you in the correct mindset to create a site that attracts and converts leads. When you understand *why* you should perform particular tasks in particular ways, the task changes from a box you need to check off to a marketing strategy. Thinking this way will empower you and excite you to create something that will bring real results.

>> Part 3, "Architecting Plans for Your Website," teaches you how to organize your content, what to include on your pages, why certain content will help you more effectively, and how to prepare these assets for the best result. You learn many of the professional tips and tricks that that "regular" people do not know. These concepts are not that difficult to understand, and I give you all of this info at once in an organized fashion.

>> Part 4, "Designing and Laying Out Your Website," is the part that most of us think is where we should start when building a website. Once you have everything organized and prepared, it is so much easier to design and lay out your website, which is why this information appears in Part 4. This section is where the rubber meets the road. If you take the time to prepare your content and work through the other parts of the book that come before this, you will be in a much better mindset to lay out and design an attractive website.

>> Part 5, "Going Live and Measuring Results," covers all things SEO (search engine optimization), including optimizing your pages for web search, measuring your results (visits, click-throughs, forms, and so on) using Google Analytics and other tools, and securing your website from fraud, malware, and hackers.

>> Part 6, "The Part of Tens," includes the "cliff notes" to building websites. If you want to read this section first, go ahead, as it might help you think about the big picture.

Icons Used in This Book

In the margins of almost every page of this book, you find icons, which are there to alert you to different types of information. Here's what they mean:

TIP

This icon saves you time and energy by explaining you a helpful method or technique for doing something.

REMEMBER

This icon points out important information you need to know as you develop your website.

WARNING

This icon points out potential problems and pitfalls to avoid, as well as positive solutions.

TECHNICAL STUFF

Feel free to skip over (and come back to) the technical information marked by this icon. However, knowledge is power, so it's wise to read them too.

AUTHOR SAYS

This icon points out sage advice I provide from my years of experience in web design. I have made some mistakes along the way, and I provide advice so you don't have to make those same mistakes!

EXAMPLE

This icon indicates the presence of concrete examples that illustrate the topic being discussed. I give you examples of situations that have happened to me over the years.

Beyond the Book

In addition to the book content, you can find valuable free material online. We provide you with a Cheat Sheet that serves as a quick checklist, including the basic supplies you need to draw, where to find inspiration, how to identify common drawing styles, and more. Check out this book's online Cheat Sheet by searching www.dummies.com for **Building DIY Websites for Dummies Cheat Sheet.**

To download the Buyer Persona Template, which you learn about in Chapter 3, go to www.dummies.com/go/buildingdiywebsitesfd.

Where to Go from Here

You don't have to go through this book in sequence, but I suggest that you do to have the best result. It is tempting to just "get some tasks done," which may be steps that come naturally later in the process. If you don't do the steps in order, and build a sitemap first, you could very well end frustrated, with a process that takes much longer. As Benjamin Franklin said, "if you fail to plan, you plan to fail."

However, there are some sections that you can skip:

>> If you have a domain name, you can skip the section on registering a domain name in Chapter 2.

>> This goes also for a platform. If you have a website up and running and you will be using the same platform to build this new site, you do not need to read the section on choosing a platform in Chapter 2.

The information in this book is the fastest route to the best website for growing your business or endeavor. A route to more sales, faster traction, better user experiences, and trouble-free website functionality.

The practices you learn in this book also translate to social media marketing, email marketing, and more. This book teaches you how to build an online presence. It's more than about websites; it's about your reputation online. *It's about that first impression — that long-lasting relationship!*

So, are you ready to get started? I'm excited for you! If you read this book and build something great, I would love for you to email me with what you built.

1

Getting Started with DIY Websites

Chapter **1**

From Groundbreaking to Grand Opening: Constructing Your Website Step by Step

Y ou've embarked on an incredible journey with a remarkable goal: to build an website for your business or endeavor that attracts visitors and converts leads.

You may have tried to build a website in the past, but were left feeling frustrated, angry, or even worse, you lost time and money. Well, that is all over now. I am here to walk with you through every step of the process.

I've been working with people just like you for several decades and I know what questions you have. I know where you can get stuck. I know where a non-technical person needs some help. Most importantly, I know that you want to get the job done and don't want to repeat the process later! This chapter helps you set the stage for building an excellent website and outlines the sequence of steps you'll follow to build an effective, compelling, and modern site that best represents your organization online.

Setting Up Your Site for Success: Foundation, Messaging, and Search Engines

Many DIY website builders worry about choosing a platform and a theme. I see it all over the Internet: "What platform should I choose?" "Which platform is the best?" "How do I choose a theme?" These are all good questions, but in the grand scheme of things, as far as your website success is concerned, the platform you use doesn't matter that much.

If you had Picasso's paintbrush, paints, and canvases, would you be able to create a masterpiece? If you had a contractor's hammers, saws, and heavy equipment, would you be able to build a house? If you had a scalpel, anesthesia, and some cotton balls, would you be able to perform surgery?

Most likely the answer to all three is a resounding no. Having the tools doesn't mean you know how to effectively use them. The same is true when building websites. Having a web host provider, easy-to-use software, and a couple of plugins doesn't mean you can build a website that will bring in thousands of click-throughs and hundreds of orders. It's more than the tools. Building a successful website includes:

>> Using the right messaging.

>> Organizing your website so that visitors can find things with the least amount of clicks possible.

>> Understanding what search engines are looking for.

>> Creating content that is easy to understand and digest.

>> Laying out your content in interesting and unique ways so that visitors understand your message.

>> Building trust so that visitors feel comfortable handing over their email addresses or their money or their time.

REMEMBER

Having the tools is a means to an end. The tools can't teach you the skills; they just provide a way to use skills you already have. This book will teach you the skills.

Picking a platform

Remember that, although the platform you choose is important, equally or *more* important is the messaging, as well as how you provide information to search engines. You should indeed choose a platform that you can use easily. However, be sure to also consider your messaging and content, how search engines work, and how to lay out your content. This is what I teach you in this book.

Having said that, you may still want some advice about which platform to pick, so consider the pros and cons of the following platforms before you decide on one:

>> **Wix:** Wix is known for its drag-and-drop interface, making it super easy to design your website without any technical skills. If you are a beginner, this may be a good option for you. Wix offers a wide range of templates and customization options, and it comes with hosting, templates, and design tools all in one place. In addition, Wix frequently updates its platform with new features and designs. Its ease of use comes at the cost of less control over more technical aspects of your website. That means you can run into a wall when you want to do more with your website. Also, it can get expensive. While it starts off affordable, costs can add up with additional features and apps. Like any other closed platform, if you decide to move your site from Wix, you most likely will need to rebuild your website from scratch.

>> **Shopify:** Shopify is ideal if you are setting up an online store, as it provides powerful tools specifically for e-commerce. Shopify also offers robust security features and reliability for handling transactions, which is important, and its platform integrates with many third-party apps and services. But there are some considerations: Shopify can be expensive, especially with transaction fees and add-ons, and it is not the best choice if your primary focus is blogging.

>> **Squarespace:** Squarespace is known for stylish and professional templates that are great for portfolios and visual presentations. Like Wix, Squarespace includes hosting, templates, and e-commerce capabilities and is user-friendly with a drag-and-drop interface. Squarespace does not have as many third-party integrations as other platforms and customization is somewhat limited compared to platforms like WordPress. While it supports e-commerce, it's not as powerful as Shopify for online stores.

>> **WordPress:** WordPress is a popular software for building websites. It come in two flavors — WordPress.org, which you download and install on your own hosting platform, and WordPress.com, which is a platform you log in to, much like the others. WordPress is the choice for many who are semi-technical or need to create a custom website, as it is highly customizable. WordPress offers extensive customization options with themes and plugins, and there is a huge global community offering support, plugins, and themes. WordPress is great for all types of websites, from blogs to e-commerce sites, and you have full control over your website and its data. While this all sounds great, for novices, WordPress has a learning curve. It can be overwhelming for beginners due to its complexity. WordPress also requires regular updates and maintenance, especially for security. You are the manager of the software, not the platform, like in the other options presented here. For example, you need to arrange your own hosting, which can be a technical challenge for non-technical users.

There are many others out there — this is just a small sample. Chapter 2 goes into more detail about choosing the best platform based on your needs and goals.

Building the foundation

Setting up the mechanics of your website involves registering your domain name, choosing a *platform* (a place to host your website), a basic understanding of how nameservers work, setting up your email, and making sure you have a few other items in place.

TIP

The good thing is that if you have already checked some of these boxes, you can skip some of the sections in this book. For example, you may have already registered a domain name. In that case, you don't need to read the section on choosing a domain name in Chapter 2. If you are starting a new business and you have not registered a domain name, then read that section. The same goes for the platform, hosting, and email sections.

Understanding your potential customers

Once you get set up with the mechanics, start thinking about connecting with your audience. Your website needs to do a lot of preselling on its own. Ask yourself, ". . . can my website presell my products or services?"

AUTHOR
SAYS

Building a successful website starts with understanding your customer. Understanding your customers' pain points and how to offer the solution to their problems is very important. When you understand your customers, you empathize with their wants and needs. *Your website should reflect your understanding of your customers and show that you have the solution to their problems.*

You want to show visitors that you understand them right away, by placing a very strong message on the homepage that talks directly to their heart. Throughout your website, you want to place content that addresses the problems that the visitor is having right now.

You might have heard that one way to create good messaging on your website is to show transformation. How will your potential customer's life be transformed after engaging with you? Chapter 3 walks you through some exercises that help you create a website that will resonate with your potential customers.

Understanding your customer helps you with other efforts as well, such as social media marketing, social media advertising, email marketing, print advertising, and more.

A Place for Everything and Everything in Its Place

This is one of my favorite sayings. When it comes to websites, this principle rings true! An organized site allows visitors to easily find whatever they need, and a *sitemap* is the tool for organizing a website.

A *sitemap* is kind of like an outline you might create for a paper you're writing. The outline ensures that the paper covers all the important points and that there is a hierarchy to the important items. Figure 1-1 shows an example sitemap that I worked on with a health club client.

MAIN MENU

ADULT FITNESS
YOUTH FITNESS
AQUATICS
GYMNASTICS
NURSERY SCHOOL & CAMPS
JEWISH CULTURE & SOCIAL EVENTS

DropDowns (Bold items are simply headers, not pages)

Adult Fitness
Fitness Center (info about the facilities, calendar of the gym)
Personal Training
Tap Dance Lessons
Zumba Class
Body Sculpt
Tai Chi Class
Yoga Class
Adult Dance (Private and classes on this page)

Youth Fitness
Gymnastics (this will have links over to all the gymnastics programs)
Preschool Ballet Class
Dance Classes
SuperSoccerStars

Aquatics
Pool Schedule
Group Swim Classes
Private and Semi-Private Lessons
JCC Stingrays Swim Team
Lifeguard Certification and Re-Certification
American Red Cross Water Safety Instructor Class
American Red Cross CPR & First Aid
Adult Swim Programs (Masters swim, aquafitness, lap)
Adult Lap Swim
Open Swim

FIGURE 1-1:
An example
sitemap built for
a health club.

For your website, you need to create an outline that includes two things:

» The *functionality* that you want the website to have, such as a shopping cart, forms to gather leads and for people to reach out to you, a calendar system to show your events, galleries of photos, databases for displaying content, or videos.

» The *information* that you want to provide, such as services you offer, product categories you offer, content that shows your credibility and authority such as degrees, licenses, or photos, and ways to reach out to you.

When considering functionality, your website can also work for you in other ways. Some examples:

» You might have some forms that clients need to fill out before they come into your office. If you move those forms online, you can decrease the amount of time that patients or customers have to spend in your office.

» You might have some videos that potential customers can watch prior to coming in to your place of business. You can place those videos on your website. Then you don't have to spend your time repeatedly explaining the basics.

You can move many administrative and repetitive tasks to your website as well. A sitemap helps you think about these issues.

When it comes to thinking about the information you want to provide, building a sitemap also gets you thinking about how can you best use your website as a tool for your business. Think about what information would be most relevant to a potential lead that would turn them into a customer. To do this, you probably want to use your website as a pre-sales tool. This means that your website should provide great information to those looking for it, and also do some of the initial screening that your salespeople would normally do when meeting with a customer. Not all customers are good for our businesses. If you can use your website to weed out the customers you don't want before they come in contact with you, that will save you time and energy. You can do this by adding specific fields to your forms, by showing photographs of the level of service you provide, and by being clear about the services you provide.

If you've already built a website or you've just started, you understand when I say that building a website can be a lot of work — there are a lot of tasks that you need to perform and a bunch of content you need to create, not to mention design!

Having those tasks organized into a list can help you focus and get things done, so it's important to create a sitemap early in the process.

REMEMBER

The great thing about creating a sitemap early in the process is that it becomes your to-do list. This will save you so much time. Sitemaps and lists go hand-in-hand!

Creating a sitemap helps you identify the tasks you need to complete and the information you want to provide:

>> You need to write the content for each page.

>> You need to find images for each page.

>> You need to think about the Call to Actions (CTAs) to include on each page.

>> You need to think about the other information that will drive people to other parts of your website and keep them engaged.

>> You need to think about the keyword phrases you want to assign to each page and some basic SEO for each page.

I like thinking this way, because it breaks up a really giant project into small tasks. You can keep checking items off the list!

TIP

There are lots of online tools that you can use to create a sitemap, or you can do this exercise in Word, Notes, Pages, Google Docs, or another word processing application. In any case, start off by brainstorming all the information you think should be on your website and the functionality it should have. Then, take all this great information and organize it so that it makes sense in terms a website flow.

Chapter 6 walks you through the process of creating an amazing sitemap for your website.

Developing a Look and Feel that Works

Once you have the mechanics, sitemap, and content gathered and ready, it's time to think about how your website will look. You want your content to look amazing and have a modem aesthetic.

>> A modern website feels good to a visitor.

>> A modern website shows that your business is up to date with current technologies.

>> A modern website shows that you are willing to invest time and money in your business, and that translates to the visitor.

>> Visitors will know that the owner of this website is willing to invest time and money in the business and its customers.

How you lay out your content is an art, but it's not rocket science. This book helps you here. There are plenty of websites that you can look at and "borrow" ideas from. For example, Figure 1-2 shows a site that's expertly designed. Some points to note on this website:

>> The fonts are modern, easy to read, and are used consistently.

>> The colors draw visitor attention to important items instead of being distracting.

>> Pleasing design elements are used, such as a slanted line dividing the rows, icons and images supporting the text, and rounded corners with a slight drop shadow to lift content off the page.

>> The rows and columns separate content into easy-to-read sections.

>> There is good use of whitespace so that visitors can read and digest one section at a time.

The look and feel of your website depends on large part on the audience you want to draw to it. For example, Figure 1-3 shows pbs.kids.org, a site for children. Notice the use of icons and images and the lack of words. Clearly a site for young children. Compare this to Figure 1-4, which shows the New York Stock Exchange site. It's a serious site for adults about trading stocks and bonds. Think about how these two sites appeal to their respective audiences.

If you provide therapy solutions, you might want to design a calming and compassionate website with muted colors, engaging and emotional photos, and rounded edges. If you provide services to hip youth, you might want to design a slick website with lots of animation, strong colors, large fonts, and more points for engagement such as videos to watch.

When you create a website that looks beautiful and modern, people want to stay on your website. And when people want to stay on your website, they begin to trust you more, and when they trust you more, they are moving down the buyer's journey and becoming a warm lead, which in turn moves the lead closer to being a customer.

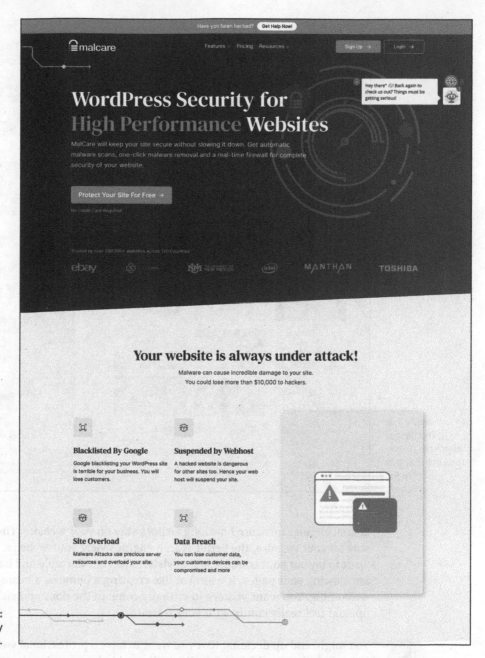

FIGURE 1-2:
An expertly
designed website.

FIGURE 1-3:
The design
elements clearly
indicate that this
is a site for
children.

Search engines measure how long visitors stay on your website. The longer people stay on your website, the better search engines view your website. Therefore, you want to lay out your content so that visitors feel comfortable and happy when they are viewing your pages. It's kind of like creating a home or a business that is very welcoming. You want visitors to virtually come in the door and sit down, snuggle up, and feel really comfy with your website.

REMEMBER

You might end up deciding that you want to have a professional web developer lay out your website, which is fine. You still need to know and understand your audience, have an understanding of your messaging, and get your content ready. A good web developer will be happy if you come to them with all of your content well-crafted, optimized, and ready.

FIGURE 1-4:
The NYSE site
conveys a more
serious and adult
aesthetic.

The NYSE is the world's largest stock exchange, offering icons and entrepreneurs the opportunity to raise capital and change the world. Our listed companies form a powerful community committed to good governance and societal impact. Industry-leading trading technology, combined with the guidance of experienced traders creates higher market quality for NYSE-market participants

If you decide to lay out your own content, Chapter 10 includes concrete tips that help you with the layout process. With the tools available nowadays, as well as other examples of beautifully laid out content, anyone can make a website that looks beautiful, appealing, and modern!

Getting and Analyzing Results

Once you have built your website and brought it live, you'll feel a huge sense of relief and accomplishment. You have completed this giant project, and you should be proud of yourself! But the process is not over.

Your website is not a project that you check off and never revisit. Think of your website as a living, breathing tool that is constantly getting potential customers through the door.

To get the best results, you need to measure your website. Just like after almost any contest that you enter, you can measure how well you performed.

At the end of the year when you are tidying up your books, you likely measure how your business performed. Did you do better compared to last year? What are your goals for next year? What changes are you going to make? Where did you have waste? Where did you excel?

At this point, you want to put software in place so that you can measure the results. You can measure so many things, such as which devices people use when they browse your website, how long people stay on your website, how far they scroll down a page, which pages are visited most frequently, where people leave your website, and more.

You can use the Google Search Console to measure results such as which search terms Google returns your website for, what position your website is returned in, and how many times people click on your listing, as shown in Figure 1-5.

Top queries	Clicks	Impressions	CTR	↑ Position
biofeedback near me	1	1	100%	1
brain waves chart	0	269	0%	1
brain frequency chart	0	24	0%	1
local guide program	0	24	0%	1
brain wave graph	0	7	0%	1
brainwave assessment near me	0	5	0%	1
how are brain waves measured	0	5	0%	1

FIGURE 1-5: The Google Search Console returns information about how visitors visit and use your website.

Just like your accounting due diligence, you can and must measure the success of your website. Remember that the longer people stay on your website, the better search engines view your website. Chapter 15 explains a few tools you should put into place now so that you can measure success later.

Your basic steps to building a great website are getting set up the equipment you need, thinking strategically about messaging and design, and remembering who is judging you (the search engines). This is your pathway to success!

Chapter **2**

Laying Your Website's Foundation

In this chapter, I show you how to set up the basics you need for your website. There are several steps you can take now that will save you a ton of time and frustration later on, as well as impact the final website and your business. Building a great foundation will make things easier later. This chapter covers those first steps.

Choosing a Domain Name Registrar

Start at the beginning: choose a domain name.

A *domain name* is like your business address, but specifically for your website. Just like you need an address to visit someone's business, you need a domain name to visit someone's website. Examples of domain names include godaddy.com, wordpress.org, and speedtest.net. Domain names chains of characters plus the extension, such as .com, .net, or .org.

An *URL* is the combination of your domain name, plus the https:// or http:// at the beginning, and sometimes more words in front of your domain name like https://mail.yahoo.com (that's called a *subdomain*). In this example, the domain name is yahoo.com and the URL is https://mail.yahoo.com.

A *registrar* is the place where you register your domain name and claim it as yours. All registrars are accredited by an organization called ICANN, which stands for Internet Corporation for Assigned Names and Numbers. This nonprofit organization manages all of the registrars — in order to be a registrar, you must be accredited by ICANN.

Domain registrars store information about your domain name in a central database, called the *registry*. All domain names need to be entered into the registry in order to be recognized.

You have many registrars to choose from, and you may have heard of some. GoDaddy is a popular registrar, and Domain.com, Network Solutions, Namecheap, and BuyDomains are examples. You can also register your domain name at a hosting company such as Bluehost or HostGator. When you are choosing a registrar, consider a few things to help make your decision easier. For example, you need to know:

>> **Registration period:** Domain names are usually registered in one-year periods. Some registrars offer a minimum of one-year registration, but some start at two years.

TIP

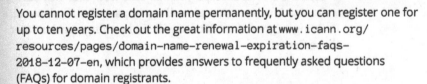

You cannot register a domain name permanently, but you can register one for up to ten years. Check out the great information at www.icann.org/resources/pages/domain-name-renewal-expiration-faqs-2018-12-07-en, which provides answers to frequently asked questions (FAQs) for domain registrants.

>> **Pricing:** Many registrars offer a discount on the first registration period and then after that, renewals can have a different price. Most domain names cost around $10 per year on average.

>> **Expiration policy:** If you forget to renew your domain, or if you have your domain set to auto-renew but your credit card changes, your domain might expire without any recourse. The registrar might auction off your domain name right away or you might have a grace period. For this reason, it is good to know the registrar's expiration policy before diving in.

>> **Available tools:** Find out what tools the registrar provides for you to manage your domain name and whether the process for making changes is manageable. Search for reviews of the registrar you are considering (enter something like "reviews of *registrar name*" into your favorite search engine). Check for reviews about the tools and whether they are difficult to access or use.

>> **Speed for implementing changes:** If you are going to use this registrar as your *nameserver* (which I cover in the section "Understanding How Authoritative Nameservers Work," later in this chapter), find out how fast changes are propagated when you make them. Try looking for reviews from other customers that indicate how quickly the registrar makes changes on their platform.

   Note: Speed is important only when you are going live or making big changes, which should not be that often, but knowing whether the changes you make are propagated to the rest of the Internet quickly is a good thing.

Registering Your Domain Name

When you register your domain name, your account must contain contacts for administrative, billing, and technical issues. These contacts will match the information of the person who registered your domain. If this is not you, you won't have control over your domain name and you will at some point run into problems with this situation. I have seen this happen many, many times.

So be sure to register your domain name in your own name. Even if someone walked you through the process of registering, your domain name needs to be under your account. You — not your web developer, a cousin, or an intern — need to own your domain name and registration. This is your business. Register it yourself so that you have these points of access to the registrar account:

>> **A valid email address:** Make sure your registration uses an email address that you can access.

>> **A verified password:** You must know the account password, save it to a password manager, and make sure it's accurate and working.

   If someone helps you open the account and they give you the password afterward, do not just assume that it's correct. Test the login by logging in with the password you were given. Make sure that you can see your domain name and that your information appears for all of the billing, administrative, and technical contact information. By the same token, if you already have a domain name, make sure that you can log in to the account on the registrar's website.

TIP

WHAT ABOUT USING A WEBSITE BUILDER TO REGISTER MY DOMAIN NAME?

If you're going to use a website builder platform like Wordpress.com, Squarespace, or Wix, they may give you the option to reserve your domain name through them in one easy process. Should you? My recommendation is that you reserve your domain name *separately* at a dedicated registrar company, such as GoDaddy.

The reason being that platforms like WordPress.com, Wix, and Squarespace are primarily platforms for *building* websites. That's what they do well, and the majority of their tools are focused on that specialty.

In the same way, a registrar company, like GoDaddy, specializes in registering domain names. That's what they do well, and they have extra tools to help you manage your domain name efficiently.

Choose each company based on what they do best, be it registrar, hosting, or site building.

WARNING

Once you register your domain name, most registrars will not allow you to change the registrar for 60 days. Hopefully you will not want to move your registrar, but you should be aware of this in any case.

Avoid the offered extras

Whichever registrar company you choose, when you go to register your domain name, you will be asked a series of questions at checkout about add-ons to your domain name registration. The questions will be something like these:

» Do you want to buy hosting for your website?

» Do you want to buy domain privacy?

» Do you want to set up a professional email address that ends with your new domain name?

» Do you want to use our website builder?

REMEMBER

You do not need to buy any of these options at this stage. You only need the domain name registration and *possibly* domain privacy. You can decide on all the extra services can later.

Again, choose companies for what they do best: registrar companies for registering domains, and hosting companies for hosting the website files.

Opt for domain privacy (or not)

By default, the information about the administrative, billing, and technical contacts is available to the public. This information might include your full name, address, and email address and is public.

This means that anyone on the Internet can inquire about who is the registered owner of any domain name. It's kind of like looking up a business at your state business registration office to see who the business owner is. In Internet-speak, it's called a *WHOIS lookup*. This is all publicly available information, by default.

If you purchase the domain privacy add-on, only your registrar can see your administrative, technical, and billing contact information. Consider these points when deciding whether to purchase the privacy add-on:

>> **You get some privacy protection when you purchase this option.** People can't get your name and email address, nor send fake domain renewal scams to your physical address. (That actually happens!)

>> **The privacy add-on usually costs about $10 a year.** Some registrar companies include domain privacy for free. It's up to you to decide if that's something you want.

>> **You may want people to know you're behind the domain.** So in that case, you wouldn't want the privacy add-on.

Choose a domain name

When choosing a domain name, you want it to match your brand as closely as possible. If you don't have a name for your company or enterprise yet, and you're flexible, you may even want to look for domain names first — *before you name your company*. Why? Because unless you have a unique business name, you'll find that a lot of domain names are taken, and some people *squat* on domains, which means they register a lot of domain names hoping that someday someone will buy the names from them and they will make some money!

Therefore, it may take some creativity to find a domain name that matches your brand *and* is available. Here are a few other things to consider when choosing your domain name:

>> **Keep it as short as possible.** The fewer characters people have to type, the better — especially on a mobile device with a small keyboard. People are much more likely to make mistakes when they're typing a longer domain name, and you don't want that!

>> **Use appropriate characters.** You can use letters, numbers, and hyphens in a domain name — that's it. No spaces or special characters such as !@#$%. Also, domain names are not case sensitive.

Even though you *can* use hyphens or numbers, you want to register a domain name with no hyphens or numbers, unless your company name has numbers in it, like 1800Flowers. Otherwise, no numbers or hyphens.

>> **Make it easy to spell.** Don't use complicated words. Even some shorter words — such as *giraffe* — may be hard for some people to spell. So make it as easy as possible.

TIP

Speaking of spelling, if a word in your domain name is misspelled a lot, consider buying the misspellings as domain names, too. Later, you can *forward* (redirect with links) those who typed the misspelled domain names to your actual domain name. For example, if you type gooogle into your browser — with three Os — you are redirected to google.com. This is because Google registered the misspelling, just in case someone adds another O by accident.

>> **Buy a domain name that contains a relevant keyword.** Adding a keyword that relates to your enterprise in the domain name can offer a small boost to your site in search results.

>> **Carefully review how the words look together.** Sometimes you'll put a couple words together and it might spell a word you don't want in your domain name. So just put together the words you're considering and look at the result. Maybe you can have someone else look at it and find out what words they see. Kind of like a word search game.

For example, suppose a company that assists with lipo operations, wants to reserve "LIPO OPS".com. That's pretty good, right? It's short, seven letters. It's pretty easy to spell. But once you put those words together, you have "POOP" in the middle. Or it might look like "L.I. POOPS," which might be a catchy name for a Long Island Wastewater company, but not for a surgical assistance company. So be sure to check for those hidden words.

Use a premium domain name

In your search for the best domain name, you may come across some domain names at a higher price point. These names are called *premium domains*, because they use short words, or valuable search words, and are popular or super easy to remember. The average price to register a domain name is $10-$20. But premium domain names cost thousands of dollars to register. You pay a bigger one-time fee to acquire it, and then it renews next year at the usual $10-20 like a normal domain name.

Is it worth it to spend the money and purchase a premium domain? It depends! If it's a perfect domain for your business and you can't imagine it being anything else, you might consider making the investment and paying the premium to obtain that domain name. After all, this name is going to last forever, and you want your business to grow. So if it is in your budget and it's important enough to you, consider purchasing the premium domain name.

Consider the extension

You must also consider domain endings (the part after the period or "dot"), also known as the *extension*. You may notice, as you search the registrar for domain names, that different domain name endings are available. These are called TLDs, or top-level domains.

Of course, the most popular extension is .com: `google.com`, `microsoft.com`, and `totocoaching.com`. Other popular TLDs include .net, .org, .gov, .mil, .edu, .us — and there are literally hundreds more. There are some restrictions as to what domains you can or cannot use. For example, these sponsored top-level domains are reserved:

>> .edu is for educational institutions only

>> .gov is only used by official government entities

>> .mil applies to military entities

These days there all kinds of other extensions, like .club and .website, even .best! So what should you choose? Without going into all the details, .com is usually your best bet, if available. That's what people expect, which makes it easier for visitors to find your website.

Understanding How Authoritative Nameservers Work

Navigating the Internet might seem simple, but behind every website visit or email, there's a complex system at play. When you want to visit a website, you usually type something like `dummies.com`. This human-readable address is the domain name and it's easier for people to remember. But computers communicate using numbers, so they require a different identification method that uses numbers.

Every root domain name has an associated number called an *IP address*, which is like a phone number for websites. Instead of dummies.com, a computer might recognize the domain as 104.18.12.160, which is its IP address; this tells the world where to find the website files.

When you type dummies.com into a web browser, your browser asks a nameserver, "What's the number (IP address) for this website?". The nameserver then sends the browser the IP address, allowing your browser to connect. Nameservers also help with other services, such as email. When you send an email to an online entity, such as support@dummies.com, a nameserver tells your email program where to send the message by translating the domain portion of an email address to an IP address where the message can be delivered.

Every domain has at least one main nameserver, called the *authoritative nameserver*. It holds many vital records, including the location of your website and email destinations. The *A Record* points to your website's IP address, and the *MX record* directs where emails sent to your domain should go.

REMEMBER

Only the domain owner (ideally, that's you) can change these records, which helps ensure security.

When you purchase a domain, your registrar will provide you with at least two default nameservers for reliability. Figure 2-1 shows an example of nameservers.

Nameservers

Using default nameservers   [Change]

Nameservers ⓘ

ns37.domaincontrol.com

ns38.domaincontrol.com

FIGURE 2-1:
GoDaddy's
nameservers.

If one nameserver is offline, the other takes over, ensuring people can always access your website and online services. If you need to change your online services, such as changing your email provider, adding Google services, or changing your website host, you log into your nameserver account to make those changes.

When you update these settings, they need to be shared across the world. This sharing is called *propagation*. This is like updating your friends when you change your phone number. It used to take days for these changes to propagate, but now, thanks to modern technology, changes can spread in minutes, especially with top-tier providers. The faster this happens, the smoother the experience for your site's visitors and email recipients. The journey from typing a website's name to viewing the site involves nameservers, IP addresses, and quick digital conversations. Even if it feels instant, you now know the magic happening behind the scenes!

Choosing a Platform and a Host

A platform is the software you use to build your website. It is also frequently called a *CMS* (Content Management System). You might also hear the terms "web authoring software" or "web publishing software" used interchangeably with website builder. All of these have one common purpose: to help you build a website. Figure 2-2 shows you some examples of platforms you can use to build your website.

FIGURE 2-2:
A few of the platforms you can use to create your website.

Examples of common website builders are Wix, GoDaddy, Weebly, Squarespace, and Shopify, and there are many, many more options available. You may have also heard of WordPress, which is popular software for building websites. These are covered in detail in Chapter 1.

TECHNICAL STUFF

Wordpress comes in two flavors: WordPress.com is the option where you create an account on their servers, log in, and begin building your website with a scaled-down version of WordPress *or* WordPress.org, where you install the WordPress software on a web host of your choice and build there. See the sidebar entitled "Wordpress Comes in Two Flavors" later in this chapter for more information.

Considerations for choosing a platform

Many people have questions and doubts about which platform they should choose. Consider these important considerations when choosing a platform:

>> **Ease of use:** This is probably the most important consideration if you are building your own website. Some people may find one software easier to use than another, so take a few web builders for a trial run to see how intuitive the software is. Be sure to find one that helps you build your site, not hinders you.

>> **Design and customization:** Look at the templates you can choose from. Do you like this company's offerings? Do any of these templates feel like your brand image? How easy is it to customize the templates? Can you add new, interesting sections to each page that look nice? If you want to change a section to have two columns instead of three, is this easy? Take a few platforms for a test drive and see how easy it is to change some things.

>> **Functionality:** Next you want to ask yourself what functionality/features you want on your website and make sure that the web builder fits your needs.

Text and images on a page are basic. If you're creating a website that's purely informational, such as an online brochure, you might not need much more than that. Or, you might need additional functionality, such as a shopping cart, an online reservation system, or a calendar. Write down all of the things you want people to do on your website and make sure that the functionality exists in the platform you choose. Sometimes functionalities are sold as paid add-ons, at a monthly price. This can add up! Make sure you compare the platform's features to what you need.

>> **Support:** Support is a good thing to consider, as you most likely will need to some help at some point. Do they offer phone support? Email or chat support? Do other customers have a hard time getting through to the support staff? How timely are their responses? You can probably find some answers to this simply by searching for reviews of the platform.

>> **Pricing:** Look at pricing for all the plans offered, because most likely you will start with the lowest plan and then upgrade as you grow. You want to know what you may be paying soon, when you bump up to the next level. Some platforms offer a low introductory price for the first year, but then jack up the

price after that. What will you be paying when it's time to renew? It's good to know these things.

>> **Closed or open platform:** When you build on a "closed" web builder platform such as Wix or Squarespace, you cannot move your website to another platform. You're locked-in to their hosting, tools, and pricing plans. If you want to move to a different platform, such as WordPress, you will need to rebuild your website from scratch. You are also stuck using whatever options the closed platform gives you. If you want your gallery of images displayed in a particular manner, or you want to have a calendar that looks a particular way, or you want to sell products online, you have only the options afforded to you by the vendor.

Open-source platforms, such as the self-hosted version of WordPress, are more flexible. You can move from one host to another and find new ways of displaying your information. The downside to these platforms is that they can be a bit more technical to use and maintain.

>> **Ongoing maintenance:** When you use a closed platform, the people who run the software do all the updating, upgrading, maintenance, and troubleshooting for you. You don't have to worry about the software getting out of date, or about two pieces of software conflicting. With an open-source platform, such as WordPress.org, you are responsible for maintaining the website software. You have to update the site, and if there is a technical issue, you have solve it on your own or hire someone to help you.

AUTHOR SAYS

There is no right or wrong platform. Think of this as your "starter home." Your goals are to get your website up and going affordably, quickly, and correctly, so choose one that is easy for you to use now! Later, when business is booming and you have new goals for your business and more income, you can rebuild the website on another platform that has more flexibility and more features, if you need to. You might find that the platform you choose now will last you for years to come!

Website hosting

This section explains website hosting — what a website host is and what to look for in a website hosting company.

What is a website host?

A website is made up of many types of files and required services:

>> There are content files, such as photos, videos, and PDFs.

>> There are website structure, style, and code files that browsers interpret, such as HTML, CSS, and JS files.

>> There are files processed on the server, such as PHP files, which generate HTML, CSS, and JS for the browser to display.

>> In the case of WordPress sites, there is also a database, which is composed of tables of information needed for your WordPress site to function.

All these files and services need a place to live on the Internet: They need to be *stored* (or *hosted*) somewhere. And that's what a web hosting service does!

Your website host is the computer or server where all the website files and services like the databases live. When you are building your website, it's the server that you either work on or upload files to. So, since this is where all your files live and are accessed from, it matters a lot who your host is! It can quite literally make or break your website.

When do you need to find separate hosting?

If you are going to build on a "closed" website-builder platform such as Wix or Squarespace, they are automatically your host. Your website files will live on Wix or Squarespace's hosting servers, and that's that. In a closed environment, everything is proprietary and decided for you. This is also a *managed host*. It's "managed" because the hosting company is taking care of things like security and software updates and backups.

REMEMBER

When you build on a platform such as Wix or Squarespace, you are using their proprietary software to build your website. Because their software is not "open source," meaning that they own the software and do not share the code with anyone, you cannot move your Wix or Squarespace website to another host.

WORDPRESS COMES IN TWO FLAVORS

When using a WordPress platform, you generally have two options:

- **WordPress.com:** A managed version or partially closed version of WordPress that comes preinstalled on WordPress.com's hosting servers. You are choosing to have WordPress host your website (similar to using Squarespace or Wix) as well as provide you with the WordPress software to build your website. They handle the server specs, location, security updates, backups, and so on. It's mostly done *for* you.

- **WordPress.org:** Open-source software that you install on a host of your choosing. WordPress.org is not a host, but simply the software only. If you choose to download the WordPress software from wordpress.org, you need to choose a separate web host.

If you use the downloadable version of WordPress, or wordpress.org, you *can* move your website hosting at any time and you do *not* need to rebuild your website from scratch. It is a fairly easy process to move a WordPress site to another website hosting company.

Considerations when choosing a web host

The most important things to consider when choosing a web host are the following:

» Platforms supported

» Support

» Security

» Location

» Uptime

» Integrated backup

» Staging sites

» SSL certificates

Each of these issues is discussed in the following sections.

PLATFORMS SUPPORTED

Some web hosts can host all kinds of websites that are built using all different types of coding. These hosts are "platform-agnostic," meaning if you have a Joomla site, you can host it there. If you have a WordPress site, you can host it there. If you have straight HTML files, you can host them there. The main point is that you can host all kinds of coded websites on these types of hosting platforms.

Some web hosts only support one platform, which can be a good thing. For example, you may come across companies like Flywheel or WPEngine. These are for

WordPress hosting only. You may also hear these companies call themselves "dedicated WordPress hosts." Their servers know how to host these files and databases, and their tools are all geared toward WordPress, and WordPress alone. If you are building a WordPress website, I suggest using one of these dedicated WordPress hosts to build your website, hands-down.

SUPPORT

If you choose a dedicated WordPress host, you can rest assured that when you call in for support or create a support ticket, the technician will most likely understand the issue you are having, will have seen the problem before, and will know the resolution. These hosting companies tout themselves as experts in WordPress, so they should be able to help you quickly resolve your issue.

If you have chosen a host that hosts all types of platforms, the support technician assigned to your ticket may not be an expert in the software you are using. This can get frustrating. I recommend that you do a quick Internet search on reviews of the host you are thinking of using.

SECURITY

As far as security goes, hosts that support one platform such as WordPress have built their entire infrastructure around supporting WordPress. Their firewalls are best at dealing with WordPress websites. Matter of fact, most of these platforms have a guarantee that you will not get hacked, and if you do, they will clean it for free. They can make this guarantee because their entire infrastructure is geared around one software package and they support that software very well.

WARNING

If you choose a hosting option that supports all types of websites coded all different ways, the firewalls are not written specifically for your platform. Some of these web hosts might not even have malware protection running on their servers. You would need to find and configure your own anti-malware solution. If your site is hacked, you might be on your own trying to recover your website. In these cases, I highly recommend that you run some malware protection on your own. Chapter 14 covers malware options in detail.

LOCATION

You want to choose a web hosting company whose servers are closest to the people visiting your website, so that the content will be delivered quickly. So, if you have a company in the United States and your customers are U.S. citizens for the most part, choose a hosting option that resides in the United States. If you are setting up a London office with a website for people in England, choose a web host in England. Sometimes you have the option to choose this with certain hosts.

UPTIME

Your website host needs to be up and running to be seen. If visitors try to buy something from your site and it goes down, panic can ensue. When your web server is up and running and you can view your website, this is called *uptime*. Nowadays, server uptime is pretty good compared to years ago. Most web host companies have a solid uptime record, but check on this before committing to a particular web host. Ideally, uptime should be above 98 or 99 percent.

INTEGRATED BACKUPS

Backups are copies of your data that protect against data loss, or in case you make a change that you need to reverse, and you need the ability to restore data from a backup version of your site. Before you choose a host, find out if daily backups are included in your hosting package. Some hosting companies offer backups, but as an add-on, meaning you need to pay more. Dedicated WordPress hosting companies such as WP Engine and Flywheel include daily backups with their hosting packages and all their backups are easy to restore. You can do the restore yourself by simply logging in and clicking the Restore button. I go more into backups in Chapter 14.

STAGING SITES

A staging site is a clone of your current website that is typically not publicly viewable.

Why would you want a clone of your website? Let's say you want to test some new software, but you don't want to do it on the live website in case it crashes the site. You can set up a staging site by creating a quick copy or clone of your website and then you can log into that staging area and test software, play around, mess it up, or whatever you like, because no one can see this staging site except for you. It does not affect your live site.

The great thing about staging sites is that you can simply "push" the staging site to the live site if you decide all the changes you made are usable. This means that you overwrite your live site with the staging site. This is a great tool if you like to try things first before you install them on your live site.

SSL CERTIFICATES

TECHNICAL STUFF

SSL stands for Secure Sockets Layer. An SSL certificate simply creates a secure connection between your computer (your web browser) and the web host using encryption.

When installed, your website will use `https://` at the beginning of your URL, not `http://`. You will also have a lock symbol near your browser bar. This does not happen automatically. You must install an SSL certificate, as it is expected by search engines, browsers, and visitors alike. Some web hosts offer free SSL certificates. Others offer a paid SSL certificate.

Find out whether the host you are looking at offers a free or paid SSL certificate and who installs those SSL certificates (as well as how difficult it is to install the certificate). Most hosting companies offer the SSL for free, and you can install it pretty easily, but this is not the case for all.

Types of hosting

Most likely you will choose shared or cloud hosting for your first website:

» **Cloud:** Cloud hosting is the newest type of inexpensive hosting and most likely the best option if you are building your own website. With cloud hosting, copies of your website are hosted on multiple servers at the same time. Your website is synched across these services, so that even if one fails, the others are available to respond. When someone requests to look at your website, this "group" of servers optimize how they send the files to the person's web browser in the most efficient, fastest way. Cloud servers can also be "scaled up" quickly, meaning if there is a website in the cloud that requires more resources because of increased traffic, it is easy to simply upgrade to the next service tier.

» **Shared:** Shared hosting involves a single server that many websites share. Each customer receives a portion of the same physical server hardware to run their website. Shared hosting is often the least expensive method, because the web hosting company houses multiple customers on a single web server, resulting in lower costs overall.

While shared hosting can seem like a great, cost-effective way to go, it is not ideal. With many customers sharing one server, individual websites are reliant on all the other customers sharing this server to play nicely in the sandbox together. For example, if you install a copy of WordPress on your shared server space, and someone else on that same server has heavy traffic to their website for some reason, the single server resources may not be enough to serve both websites efficiently at the same time. This could happen if a website on the same server as yours becomes infected with malware, or if another company's website is picked up with a huge news story. If there is a surge of traffic going to the other website, the server will not have enough resources to deliver your website quickly and efficiently. Your website will slow down. Sometimes this is called having a "noisy neighbor." Well, we don't like noisy neighbors.

WARNING

If you choose shared hosting, you can't predict your website's performance because you are not privy to which other websites are hosted on your same server and you can't control their traffic or security settings. With cloud hosting, you have a much better chance of your website being delivered quickly and efficiently to your visitors.

In addition to these two options, there is also dedicated hosting and VPS hosting. If you are building your own website, you will not need either of these options, but they are covered here for completeness:

>> **Dedicated:** With dedicated hosting, your website is hosted on your own server. The amount of processors, memory, and space that you pay for is yours and yours alone. You don't share your resources with any other websites. This is generally more expensive because you are paying for the entire server instead of just a portion. This is a good option when you have a very busy online store or a blog with lots of web traffic, or when your website runs a lot of databases.

>> **VPS:** VPS hosting stands for Virtual Private Server. A VPS hosts multiple customers on the same server and uses software to "virtually" split the physical server into several smaller virtual servers. Although the users share the same physical server, it's as if they each have their own dedicated server. Each user on a VPS receives a dedicated segment of the parent server's hardware resources. These are less expensive than dedicated servers because you don't have to purchase a separate physical server for each website.

Deciding Where to Build Your Website

You need to plan where to build your new website. You have three basic options:

>> Build on a temporary URL

>> Build on a live URL

>> Build on a staging URL

Build on a temporary URL

When you sign up for a website building platform or a hosting service, you may be given what is called a temporary URL to build on. Depending on your host or platform, the exact URL will look different. It may be an IP address or some funny words, or you might get to make it up yourself. Here's an example of a temporary URL:

```
https://wordpress-291351-2757964.cloudwaysapps.com/
```

Whatever it is, it is *not* your main business domain name. It's an odd and fairly hard-to-guess URL because it's only meant to be temporary — used or accessed only while you are building your website. You can build your website by logging into this temporary URL and keeping it on that weird-looking domain while you build your website.

People use temporary URLs to upload images and content on their own time, and pages can be half completed, broken, or even missing completely and it doesn't matter because no one can access these websites. Typically, hosting companies tell search engines to not list such a site, so no one will happen upon it when they are searching for something. It's like you're working on something behind a curtain, and when it's exactly how you want it and you're ready to show the world, you simply pull back the curtain (or *go live*) to reveal the finished, polished website!

Build on a live URL

If you've already purchased a domain name, you can point it to your new hosting server or platform and then build your website using your actual business domain name. That's what is called building on a "live" URL, a production server, or live server.

Search engines can see these live URLs and might even index the website, depending on certain settings. If you already have a website up and running and are making changes to it using this book, you may be making the changes on your live website, meaning that people can see the changes if they visit your website. In this case, they will see any missing and dummy content, broken links, and all of your mistakes while you're building. It's like building in front of the curtain, on stage, while everyone watches.

AUTHOR SAYS

I want you to appear as professional as possible, so I do not recommend building on a live URL unless you are somehow able to put up a "Coming Soon" or "Under Construction" page and then build behind the scenes. This can be tricky, because you need to make sure that your "Coming Soon" page does not show the real header or the real footer because those might contain links to pages that are not yet ready.

If you can put up some sort of "Coming Soon" page, don't just put up a background with those words on it. You can use this page to your advantage. You can put a form on the page to gather email addresses of people who want to be notified when you go live. You could put up a video about what you are planning to launch. You could add your social media links encouraging people to find out more about you. How about a countdown? Add a beautiful graphic to the page and a nice big headline so the page is working for you!

TIP

If you are using WordPress, there is a checkbox in the Dashboard under Settings --> Reading that says: Search Engine Visibility: Discourage Search Engines from Indexing This Site. If you look below this checkbox, shown in Figure 2-3, you'll see that it says, "It is up to search engines to honor this request." Use this option while you are building the website, and make sure you uncheck it when you go live.

FIGURE 2-3:
The WordPress setting that tells search engines not to index your website.

Search engine visibility	☐ Discourage search engines from indexing this site
	It is up to search engines to honor this request.

REMEMBER

You can check that box while you are under development, but you *must* remember to uncheck that box when you go live.

Build on a staging site

What if you have a live website that you want to modify, but you also want to keep the website up while you make changes to it? There is an amazing way to do this.

It's called a "staging site" and this is the *preferred method* for making changes to a website that has been live. This may sometimes also be referred to as a "test site" or a "development site" or a few other terms, depending on your platform or the tools you are using. A staging, test, or development site is simply a copy of your current website, and you access this copy using a temporary URL.

Most of the time, you need to manually create this staging site through your host or platform. You tell the software to create the staging site and then the software sends you a new temporary login URL to log in and make changes.

If you do decide to set up a staging site, you must find out and plan for two contingencies:

>> *How long you have access to this staging site.*
Some platforms let you keep your staging site up and running indefinitely, until you choose to publish the changes. Other companies offer access for a

limited time only. You want to know how long you have access to this staging site so that you do not lose all of your work. Find out that information if you are going to build on a staging site.

>> *What changes need to be made to the live site while you are building on the staging site.*

You need to think about the live site while you are working on the staging site. Is your live site a busy one? Do you add blog posts or new products on a regular basis or make edits to a directory all the time? If you do, you must establish a fail-safe process so that when the live site is updated, the staging site gets the update as well. Add an SOP (standard operating procedure) so that you do not have missing information once you overwrite the live site. If you have an online store, this is the trickiest option, as you need to retain the orders in the backend of the website. If orders come in while you are building on the staging site, when it is time to go live (depending on the software), you can't simply overwrite the live site with the staging site, because all the new orders will be gone!

You need a good plan for integrating these changes going in, so make sure you ask those questions of your platform, or research how you will handle this.

Going Live with Your Staging Site

For the most part, when you build on a staging site, it is super easy to make the staging site the live site when you are ready. Most platforms have a button that you press and then you confirm that you want to overwrite your live site with the staging site. You press that button, go have coffee or take the dogs for a walk, come back, and the live site now shows all of your work! Figure 2-4 gives you an idea of this overwriting process.

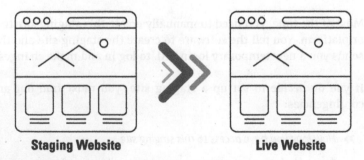

FIGURE 2-4:
How staging sites overwrite live sites.

Staging Website

Live Website

WARNING

No matter where you are building your new website, make sure you have backups of your temporary staging and live sites running automatically on a daily basis. Your backups should be retained for at least seven days in case you need to restore to an earlier time. You do not want to lose all the work you are doing. Do not take backups for granted. Decide where you will build your website, have a plan for backups, and have a plan for going live without losing information.

Get this area ready now so that when you are ready to create your menus and pages, you don't have to worry about this part, because you'll already have a plan in place.

Setting Up Your Business Email

You need a professional business email address so that you look professional to the world — to your potential clients and your current clients. This means having business email addresses ending in your business domain name, which help give your business authority and legitimacy. In other words, this makes you look like a real company. An example of this is jennifer@totocoaching.com or jderosa@totocoaching.com or jennifer.derosa@totocoaching.com. Those are all professional email addresses that look official because they end with your domain name.

Now, do you really have to do this step? No, you can use your personal Gmail, Me, Yahoo!, or Outlook address and you'll probably receive the emails just fine. But from a client's point of view, does it look professional? No. It looks hokey and homemade.

How many email addresses should you have?

You most likely want to set up at least two email addresses: a personal and a generic email address.

>> The *personal email* address will go only to you and has some form of your name in the address. You want to keep control over this email inbox. You don't want to give access to this email inbox to others, as you may end up having sensitive HR information sent to you, or private information about the business or financials. . . so set one up for yourself, personally.

>> Next, set up at least one other email address that is used to do "business stuff." This email address should be generic. Something like info@yourbusiness.com. This address should be used for anything business related that is not sensitive material, and that other employees can look at safely.

Use the generic address to sign up for software or a platform so that your employees can log in with that email address on behalf of the company. You should also set up most of your public contact forms on your website to forward messages to this generic email address so that you are not personally checking all the forms coming from the website. Even if that is what you're doing in the beginning as a small company, having the generic email address will give you the flexibility in the future to delegate the responsibility of checking email to somebody else as you grow.

**AUTHOR
SAYS**

Imagine this: one day you want to go on a three-week vacation. Your employees will "run" your company while you are gone. If you sign up for services with your personal email and you leave for vacation, one of two things will happen: one is employees will call and bother you while you are on vacation. That is not fair to your family or your mental health. Or, two, things simply won't get done and balls will be dropped. When you come back from vacation, you will have a huge mess on your hands.

Generic email address can start with something like info@, support@, orders@, sales@.

Where should you host your email?

Now that you know you are setting up two email addresses, you need to find a place to host your emails. Just like finding a host for your website files, you need a host to host your emails. The email host is the company that has software that allows you to set up your professional email addresses and receive email there.

Email hosts can be:

>> Your registrar (where you registered your domain name)

>> Your host (sometimes where you host your website)

>> A dedicated email host

I don't have strong recommendations on where to host your email, but I do offer a few suggestions. Each host will most likely have a few different plans you can choose from. The difference in their plans include how much space you have for your emails and documents, the level of support you receive, and other options. You can always start off with the lowest plan and then move up as you grow your business.

>> **Gmail:** Some people already have a Gmail account and they like the way that Gmail works. If you are comfortable with its interface, you can use Google to host your professional domain name's email using Google Workspace.

>> **Zoho:** Zoho offers a suite of online business applications. They have email hosting as well as CRMs (*customer relationship management* software) and other software to run your business. You can host your email at Zoho and integrate your email with other software as you go along.

>> **Microsoft 365 (formerly Office 365):** If you're used to using Microsoft products like Word, Excel, PowerPoint, and Outlook, hosting your professional email through Microsoft 365 might be a good idea.

Once you set up your email addresses, you need to tell your nameserver about the email. At some point while you are setting up the email addresses, you will see some information that you need to add the *MX records*.

TECHNICAL STUFF

MX stands for *mail exchange record* and it simply tells the Internet, "When someone sends an email to a user at this domain, send that mail to this company that hosts my email."

Setting this up is pretty easy. The email host either has a tool that automatically configures the MX settings for you, or you need to enter them on your own. Zoho has such a tool integrated with GoDaddy. If you are logged in to both platforms, you will see a button that enables Zoho to do the configuration for you.

Entering MX records might sound scary and nerdy but it's not. Every mail host gives you step-by-step instructions. Basically, you log in to your nameserver and find your DNS records. Examples of GoDaddy's DNS records are shown in Figure 2-5. Yours will look similar.

Then you add a new record. This will be an MX record. The email host will tell you what to put in the name, priority, and value areas. They might show you something like Figure 2-6.

Don't worry about the TTL (Time to Live) for now. You will most likely enter at least two MX records. One is the primary record; it will have a lower priority number like 10. This is the first server the system tries; if it's down for some reason, the system tries the second server. That entry will have a higher priority number, like 20. You may need to enter three or four MX records.

Type ⓘ	Name ⓘ	Data ⓘ	TTL ⓘ	Delete	Edit
☐ A	@	Parked	600 seconds	🗑	✎
☐ NS	@	ns19.domaincontrol.com.	1 Hour	Can't delete	Can't edit
☐ NS	@	ns20.domaincontrol.com.	1 Hour	Can't delete	Can't edit
☐ CNAME	www	aipromptperfect.com.	1 Hour	🗑	✎
☐ CNAME	_domainconnect	_domainconnect.gd.domaincontrol.com.	1 Hour	🗑	✎
☐ SOA	@	Primary nameserver: ns19.domaincontrol.com.	1 Hour	🗑	✎

FIGURE 2-5:
The account admin can add, delete, and edit the DNS records.

Priority	Address
10	mx.zoho.com ✓
20	mx2.zoho.com ✓
50	mx3.zoho.com ✓

FIGURE 2-6:
You need to enter these MX records so that your email works.

How do you access your business email accounts?

There are four main ways to access your email:

» You can access your email by going to the website and logging in. You open a browser and navigate to something like `workspace.google.com` or `mail.zoho.com` to log in. Then you can see your emails in your browser. This is a good option if you work at a desk all day long.

» You can use the POP (Post Office Protocol) delivery method to install your email on your phone or desktop software, like Outlook or Apple Mail.

>> You can IMAP your email on your phone, desktop, or other device. IMAP stands for Internet Message Access Protocol and it's the newer of the two methods.

>> You can download an app if one is provided and open the app on your device.

POP and IMAP allow you to use software on your desktop (such as Outlook or Mail), tablet, or smartphone device (like the mail application) to access your email. When you set up your email addresses, you get instructions on how to set up your email application. These instructions include things like login name, the incoming mail server and port, the SMTP server and port, and so on.

Figure 2-7 shows the Zoho Mail options. It's a good idea to record this information so that you can set up new devices quickly.

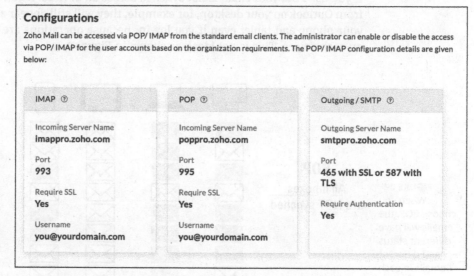

Configurations

Zoho Mail can be accessed via POP/ IMAP from the standard email clients. The administrator can enable or disable the access via POP/ IMAP for the user accounts based on the organization requirements. The POP/ IMAP configuration details are given below:

IMAP ⑦	POP ⑦	Outgoing / SMTP ⑦
Incoming Server Name **imappro.zoho.com**	Incoming Server Name **poppro.zoho.com**	Outgoing Server Name **smtppro.zoho.com**
Port **993**	Port **995**	Port **465 with SSL or 587 with TLS**
Require SSL **Yes**	Require SSL **Yes**	Require Authentication **Yes**
Username **you@yourdomain.com**	Username **you@yourdomain.com**	

FIGURE 2-7: Your email host provides these settings so that you can set up Outlook, Mail, or other email applications on your devices.

While you are setting up your accounts, you can choose to POP or IMAP your email. Whenever you have the option, choose IMAP, the newer protocol. The reason is that IMAP syncs your email across all of your devices. If you delete 30 emails on your phone, when you look at your email box on your iPad, you will not see those emails, because they will be deleted there as well. IMAP performs operations on the central email box. So, if you read an email in Outlook on your desktop and then you look at your email box on your phone, the email will appear as read. Figure 2-8 shows how all the devices reflect the read status when you use IMAP.

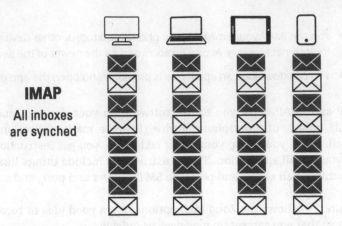

FIGURE 2-8: When you are setting up your devices to receive mail, choose IMAP so that your devices will be synched.

IMAP
All inboxes are synched

If you use POP, your email is not synched across all devices. If you delete 30 emails from Outlook on your desktop, for example, they will still appear as new emails on your phone and tablet even if you log in, because operations are performed only on each device. This is not ideal, as shown in Figure 2-9.

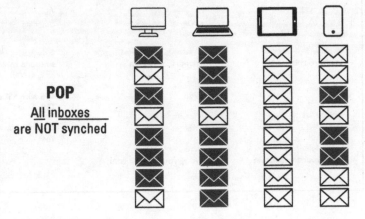

FIGURE 2-9: When you choose POP, the emails will have different status and different emails in each application.

POP
All inboxes are NOT synched

AUTHOR SAYS

Choose IMAP whenever possible.

One last thing: It may sound simple, but is also important: When you set up your emails on the email host, there's also a space for you to put the sender's first and last name in plain text. Make sure that you type the first name and last name correctly, with proper capitalization and punctuation, so that when people receive emails from you, they look professional: Don't use all lowercase letters. Use capital J for John — these small details show that you're professional and care about the details. Don't you want to put your most professional foot forward? Of course, you do! And that's what I want for you too!

2

Creating a Site That People Will Visit

Creating a compelling site that visitors will return to

Learning how search engines rate content and using that knowledge to your benefit

Using keywords strategically

IN THIS CHAPTER

» **Defining a buyer persona**

» **Triggering an emotional response from your visitors**

» **Considering UI and UX when designing your site**

» **Designing with the modern website in mind**

» **Selling the why to your visitors**

Chapter **3**

Resonating with Visitors

When creating your website, it's important to appeal to your target audience with a *UI* (user interface) and *UX* (user experience) that speaks to their aesthetic and solves their pain points. Your website needs to resonate with your customers' real pain points. When you get an emotional response from your visitors, you are more likely to see them coming back and spending more time at your site. This chapter explains how to do all this. You start by defining your buyer personas.

Defining Buyer Personas

Buyer personas, often simply referred to as personas or avatars, are fictional, generalized representations of your customers. They can represent your ideal customer, your worst customer, and all in between. They help businesses better understand their target audience. These personas are usually based on research, data, and educated speculation. In essence, buyer personas allow businesses to humanize their target audience segments, leading to more empathetic, effective, and strategic decisions across various facets of the business.

The process of creating buyer personas often involves collecting data from customer-facing team members. It's essential to ensure that the personas are grounded in real-world information and not just based on assumptions. You should also regularly update and refine these personas as markets change, new products are developed, or the company's direction shifts.

You need to document your persona's demographic details, interests, and behavioral traits. You'll then understand their goals, pain points, and buying patterns. You will have multiple buyer personas, and you should create multiple ones.

The importance of buyer personas

If you want to be successful, you should understand your customers and what motivates them. Creating buyer multiple buyer personas can help you fine-tune your marketing messages. They allow you to speak directly to the heart of your customer. Buyer personas provide many benefits:

>> They help you identify different types of customers right away, so that you have a more defined and better way to communicate effectively with each type.

>> You can quickly and easily react to key topics that matter most to your customers. This can help keep customers loyal and happy.

>> You are better able to spot a terrible customer right away, so you don't continue to make mistakes taking on customers who are not good for your business.

>> You can "categorize" your customers. This will allow you to attract the most valuable visitors, leads, and customers to your website and business.

WHY THE BUYER PERSONA IS SO IMPORTANT

EXAMPLE

As a real-life example of creating a buyer persona, I had a customer that designed, built, and maintained organic gardens for high net-worth individuals' homes. The gardens were not inexpensive; they started at around $10,000. When my company first engaged the client, they talked about their juicy tomatoes and their crunchy red bell peppers and how yummy and fresh their vegetables were. We assumed that their messaging on their website should convey the quality of their produce and show lots of beautiful photos of their amazing veggies. We assumed people visiting the website would get excited about seeing these crunchy, colorful, delicious vegetables and they would spring into action to purchase a $10K garden because of the quality of the veggies.

Then we created buyer personas with the client. The buyer personas were representative of wealthy, stay-at-home moms who cared for their children, but also were very social. They played tennis and golf with friends and spent time practicing yoga or on self-care. We found this out by having the client walk us through a typical day in the life of these women, from the moment they woke up until the moment they went to bed. We found that the women who purchased these gardens were proud that they were helping combat climate change with their gardens. The gardens gave them a sense of being part of a global community and tapped into their desire to give back. They proudly told their friends about their gardens and showed them photos. When their children were home, they loved that they were providing a non-screen experience for their children: that they were teaching their children where food came from and encouraging them to be part of the process.

These people could go to a farm stand each week or to Whole Foods and buy all the organic vegetables they wanted for *much* less than the cost of the garden. Going through our exercise, we realized quickly that our client was not selling organic vegetables to these people, they were selling a *lifestyle*. We needed the website to have *lifestyle* messages, tag lines, videos, and photos of families and children in their gardens in beautiful back yards.

This also helped us realize the garden's competition. The garden was in competition with adding a pool. A pool is something that provides a family experience, the same with the garden. So, the primary motivator for having one of these gardens was not the actual produce, but the experience. The experience that a beautiful, organic garden gives the client: how the organic garden eased their mind, because they were helping to combat climate change. The garden also gave them a sense of power and control.

Determining these prime motivators changed how this client markets to potential new customers.

To talk to the very heart of potential customers, you need to find their central pain points, and their central reasons for purchasing, which may not be what you think they are. Digging deeper, you can find their true motivators and resonate with them. That way, they will at least reach out to you to find out more.

TIP

This may be the most important takeaway from this book: Resonate with your customers' real pain points and motivators and you will find success. Build your online presence around these motivators.

Create a buyer persona

There are tons of templates and guides on the Internet to help you create a buyer persona, and I provide a template in Figure 3-1. To download the Buyer Persona Template, go to www.dummies.com/go/buildingdiywebsitesfd. It helps to have someone else do this exercise with you.

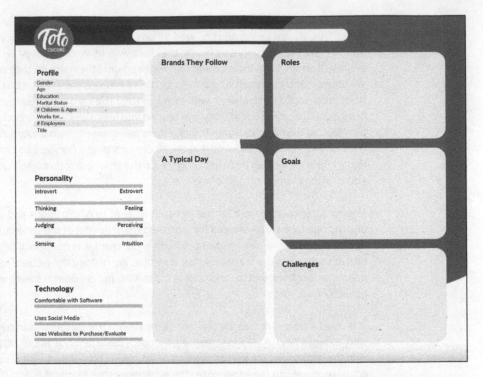

FIGURE 3-1:
You can use this buyer persona template to create your own buyer personas.

Start by thinking of a typical client that you love working with. You might have a few types of clients that you love working with; if so, you can eventually create a separate buyer persona for each type of client. However, to begin, think of one client who you love and base the answers on this client.

First, determine the basics:

» Person's age, working status, and title

» Education status, marital status, and children, if any

» Information about where they work, including the size of the company and the dynamics

One of the most important parts of creating a buyer persona is creating a timeline of a typical day. What time do they wake up, what do they do in the morning, afternoon, and evening, and then what they do until they go to sleep? A timeline provides insight into their priorities and pain points.

Also answer questions about what worries them daily, even if it has nothing to do with your business. This can certainly help you understand why they may purchase from you. Consider these questions:

- » Do they not have enough time?
- » Do they not have enough money?
- » Do they not have enough expertise?
- » Do they care about what others think of them?
- » Are they worried about doing a good job or keeping their job?
- » Are they worried about the health and well-being of their children or family?

Understanding your client's motivators can help you understand why they are buying from you. It may not have anything to do with what you are offering.

Part of creating buyer personas focuses on the roles, goals, and challenges your customers have:

- » The *role* that a buyer persona plays can tell you a lot about how to market to that persona. Once you know what their role is (volunteer, parent, manager, caretaker, CEO) and you know what they do and their worries, struggles, and pain points are in that role, you can create content that speaks to those specific roles.

- » Understanding your buyer personas' *goals* is a huge step forward to understanding your customer on a deeper level so that you can connect with them. You can offer a product or service to help them achieve their goals. Are they trying to impress their boss so that they don't lose their job and are relying on you to support them and make them look like a star? Are they trying to grow and scale their business so that they can sell it? Are they trying to get their children's friends to hang out at their house so that they can keep an eye on them? Understanding your buyer persona's goals helps you connect and resonate with them.

- » *Challenges* are the crux of the buyer personas: what are each persona's pain points? What keeps them from attaining their goals? Do they not have enough time? If so, marketing your service or product as a time saver is a great idea. Do they not have enough expertise in this area, and they need to get a job done? Marketing your service or product to support them in their job would be right on target. The more challenges you can identify, the more opportunities you have to deliver solutions. Delivering those solutions helps you not only bring in more leads but close more sales.

Some of this information may be difficult for you to determine, especially if you are a new company or you personally do not work directly with customers. Talk to the customer–facing employees at your own company to get a better sense of the people your company is already working with. Account managers and salespeople have the best insight into the lives of your clients, since they're in direct contact with them. If it's feasible, it's also a great idea to talk to some of your existing clients. Consider sending out a short survey to your main points of contact, asking them a little about themselves. You might have to send along a small incentive to get them to fill these out, but it's worth it.

At the end of the exercise, give each buyer persona a fictional name with an adjective. This makes them more relatable and helps teams easily refer to them. These names often reflect key characteristics or demographics of the persona. Examples include Supercharged Suzanne, Budgeting Bill, Gourmet Gary, Caviar Cathy, Eco-Friendly Ellie, Corporate Carla, or Time Consuming Tim.

REMEMBER

Don't forget to create buyer personas for your least favorite clients. Running through this exercise helps you determine why you are appealing to these types of customers. You will be better able to spot a potential bad fit right away so you don't waste time, money, and energy on these customers. You'll also learn how to avoid marketing to these types of customers.

As you can see, developing these buyer personas can be challenging, but this process is invaluable to growing your business.

Triggering Emotional Responses

Whether you like it or not, when visitors come to your website, they will have an emotional response.

REMEMBER

If you don't remember anything else from this book, remember this: You want people to come to your website and sigh out loud and say to themselves, "Yes! I have found what I am looking for!" *That*, my friends, is the ultimate goal of building a website.

Evoke emotional responses

If you have a website right now, think about what your visitors are feeling when they look at it. Does it evoke positive or negative feelings?

Website visitors translate feelings that they have about websites to actual companies, as well as to the services they sell. If visitors have a good emotional response, they are more likely to have a good initial impression of the company. If they have a bad emotional response, the opposite is true.

The *user experience* (UX) refers to the entire interaction visitors have with the website, including how they feel about the interaction. Emotions play into the UX in two main ways:

>> *They can motivate people to engage with you and make a purchase, or discourage them from doing so.* You want people to have a positive experience when viewing your website and feel a huge sense of relief that you are going to solve their problems.

>> *They affect the consumers' memory.* Each purchase is associated with some kind of emotion. You want people to remember your website and think thoughts such as "That was easy" and "I am excited to hear back from these people." You do not want them to feel frustrated, confused, misguided, stupid, and so on.

Good design and ease of use are both critical to creating a great UX. You can design better websites by simply making choices that lead to better design. You learn bits and pieces of better design throughout this book.

REMEMBER

You also may be nervous to put a website out for the world to see because you feel it is not perfect. Done is better than perfect. When you are building your website, do your best, but plan on making it better over time by incorporating good feedback. Remember: Your website is a work in progress!

The great thing about websites is that they are easy to iterate. If you want to make a change, you can make it right now and the change can be live for the world to see in a few minutes! If you gather feedback from your customers and others who view your website and implement changes based on that feedback, you are making new versions of your site, hopefully for the better.

Evoke positive responses

Here are some suggestions for the types of emotions you might want to elicit from your viewers, but you should think about any additional emotions that you want people to have when they visit your website. A great basic list of emotions your site should evoke might include these:

>> Relief/serenity

>> Trust/confidence

>> Satisfaction/happiness

>> Some level of excitement

The following sections cover some tips that can help you create a website that elicits a positive emotional response.

Be consistent

Consistency is a large part of sending a clear message as well as creating simplicity. Your UI (*user interface*) — which includes the screens, links, tabs, buttons, icons, and other visual elements that you interact with when using a website — should be consistent.

>> Choose one body font and one heading font and stick to them.

>> Choose a body font, size, and weight and stick to that font for most of your website (*size* is how big the font is and *weight* is how thin or thick the font is).

>> If you want to have a rounded edge on your buttons, say 30 pixels or so, then make sure that all of your buttons have a 30-pixel border radius.

>> If you want the font on your buttons to be bold and the letters in all upper-case, make sure this is consistent across your entire website.

>> When you choose images for your website, make sure they are all the same style of image. Images can be dark and mysterious, they can be blurred and give an "idea," they can be illustrations, sketches, and more. You don't have to use the exact style for all images but try to be consistent.

>> If you are adding *padding*, which is the space between an element's border and content, to your rows, keep that consistent as well — don't add 100px of padding on one row and then on the next, bump the text right up to the top of the row.

Be simple

You want a website that is simple to use. You want the site to logically guide viewers on how to use it. You don't want visitors spending energy trying to figure out where to find some piece of information.

Visitors expect certain kinds of information in certain places — in other words, they expect the UI to be simple. Make sure you put that content where it is expected. For example, if you receive a lot of calls, add your phone number to the top bar of your website. Also, add a Contact link to the footer of your website. If you have a Careers or Employment page, add that to the footer of your website. Add your logo to the top of each page, either on the top left, top right, or top center of your website. Your menu can be at the top, down the side, or behind a *hamburger menu* (the menu you sometimes see hidden behind three bars that looks like a hamburger bun), but add it somewhere so people can find it where they expect it.

Be exciting or inspirational

If you follow best practices when laying out your web pages and include content where it is expected, and if you guide people to the information they should look at, the next step is to add a touch of surprise and a wow factor. You can do that by adding design elements such a borders, icons, and images. Be sure you have the user experience basics down first — design consistently and simply — before moving on to these wow factors. You can go back over your pages and add elements that boast a bit of wow factor. . . and then you have an exciting and inspirational website! Thinking about UI and UX help you create a website that is easy to use, simple, and awe-inspiring!

Start thinking about any "wow" elements. Pay attention to what other websites are doing. Then, when it comes time to design and lay out your web pages, you have some ideas at the ready. This is a great time to bookmark websites that you like. If you start gathering these websites now, you will be way ahead of the game when it comes time to design your site.

Incorporating Modern Design Techniques

Modern website design is generally a good place to start when trying to make a website that is attractive and evokes positive emotions. Modern design also invokes trust because visitors assume that you are a modern company and that you stay up to date with the industry. You are not outdated and, therefore, you are more trustworthy.

One good way to see what is considered "modern" is to look at what the best companies out there are doing and build from those ideas. You can study how they do it and apply those strategies to your own website.

Start with larger companies. They have deeper pockets and are constantly iterating based on new data they gather from user interactions. They measure and use real data such as how far down a page users scroll, what they click on the most, which button colors are more effective, how long a visitor stays on a page, and so on.

There are many features that are considered part of "modern design," but this section sticks to ones that you can implement easily. Start by looking for websites that handle these elements well and think about how you can include some of these elements on your website.

Choosing a theme or page builder that has these built-in elements will give you a huge head start on creating a positive, emotive, and modern website.

Add vivid imagery and graphics

The power of great images cannot be underestimated. Take amazing photos when you can, or better yet, hire a professional photographer. Professional photographs are almost always much better. The best professionally taken photos are bright and crisp and colorful; they show off the service or product in an amazing way, so that visitors want the product innately. When your visuals are stunning, people will picture themselves in your photos and images. If you have the money, spend it on a photographer. It is worth it, and you can use the photos not only on your website, but in print material, social media posts, ads, and elsewhere.

You do not have to hire a photographer or take your own photos. You can use stock photography very effectively. If you use stock images, choose the best ones that do not look like stock. Stay away from stock images that are trite and overused, such as the typical example of a customer service agent smiling and wearing a headset or smiling coworkers around a desk. These are clearly stock images and will turn off visitors and could very likely erode trust in your site.

AUTHOR SAYS

Collages with illustrations and shapes

Layering images and shapes of all transparencies over each other can be pleasing and entertaining. This is modern technique that was only recently developed — it's sometimes called Memphis design. Figure 3-2 shows an example of layering an image with shapes.

FIGURE 3-2:
You can combine elements and place them on top of or behind other elements for a modern look.

Handmade graphics

Handmade graphics are images or graphics that are created just for your site. They can be fun and unexpected, and you can use handmade graphics in different, creative ways. For example, a few of my clients did not want to put real photos on their team page so they hired an illustrator to illustrate all the team members. Figure 3-3 shows these avatars created just for this company.

Meet Our Management Team

Marlo Schoeneman
President

Jonathan Bottoms
Vice President

Justin Eisenhaure
Director of Strategic
Development and Sales

FIGURE 3-3:
This client hired an illustrator to draw their team members as avatars.

I also have clients who have "mascots" on their websites, so they hired an illustrator to draw their mascots. Mascots can convey an idea in a fun and non-threatening way. Figures 3-4 and 3-5 shows these mascots.

TIP

You can easily find an illustrator on websites such as Fiverr or Upwork to create some custom illustrations just for you. It does not need to cost a fortune. They can make your website stand out and differentiate you from your competition. In addition, they show that you took the time and you care about your brand and company and website to spend a little time and energy on something different.

Videos

Using quality videos to explain the benefits of your product or service, or to show testimonials, can be just the push visitors need to reach out to you. Videos are great for showing how a product is used and assembled, for step-by-step processes, for telling a story, and for getting the visitors to like and trust you.

REDUCE RISKS & PROVIDE SUPERIOR SERVICE

Small business owners know that one job for a less-than-ideal customer can make the difference between a great business year... and re-considering our career choices.

How many times have you wished you could know just a bit more about a potential customer before agreeing to work with them? Will they demand endless changes? Will they pay on time? Will they pay at all?

With Report Customer^{SM}, you have the tools and information you need to build better customer relationships and avoid the headaches.

⊕ JOIN TODAY!

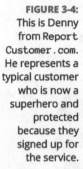

FIGURE 3-4: This is Denny from Report Customer.com. He represents a typical customer who is now a superhero and protected because they signed up for the service.

FIGURE 3-5: This is Rhody from 442lowe.com. Rhody makes dumpster rentals, junk removal, and moving fun and lighthearted.

Other modern typographic tips

Consider incorporating these tidbits into your site as well, to give it a modern feel.

> **Full width rows:** Designs that fill up the entire screen left to right are modern. Of course, they should be filled with the right message and imagery. They can

really make a great impact! One of the reasons full width rows indicate modern design is because it has only been recently that designers had the ability to code web pages this way.

» **Oversized typography:** Oversized typography is a fancy way of saying huge fonts! Try using huge fonts for headings or maybe a row with a call to action, as shown in Figures 3-6 and 3-7. Oversized fonts are fun, unexpected, carry a strong message, and make the visitor excited. They draw the user's attention to that section, so they can be used for vital sections and calls to action (CTAs). Also, when you use fonts that are really giant, all of a sudden, the letters become art.

SAVE TIME BUILDING YOUR WEBSITE AND AVOID FRUSTRATION

#TOTOCOACHING

FIGURE 3-6: Oversized typography can deliver a strong message when used properly.

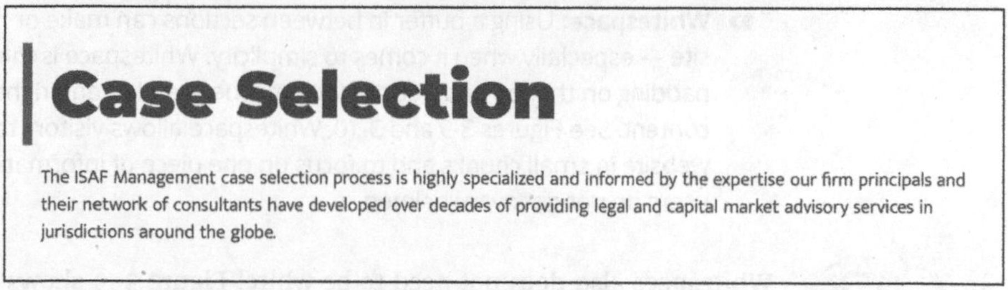

FIGURE 3-7: Oversized typography is also great for calls to action.

Case Selection

The ISAF Management case selection process is highly specialized and informed by the expertise our firm principals and their network of consultants have developed over decades of providing legal and capital market advisory services in jurisdictions around the globe.

» **Typographic heroes:** Rather than use sliders, where images slide and change, the modern approach uses a single, static, strong image that fills up the entire row. It's overlayed with a strong message. Figure 3-8 shows an example.

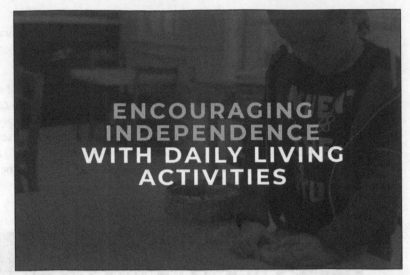

FIGURE 3-8:
A typographic
hero is an image
that fills up the
background of a
row on your
website,
overlayed with a
darker color and
a strong
message.

**ENCOURAGING
INDEPENDENCE
WITH DAILY LIVING
ACTIVITIES**

>> **Scrolling experiences:** An example of a scrolling experience is when the photo stays in one place and more of it is revealed as you scroll down the page. This may be a bit more difficult for you and you may not have the tools to create scrolling experiences. This can be called "parallax" or a "fixed" image placement.

When you are adding a background image to a row, column or module, you might see an option to add a parallax or fixed image. Try to implement some of these. Don't worry too much if your platform or page builder does not support it. But if you see this option, implement it on your website to see how it looks.

>> **Whitespace:** Using a buffer in between sections can make or break your site — especially when it comes to simplicity. Whitespace is the margins and padding on the top and bottom (and maybe even left and right) of your content. See Figures 3-9 and 3-10. Whitespace allows visitors to digest your website in small chunks and to focus on one piece of information at a time so users do not get overwhelmed

TIP

Whitespace also does not need to be white! Figure 3-9 shows the use of gray. It can be any color at all. Whitespace simply refers to the buffer you place around an element such as text or an image.

There are many more "ideas" about modern design — some are good and some are over the top. If you have ever looked *Vogue* magazine or watched models on a runway, you know that "modern" can get a bit carried away.

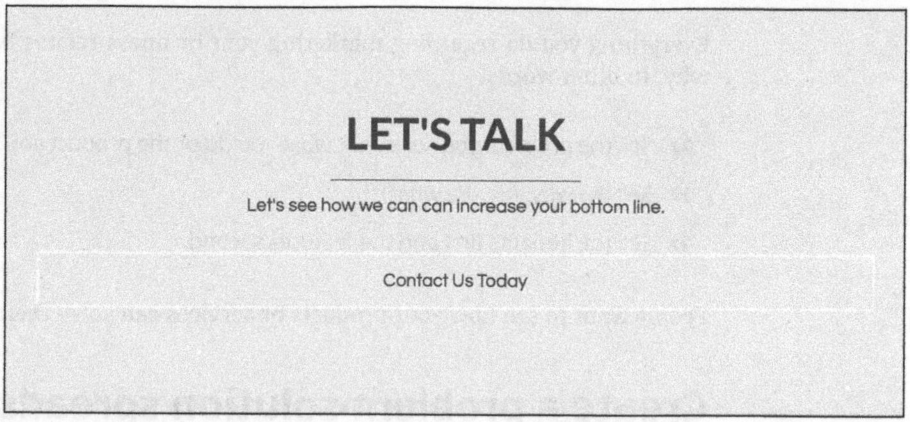
LET'S TALK
Let's see how we can can increase your bottom line.
Contact Us Today

FIGURE 3-9: Whitespace is simply blank padding added to the top, left, right, and left of any element on your page.

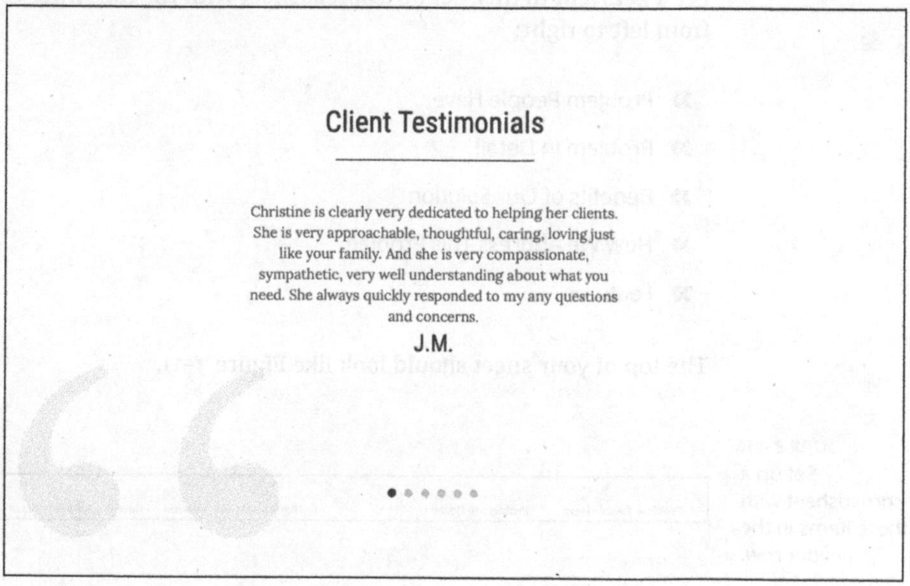
Client Testimonials
Christine is clearly very dedicated to helping her clients. She is very approachable, thoughtful, caring, loving just like your family. And she is very compassionate, sympathetic, very well understanding about what you need. She always quickly responded to my any questions and concerns.
J.M.

FIGURE 3-10: You can use a lot of whitespace for a dramatic look. The visitor can then concentrate on the message you are trying to convey.

You don't need to go there (unless you want to). The ideas in this section are a great start. If you focus on these, you will create something beautiful and resonate with visitors.

Selling the Why

This section contains a working exercise. Completing this exercise will save you so much time later on! If you have created a buyer persona, you are in the perfect spot to complete this exercise. This exercise ties all of these things together.

Everything you do regarding marketing your business relates back to selling the why. In other words:

>> Sell the problem you solve, not what you do or the product you sell.

>> Sell the why, not the what.

>> Sell the benefits first and the features second.

People want to see how your products or services can solve their problems.

Create a problem-solution spreadsheet

Let's get right to this. Set up a spreadsheet with the following columns at the top, from left to right:

>> Problem People Have

>> Problem in Detail

>> Benefits of Our Solution

>> How We Address This Problem

>> Features

The top of your sheet should look like Figure 3-11.

FIGURE 3-11:
Set up a spreadsheet with these items in the header row.

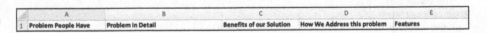

A	B		C	D	E
1 Problem People Have	Problem in Detail		Benefits of our Solution	How We Address this problem	Features

In the first column, Problem People Have, add 3-10 problems your product or service solves, one per row, in just a few words. Think about the problems that your customers have before they engage with you. Use a few words.

If you don't know your customer's problems or you are having trouble verbalizing them, find a mentor, spouse, friend, colleague, or someone you can talk to who is intuitive and ask them to help you answer this question. You can also read over your buyer personas and glean some great knowledge.

Another way to figure out the problems your customers have is to read your reviews. See what people say about your product and then add those items to your list.

Here are some ideas I came up with for my website-building business — note that they are short and to the point:

>> Not enough time

>> No budget

>> Frustrated

>> Don't know what to do first, second, and so on

>> Feeling of uncertainty

>> Website is coming out terrible

Once you have a few problems listed, fill out the second column, Problem in Detail. Next to each problem, provide more detail around this problem. My list is shown in Figure 3-12.

Now fill out the Benefits of Our Solution column. This should list the benefits of your solution or product that address each problem. These should be simple answers. My column is shown in Figure 3-13.

Finally, fill out the How We Address This Problem column. Take a minute to answer how your product or service addresses the problem that your customer is having in more detail. Your answers might look similar to Figure 3-14.

Now you need to fill out the last column, which is Features. Which specific features of your product or service help solve the problems? These should be short answers here. You might have multiple features that address the problems and provide the benefits. Figure 3-15 shows my list.

Utilize this information

Now that you have this amazing list of the problems your customer is facing, the benefits of your solution, and the features of your solution, you can do so many things!

>> Keep this information handy when building your pages and writing your content. If you have done a thorough job here, you just wrote a bunch of your website content. That is exciting because the place where most people get hung up when building a website is writing the content. And you are way ahead of the game here! If you did a really good job, you will be able to copy and paste what you wrote onto your Features or Service pages or maybe even your homepage. Amazing.

	A	B
1	**Problem People Have**	**Problem in Detail**
2	Not enough time	They don't have to research online blogs and videos on how to do something. The videos can be too fast, too slow, hard to understand, or not helpful in any way. Also, people do things out of order and this wastes time because if you don't do things in a building block style, you will spend time working on something and then going backwards, changing someting, and then you need to undo what you started.
3	No budget	Money is time so in that way we save money. Also, hiring a cheap developer will not give you the results you get in our course so you will be need to spend more money to get better results over time.
4	Frustrated	We get frustrated when we don't know how to do something that we either need to do or feel like we should know how to do. We also get frustrated when the steps for what we need to do are not clearly laid out like if we purchase build your own furnitre and the instructions are not included.
5	Don't know what to do first, second, etc	People love checklists, guides, and advice. When someone tries to build a piece of furniture without the order of what needs to happen in what order, most likely they will end up with extra parts and/or the unit will fall apart after a little while.
6	Feeling of uncertainty	When we do something new we don't have background experiece to know if we are doing something right or wrong. Lifting weights for example, if you do not have good form, you will hurt yourself. Once you know the form taught by an expert, you have confidence that you are lifting correctly. Same with websites, if you have never built one before, you do not know if you are doing it correctly.
	Website is coming out terrible	Everyone wants great results when they put in time, effort and money, otherwise why do anything? Also, we want to grow our business and the website is a tool to grow the business.

FIGURE 3-12: The Problem in Detail column describes the problem that people have before engaging with you.

FIGURE 3-13:
The Benefits of
Our Solution
column should be
short and should
directly address
the problems
people have.

	A	B	C
1	**Problem People Have**	**Problem in Detail**	**Benefits of our Solution**
2	Not enough time	They don't have to research online blogs and videos on how to do something. The videos can be too fast, too slow, hard to understand, or not helpful in any way. Also, people do things out of order and this wastes time because if you don't do things in a building block style, you will spend time working on something and then going backwards, changing someting, and then you need to undo what you started.	Saves people time
3	No budget	Money is time so in that way we save money. Also, hiring a cheap developer will not give you the results you get in our course so you will be need to spend more money to get better results over time.	Saves people money
4	Frustrated	We get frustrated when we don't know how to do something that we either need to do or feel like we should know how to do. We also get frustrated when the steps for what we need to do are not clearly laid out like if we purchase build your own furnitre and the instructions are not included.	Lessens frustration
5	Don't know what to do first, second, etc	People love checklists, guides, and advice. When someone tries to build a piece of furniture without the order of what needs to happen in what order, most likely they will end up with extra parts and/or the unit will fall apart after a little while.	People are given a path to follow
6	Feeling of uncertainty	When we do something new we don't have background experiece to know if we are doing something right or wrong. Lifting weights for example, if you do not have good form, you will hurt yourself. Once you know the form taught by an expert, you have confidence that you are lifting correctly. Same with websites, if you have never built one before, you do not know if you are doing it correctly.	Feeling of confidence that they are doing this right
7	Website is coming out terrible	Everyone wants great results when they put in time, effort and money, otherwise why do anything? Also, we want to grow our business and the website is a tool to grow the business.	Great results

	A	B	C	D
1	Problem People Have	Problem in Detail	Benefits of our Solution	How We Address this problem
2	Not enough time	They don't have to research online blogs and videos on how to do something. The videos can be too fast, too slow, hard to understand, or not helpful in any way. Also, people do things out of order and this wastes time because if you don't do things in a building block style, you will spend time working on something and then going backwards, changing someting, and then you need to undo what you started.	Saves people time	No more seraching online for information wasting time watching videos that are not answering your questions, are too technical, not technical enough, etc!
3	No budget	Money is time so in that way we save money. Also, hiring a cheap developer will not give you the results you get in our course so you will be need to spend more money to get better results over time.	Saves people money	All of the lessons we are teaching is what web developers would charge you thousands of dollars to do and you are doing this yourself.
4	Frustrated	We get frustrated when we don't know how to do something that we either need to do or feel like we should know how to do. We also get frustrated when the steps for what we need to do are not clearly laid out like if we purchase build your own furnitre and the instructions are not included.	Lessens frustration	Our program gives clear instructions in order and you breaks large tasks up, explains them clearly in non-technical language so you are not frustrated any more. Most of all, you are not trying to do this alone, you have a coach.
5	Don't know what to do first, second, etc	People love checklists, guides, and advice. When someone tries to build a piece of furniture without the order of what needs to happen in what order, most likely they will end up with extra parts and/or the unit will fall apart after a little while.	People are given a path to follow	it is helpful to have checklists, guides and advice and overall get a better product/result, which is what we provide.
6	Feeling of uncertainty	When we do something new we don't have background experiece to know if we are doing something right or wrong. Lifting weights for example, if you do not have good form, you will hurt yourself. Once you know the form taught by an expert, you have confidence that you are lifting correctly. Same with websites, if you have never built one before, you do not know if you are doing it correctly.	Feeling of confidence that they are doing this right	This course is taught by experts in web development, so students have confidence that they are building their site right.
7	Website is coming out terrible	Everyone wants great results when they put in time, effort and money, otherwise why do anything? Also, we want to grow our business and the website is a tool to grow the business.	Great results	Your wesbsite will be built correctly so that Google understands it and returns it in search, as well as visitors understand it and trust you and engage with you!

FIGURE 3-14: If you do this right, you can simply copy and paste this text on to your website where appropriate!

» If you choose to write a blog, you can think of a lot of blog posts that you could write around these topics.

» If you are launching a social media or ad campaign, you can use this sheet to talk directly to your customers.

Remember, instead of talking about how great your product or service is and addressing all the features it has, you should talk about how it can change lives and then back that claim up with the features that fix these problems.

	A	B	C	D	E
1	Problem People Have	Problem in Detail	Benefits of our Solution	How We Address this problem	Features
2	Not enough time	They don't have to research online blogs and videos on how to do something. The videos can be too fast, too slow, hard to understand, or not helpful in any way. Also, people do things out of order and this wastes time because if you don't do things in a building block style, you will spend time working on something and then going backwards, changing someting, and then you need to undo what you started.	Saves people time	No more seraching online for information wasting time watching videos that are not answering your questions, are too technical, not technical enough, etcl	All videos are in one place. All teachers are easy to understand Everything is already organized
3	No budget	Money is time so in that way we save money. Also, hiring a cheap developer will not give you the results you get in our course so you will be need to spend more money to get better results over time.	Saves people money	All of the lessons we are teaching is what web developers would charge you thousands of dollars to do and you are doing this yourself.	Course is affordable
4	Frustrated	We get frustrated when we don't know how to do something that we either need to do or feel like we should know how to do. We also get frustrated when the steps for what we need to do are not clearly laid out like if we purchase build your own furnitre and the instructions are not included.	Lessens frustration	Our program gives clear instructions in order and you breaks large tasks up, explains them clearly in non-technical language so you are not frustrated any more. Most of all, you are not trying to do this alone, you have a coach.	Large Tasks are Broken Up into Smaller Tasks. You are not building alone
5	Don't know what to do first, second, etc	People love checklists, guides, and advice. When someone tries to build a piece of furniture without the order of what needs to happen in what order, most likely they will end up with extra parts and/or the unit will fall apart after a little while.	People are given a path to follow	it is helpful to have checklists, guides and advice and overall get a better product/result, which is what we provide.	Classes are laid out in an organized fashion
6	Feeling of uncertainty	When we do something new we don't have background experiece to know if we are doing something right or wrong. Lifting weights for example, if you do not have good form, you will hurt yourself. Once you know the form taught by an expert, you have confidence that you are lifting correctly. Same with websites, if you have never built one before, you do not know if you are doing it correctly.	Feeling of confidence that they are doing this right	This course is taught by experts in web development, so students have confidence that they are building their site right.	Guidance given by seasoned experts
7	Website is coming out terrible	Everyone wants great results when they put in time, effort and money, otherwise why do anything? Also, we want to grow our business and the website is a tool to grow the business.	Great results	Your wesbsite will be built correctly so that Google understands it and returns it in search, as well as visitors understand it and trust you and engage with you!	Your website will be built correctly

FIGURE 3-15: These are short headlines that you can use all over your marketing materials: social media posts, brochures, videos, and of course, your website.

AUTHOR SAYS

The key is to educate your consumers. Teach your consumers. Have the heart of a teacher. When you educate others from your heart, people will see this, understand this, and will not even realize that they are learning.

When you approach your messaging from this perspective, it not only speaks directly to the pain points you are solving, but it also establishes you as an authority in your field, so it builds trust. Speaking to the consumer's heart and developing trust presell your product or service!

If you do this right, by the time a person reaches out to you, they are already partway sold. Now it is up to you to live up to those expectations and close the deal. That part is on you!

IN THIS CHAPTER

» **Thinking like search engines**

» **Learning how search engines rate content**

» **Doing things the right way (as a white hat)**

» **Gaining popularity and getting in with the "popular" group online**

» **Using structured data to your advantage**

Chapter **4**

Nailing SEO Basics: Search Engine Optimization 101

G rasp ing the concepts in this chapter and applying them to your online ventures will exponentially increase your chances of building a successful website that users can find when searching. The insights in this chapter form the foundation of how websites gain visibility online, and undoubtedly, you want your site to be discovered.

Many self-made website creators, who aren't professional developers, often over-look the information presented in this chapter. That's a shame, because it doesn't matter how fantastic your site looks or how great the information on it is if your potential customers/users can't find you. This chapter explains how to make sure that doesn't happen. For lots more about SEO, turn to Chapter 12 after you've mastered these basics.

Grasping Search Engine Basics

When most people think of a search engine, they think of Google because it's by far the biggest and most popular search engine, but there are many others as well. It's so popular, people even use the name of the search engine as a verb: "Google it!"

You are probably familiar with how a search engine works: You navigate to a search engine like Google, DuckDuckGo, Firefox, or Bing, and you type in the problem you are having or the question you want to ask into the search box.

You are then presented with a list of options that relate to your search term(s). This list is called your *search results* and the page that comes back with the search results is called the *SERP* (the *Search Engine Results Page*).

Websites are also ranked by popularity, often using SEO tools (such as Moz, Ahrefs and Semrush). The more popular a website is, the higher the rank it gets.

If your website is considered by search engines to be very popular, it is more likely to be looked upon in a favorable way because a search engine's business model is to give people the best answer to their questions. When searchers are satisfied with the search results, they will continue to use that search engine.

Popularity, in the Internet world, is judged by a few factors — one of those is by looking at what other websites link to your website. These are called backlinks and are covered in more detail later in this chapter.

The ranking scale that Moz developed, *domain authority*, is referenced most often when talking about this concept. A higher domain authority score indicates that a website is more popular, and there is a higher likelihood of that website ranking higher in the SERP. If search engines can also somehow associate your website with other "popular" websites that have a high domain authority, this is a good thing for your site.

All this is to say that the art and science of SEO is important if you want your site to be seen by potential customers/users.

Unraveling the Essentials of Search Engine Optimization

Search Engine Optimization (SEO) is the process of making specific modifications to your site so that it is returned in the SERP when people search for certain terms (called *keywords*, and covered in more detail in Chapter 5). You want the best results in the SERP, which means you want your website to be returned near the top when someone searches for a term that is related to your offer/product.

You want search engines to match your website with the searcher's intent. That's where SEO comes in. When you "optimize" your website for search engines, you do a few specific things that make your site more understandable and readable by them.

There are specific places where Google and other search engines look for keywords. You want to put those keywords and phrases in your headlines, the title of the page, the URL of the page, the filenames of the images you upload, and more. When you use these keywords in strategic places on your website, search engines can interpret your content accurately.

When search engines understand your website and view your website as a trusted source, they are more likely to return your website higher in the SERP.

AUTHOR SAYS

Do you *have* to optimize your website? No, of course not. Many websites are not optimized for search at all. But, if your competition is optimizing their website for search and you're not, there is a pretty good chance your competition will get more leads than you. If most of your business originates from the Internet, you should be optimizing for search.

Think like a search engine

If you were to enter a competition, one of the first steps you most likely would do after registering would be to determine the criteria for first place. You would then make sure that you practiced for the competition, and you did the things that you needed to do to have a shot at first place.

Think the same way about your website! If you want to be returned in a top position on the SERP, you need to know the rules and criteria so that you can add those things to your website.

In addition, remember that search engines such as Google, Bing, Yahoo!, and DuckDuckGo are businesses. They have a business model, just like you do. They want to attract Internet users to their search engines and keep them coming back. To do that, they need to provide a great experience. It's in each search engine's best interest to be the industry leader at indexing (or in other words, making a searchable record of) every website. They must produce the most relevant search results to their users. Otherwise, users won't come back.

In the early days of the Internet, many websites used to be full of links to other websites. There was no unique content or valuable information on those pages; they were just a sea of links, or even just a big list of keywords, without any helpful information. Figure 4-1 shows a current example of this. Imagine if you were looking for information and you got to a page with just links, or just a paragraph that had the words that you typed in repeated many times. You would feel cheated and frustrated, and you would probably start using a different search engine. This is the foundation of the search engine business model.

| 22,300 | With | 2,724,400 | And | 243,912,200 | For | 2.8 Million USD |
| Domains sold since 2014 launch | | Referring domains in total | | Visits for all domains ever owned | | To 2200+ happy buyers |

yammet.com   mymercy.net   mag20.com   lawebcenter.com   sedopropartnerforum.com   bentonharborlibrary.com   910jr.com

prosolutionreviews.net   caravan-park-anglesey.co.uk   turnmeon.co.uk   action4life.com   fgmlandscaping.com   hess-timber.com

harpethtechnologygroup.com   sky-is-falling.co.uk   gets.com   madebyarchetype.com   allstunt.com   music-soul.com   877paduilaw.com

situk.org.uk   dawnstitches.com   acbscare.co.uk   bvjhotel.com   cinemarenefallet.fr   noniecrete.com   nittanyvillage.com   pixelsmithy.com

autenticoecuatoriano.com   cafe-stein.com   holidayonlinerentals.com   publicip.net   valdresflya.com   homeprc.com

bluewater-solutions.com   trinitystudio.com   weddingcliqs.com   osakaflights.com   notepc-repair.com   gmcmidwestclassics.org

terra-form.org   mindenmemories.net   doll-doll.com   movierange.com   cheappiercings.com   scgolfcenter.com   dpnkh.com

theslumflower.com   languageoflightmusic.com   customerchampions.co.uk   studiosource.com   justwaterpumps.com.au   voipits.com

FIGURE 4-1:
Link-filled pages still exist today but you rarely see them in the search results.

The search engines realized that those link-filled or keyword-filled pages were not valuable, so they created their own algorithms (their own computer formulas) to decide which websites were relevant to a particular search term. They've spent many years and billions of dollars improving and perfecting those algorithms, and their algorithms are very closely guarded secrets.

Nobody knows each search engine's exact algorithms, but the search engines do share some information about how they work. For example, they do reveal what information the search engine is looking for and where they look for that information. This is so that web developers (like you and me) can set up their websites in a way that plays nicely with the algorithms.

TIP

You want to set up your website so that the search engines understand what you are offering, consider it to be valuable and relevant to a searcher's keywords and phrases, and return your website high in the SERP, hopefully above your competitors.

Understand search intent

Returning great quality websites comes down to the search engines understanding the searcher's *search intent*. They need to figure out the *why* behind each search so that they can return the best results. You need to understand search intent as well.

Search intent is *the reason why* someone types a query into a search engine. Imagine you're looking for "how to make pancakes." Your intent might be to find a recipe, rather than learn about the history of pancakes. Search engines, like Google, try their best to figure out your intent so they can show you the most relevant results. It's all about understanding what you're *really* looking for!

Remember this as you build your website and write your content. If you want search engines to return your website, you need to understand the searcher's search intent.

Provide complete content

After a search engine figures out the search intent of a searcher, it needs to return the best websites. One of the factors that determines the "best" website is how thorough the content on the website is. Search engines want what is called complete content. This is content that fully answers the searcher's question, as well as the every possible follow-up question. The goal is to ensure that the user is satisfied when they visit your site.

Eating the Acronym Soup: HCU, YMYL, and E-E-A-T

If you want to create a website that returns high upon searching, you need to focus on a few things:

>> HCU (Helpful Content Update or Unhelpful Content Classifier)

>> The YMYL concept

>> The E-E-A-T concept

Helpful content update

Google's Helpful Content Update (HCU) is part of their algorithm that helps them rank pages on the SERP. It reinforces the idea that Google wants you to provide thorough, complete, helpful content on your website. Search engines are more likely to return a website if the content answers the following questions, which you can find directly on Google's website (see https://developers.google.com/search/blog/2022/08/helpful-content-update):

>> Do you have an existing or intended audience for your business or site that would find the content useful if they came directly to you?

>> Does your content clearly demonstrate first-hand expertise and a depth of knowledge (for example, expertise that comes from having used a product or service, or visiting a place)?

>> Does your site have a primary purpose or focus?

>> After reading your content, will someone leave feeling they've learned enough about a topic to help achieve their goal?

>> Will someone reading your content leave feeling like they've had a satisfying experience?

>> Are you keeping in mind our guidance for core updates and for product reviews?

The HCU is in place now. If you are simply posting articles with points that other articles have pointed out, this article is not helpful and will be tagged as such. In a nutshell, you need to write something new and different, and not regurgitate information.

TIP

Many people are using a large language model (LLM) such as ChatGPT to write articles these days. If you use content provided by an AI writing assistant such as ChatGPT without adding your own information or your own perspective, you are simply regurgitating other information found on the Internet, which lowers your HCU. It's more valuable to go beyond what anyone can find on the Internet and provide your unique business perspective. Chapter 8 talks more about using AI to write content.

The YMYL concept

This stands for Your Money Your Life and is a term that Google uses to describe concepts, topics, and websites that impact a person's health, happiness, safety, or financial stability. YMYL topics are ones where a person viewing the content may be harmed.

Some examples of YMYL websites include:

>> **Medical information sites:** Think of health advice, symptoms, treatments, and so on.

>> **Financial advice sites:** Information about investments, taxes, retirement planning, buying insurance, and so on.

>> **Legal advice sites:** Details about laws, legal procedures, rights, and so on.

>> **News and current events:** Especially those that provide information about critical topics like politics, business, and science.

>> **Safety information:** Tips or guidelines on ensuring personal and public safety.

Google applies very high page quality (PQ) standards to websites containing such topics because of the stakes involved.

Sites that do not fall under YMYL are fashion sites, entertainment sites, traveling, hobbies and more. If you are building a site that does not fall under YMYL, you don't necessarily need to adhere to these guidelines. However, if you do you will have a better chance at making a great website.

WARNING

If you have a blog or a website that is in a YMYL industry, you must be an authority on this subject and be very careful to document and cite your research, discoveries, opinions, and advice. Be transparent with who created the content on your website, how that content was created, and why the content was created. If you do not do this, Google may flag your content for having low-quality YMYL advice and you will drop in the SERP.

I just saw an example of this. A potential client in the financial industry came to me wondering why in 2018/2019 they dropped tremendously in the SERP. They were not following the YMYL guidelines, so they needed to make the required changes to move back up in the SERP.

The good news is that if you fall under the YMYL category and your information is reliable, Google will give extra weight to your pages. This can actually boost your SEO results!

The E-E-A-T concept

E-E-A-T (Experience, Expertise, Authoritativeness, and Trustworthiness) is a set of criteria used by Google's human quality raters to evaluate the quality of web pages.

Google rolled out this update in 2018 in a core update for their Quality Raters (these are human beings who spot-check websites). The raters rate not only the websites themselves, but also the authors or content creators. The Quality Raters give this information to Google to make their indexing and search algorithms even better. E-E-A-T helps them do this.

While E-E-A-T applies to all websites, it's especially critical for sites that fall under the YMYL category. High-quality content that showcases experience, expertise, authoritativeness, and trustworthiness can lead to better user trust and potentially better search engine performance.

Experience

The first E stands for *experience*. You want to show your experience on your website. Imagine a seasoned architect who has overseen numerous building projects over the years. That hands-on involvement and accumulated knowledge from real-world scenarios is what Google means by experience. It's the practical insights and understanding gained from actively engaging with a particular field or discipline.

Expertise

The second E stands for *expertise*. In the context of evaluating website content, especially from the perspective of search engines like Google, expertise refers to the depth of knowledge or skill in a particular subject demonstrated by the content. If the content is from someone with a deep understanding or proficiency in a certain topic, it's considered to have high expertise. This becomes important in topics where accuracy is vital, such as medical or financial advice. Basically, it's like asking, "Is the person behind this content knowledgeable in their field?"

Are you an expert in your field? You need to show that. This can include also what is called "everyday expertise," meaning that you have first-hand experience with something. For example, my previous dentist filled some cavities that I had. Then I found out that he had never had a cavity in his life! So, he had no idea what it felt like to be in the chair getting one filled! He knew what it felt like to be a dentist filling the cavity, but I was more of an expert than he was on getting a cavity filled. That is considered everyday experience. Let Google know that you are qualified to provide valid and important information to others. List all your certifications, degrees, memberships, awards, speaking engagements, anything at all that shows you as an expert in your field. You also want to place a detailed author bio on your website and give it to other websites where you may guest blog.

Authoritativeness

The A stands for *authoritativeness*. This is all about the credibility and respect that a content creator or website has earned in its field or topic area. It's like when you think of a top expert or a go-to source in a particular domain; that's authority.

Search engines look at things like backlinks from reputable sites, mentions of the author or site in respected publications, and other signals. In simple terms, it's like asking, "Is this source recognized and trusted by others in the industry or topic area?". Post your formal education and qualifications on your website to back up what you say. Do you have a formal degree or certificate in this area? How about work experience? You can also include relevant life experiences if you do not have a formal degree or work experience, although you need to make sure it is legitimate. Do you have reviews you can post? Conferences where you have presented? Articles you have written? Start documenting what makes you an authority in your field.

Trustworthiness

The final letter, T, stands for *trustworthiness* and is indicated by how dependable and credible a website or content source is. It's not just about accurate information, but also about the site's security, transparency in its dealings, and its history of user trust.

In the online world, search engines gauge trustworthiness through things like secure browsing (SSL certificates), user reviews, and transparent business practices. It's like asking, "Can I rely on this information without any doubts?" Google is answering this question: Is this source giving not only accurate information but are they also identifying themselves and are they a true resource to be trusted? Provide information on your website on the about page or on each article in an author bio that lets visitors know who you are, what you have done in this field, how you are qualified, and how to reach you via email or phone or another method like social channels. Google is going to look at your content and see if you are who you say you are.

TIP

In a nutshell, if you are an expert in your field, show it, and if you are not, do not write authoritatively as if you are. Be transparent. Be honest. Make your site secure (see Chapter 14). Document and cite your sources. If you do all this, you will be fine.

Wearing the Right Hat: Black Hat versus White Hat SEO

When building your website, it's essential to understand the distinction between black hat and white hat SEO practices. These terms represent two fundamentally different approaches to search engine optimization.

>> *White hat SEO* involves using ethical and legitimate techniques to improve your website's visibility in search engine rankings, focusing on high-quality content, user experience, and adhering to search engine guidelines.

>> *Black hat SEO* employs deceptive, manipulative, or unethical tactics that can result in short-term gains but often lead to penalties or long-term damage to your website's reputation and rankings.

Making the right choice between these approaches is crucial for the long-term success and sustainability of your online presence.

Black hat SEO techniques

You can think of black hat techniques as cheating. Cheating usually *seems* easier and gets you a better and faster result, while playing by the rules can harder and take longer.

Black hat SEO techniques are unethical and violate search engines terms of service and guidelines. Some try to manipulate algorithms, which can lead to greater visibility in search engine results pages (SERPs) in the *short term*, but in the long term this can be detrimental to website ranking and result in a penalty, or even worse, a search engine ban.

Other examples of black hat techniques include keywords stuffing and duplicate content:

>> *Keyword stuffing* is when you enter keywords into pages, page titles, or other places by placing (sometimes hidden) keywords in an unnatural way that don't read well or make sense. I am sure you have seen examples of this. Keywords are discussed in more detail in Chapter 5.

>> *Duplicate content* occurs when text is copied from another website. If you have thought maybe you will copy text from another website, just get that idea out of your head right now.

WARNING

Trying to cheat your way to the top doesn't work. Google will catch on eventually, and the consequences will be terrible for your business.

White hat SEO techniques

White hat SEO techniques are ethical approaches that adhere to search engines terms of service and guidelines. Here are the most important things you want to concentrate on when you are working on your website:

>> Provide unique, quality content

>> Include relevant keywords (Chapter 5 covers keywords)

>> Cite high authority backlinks (see the next section)

>> Link internal links to other content on your website

>> Develop structured data markup (see the section titled "Recognizing Structured Data Opportunities" in this chapter)

>> Check your page speed (see Chapter 12 on optimizing your images and content)

Realizing the Importance of Backlinks

As mentioned, one of the important ways that a search engine can determine how popular your site is by any *backlinks*.

A backlink is simply a link to your website from another website. You might also hear backlinks also called "incoming links" or "inbound links" and the sites that link to your website are called "referring domains."

Other websites or referring domains will link to your website if they view your website as important. You can think of a backlink to your website as a vote of confidence! Search engines use backlinks to determine the value of your website.

REMEMBER

The quality of the backlinks your website has is more important than the sheer number. If you have backlinks from quality sites, search engines will associate your site with these quality websites and these sites will pass some authority over to your site. Likewise, if you have links from low-quality websites, search engines will associate your website with low-quality websites and not look as favorably on your site.

The great thing about having good backlinks is that most of the time once they are added to a website, they exist forever (as long as the referring website page and the page they link to on your website remain active), and having backlinks that are older are even better.

TIP

Your website has what is called a *backlink profile* even if you have no links yet to your website. Focus on developing a strong backlink profile, as this will help your site rise to the top of the SERP.

REMEMBER

Backlinks are one of the most important signals that search engines consider when they are ranking your website! Another website that is reputable will not link to a terrible website; they will only link to other reputable websites.

For example, if the BBC or *Forbes* were to write an article and include a link back to your website, this would be a really good thing, because these two websites have a domain authority in the 90s. Figures 4-2 and 4-3 show their domain authority scores from Moz. Links from .edu or .gov sites tend to carry a lot of authority as well, as do news domains.

USING ANCHOR TEXT

In addition to the importance and score of the domain providing the backlinks, the text that is linked to your website is important as well. The anchor text is the clickable word, and there is a correlation between keyword-rich anchor text and higher SERP rankings. If the referring website can link keywords that match your keyword list, this will help your position in the SERP even more. The anchor text passes relevance signals, meaning that it can help people and search engines understand why the link is there in the first place, and explain how this other website is relevant to this topic.

TIP

Years ago, many people realized how important the anchor text was, and a practice called "Google Bombing" was started. Basically, you could get any web page to rank for a phrase that you chose by simply putting a link to that page on many referring websites with the same anchor text. If you're old enough, you may remember the "miserable failure" example of this! Many websites around the world posted a link to President George Bush's official bio page and used the search term "miserable failure" as the words that were linked: the anchor text. If anyone typed "miserable failure" as a search term into Google, George Bush's bio page would come up. Google realized this and added precautions to one of their updates, but this is an example of how the text that is linked, or anchor text, is important. Ideally, you want the anchor text to be keyword-rich text. For example, a link to this book that contains words such as How to Build a Website or "Web Building Book" would be much better than just the URL to the page on Amazon or to Wiley's website.

FIGURE 4-2:
The authority score given to Forbes from Moz. This is a very high number and is extremely difficult to achieve.

FIGURE 4-3:
The BBC's website has a very high authority score. If you were able to secure a link from this website, it would help your authority score immensely.

Types of backlinks: follow and nofollow

There are a few types of backlinks. The ones you should know about now are follow and nofollow links.

A *follow link* is the most popular type of link and is a simple link back to your website with no parameters. When the follow link is created, the text, button or an image is linked to your URL. This is the default way of linking. Most of the time you make follow links when you link to another page on your website or if you link to another website. With a regular follow link, the domain authority or page authority from the referring website, the one that creates the link, is passed to the target website.

There is a way to create a link and not pass trust or authority to the target website. This is called a nofollow link. A *nofollow link* supposedly does not pass any authority over to the referred domain. The `nofollow` tag tells search engines to ignore that link. To create a nofollow link you simply add this code to the link: `rel="nofollow"`.

When you obtain links to your website from other referring domains, find out whether they will give you a follow or nofollow link. If this is a reputable website with a high domain authority, you really want a follow link. If you are trying to build links to your site and you are doing research, you may see that the referring website will offer a nofollow link. If you have only so much time and effort for link building, you want to focus on websites that will give you a follow link.

Black hat vs white hat backlinks

There are black hat backlinks and white hat backlinks. Black hat backlinks are spammy and frowned upon by search engines. They can lead to not only lower rankings in the SERP but also to a search engine ban. You do not want black hat backlinks.

On the other hand, white hat backlinks help you rise in the SERP. You want white hat backlinks.

WARNING

Many companies claim that they can give you tons of backlinks for a fee. Find out what types of links you'll get and determine where they are placing links to your site. There is a pretty good chance that they will try to take advantage of your lack of knowledge and give you horrible black hat links that can be unrecoverable. There are different ways that companies do this, for example they may build a lot of websites and create links between them in wheels or a hierarchy to try to trick Google.

EXAMPLE

A few years ago, I was hired by a landscaping company in Reading, PA to help them with their website. The owner was not getting any traction, and in addition, he was paying $600 a month to a company that was supposed to be helping him with SEO and rank for the words "residential landscaping Reading." I met with his account rep at the SEO agency over the phone and asked him where he was getting the backlinks placed — I wanted a list of websites. The rep answered me, "That's our secret sauce." This was a huge red flag! I used a tool to find some of the links to his website. What I discovered was horrible. This company was creating fake blog posts and then linking to his website. Figure 4-4 shows some of these pages.

I found example after example after example of this. They were not only doing this to my client, but they were also doing this to hundreds, if not thousands, of other unsuspecting, uninformed businesses. If are planning on hiring someone to help you with backlinks, do your research and make sure they are legit.

Discover More About The Mounting Relationship In Residential Landscaping Reading

By Andrew Ward

Recently, maintainability offers possessed the unmistakable anyway challenged put on people in general arrangement. While couple of inquiry the basic thought person life on planet should in the end be enduring, the exact related with this expression, particularly in metropolitan scene keeps on being liable to substantial contradiction. Therefore there should be a phenomenal requirement for substantially more explicit edges for understanding and applying urban view manageability like in residential landscaping reading.

Therefore, sustainability within urban surroundings has become an essential topic due to perceptions associated with environmental destruction. However, they have also turn out to be salient individuals have using quality of life within their communities. Confronted with diverse and frequently contradictory objectives, many interests have took on indicators regarding urban panorama sustainability being an approach to creating a more particular definition as well as implementation which are of importance inside their context.

FIGURE 4-4:
If you purchase backlinks, your website might be linked from a website like this.

Discovering your backlinks

One good way to see your backlinks for free is to log into Google Search Console and, on the left menu, click the tab called Links. You can then see your backlinks.

There are also a lot of tools — some free and some paid — that you can use to discover your backlinks. Ahrefs has a popular Free Backlink checker, and Semrush and Moz have legitimate tools that can help you find your backlinks.

Ridding your site of toxic backlinks

Now, what if you find out that you have a ton of backlinks to your website from spammy, low domain authority websites? You can tell Google to disavow your links. Create a file that includes all of the toxic domains or toxic pages you have links from and upload it to Google Search Console. This tells Google that your site is not associated with these websites so they should not pass their low authority over to your website.

WARNING

Check out this article on how to disavow toxic links: https://support.google.com/webmasters/answer/2648487?hl=en. However, use this tool with caution. If you use this incorrectly, you can potentially harm your site's performance in Google Search results. Keep in mind that part of Google's job is to assess which links to trust without your guidance, and Google claims that most sites do not need to use this tool.

Obtain white hat backlinks

There are some quick and easy ways you can get some backlinks — the rest is hard work! The process of getting links is called *link building*. You get backlinks by either outright asking for them or because your content is good enough that another site chooses to link to it.

Here are some ways you can obtain backlinks to your website:

>> Include links to your website from your social media channels. Set up social media profiles on all the platforms and then link back to your website.

>> Many associations have a public online directory where they list a link to your website. Chambers, networking groups, clubs, and associations are good places to look.

>> Ask blog owners of reputable, informative blogs in your industry if you can write a guest post. Then, write an amazing article with an author bio and ask for a follow link back to your website.

>> Ask your local paper or better yet, a regional or national paper to do a story on your company or organization. This is a great way to obtain a backlink that is high authority.

>> Write amazing, complete how-to guides or other content, and then ask other websites in your industry to link to your valuable content. This is sometimes called *reverse outreach*. This needs to be a comprehensive guide with great, valuable information. It is even better if there are not a lot of articles already online about this topic.

>> Publish free guides or a free tool is great, as other websites might want to link to your free guide or tool to help their visitors.

>> Check if there are unlinked mentions of your brand on the Internet, meaning your brand was mentioned but they did not link to your website. When you find these, ask the websites to include a link.

>> Check with your suppliers or those you supply to. Will they link to your website? Do a bit of research on their websites and see if there is a natural spot where they could link or ask your rep.

>> Many industries grant awards. Find those websites behind the awards and see what the application process is like. Determine if you can receive a follow backlink to your site.

>> Some people use the broken link method and this can be effective but takes some time. If you install the Chrome extension called Check My Links and then visit websites in your industry, you can see using this tool to identify links that the website has provided that are broken. Then, write a great alternative to the broken link. Reach out to the webmaster that takes care of the site with the broken links. Tell them how much you love their content and that you found a broken link, but that you have created an alternative and they should link to your site.

>> Local directories and citations are important. If you provide services or products to a local area or if you are a brick and mortar store, you are known as a local business. You should set up directories and citations. There are two ways to do this: You can create your own directory listings or you can pay a service to set these up for you. Either way, this is very important.

>> HARO (Help a Reporter Out) is a website that matches experts and writers with journalists. Many journalists are looking for experts in fields to help them with their articles. You can create an account on the HARO system and you will be sent requests for articles.

>> Find influencers who like what you have to offer and see if they will link to your website. This is becoming a completely new and vibrant industry. There are influencer brokers you can contact as well.

>> Interview people, post the interview on your website, and then place a link to their website. They will most likely link back to this article.

There are many other ways to get backlinks, but you can see that it is not easy. It requires a bit of work on your end, but the results can pay off in the long run.

Recognizing Structured Data Opportunities

Structured data, schema markup, rich results, and Schema.org are helping search engines understand and present information on the web. You can implement structured data on your website, and you should!

Structured data does three main things:

>> It helps search engines understand your website and your content.

>> It helps your website get returned higher in search results.

>> It can lead to rich results, which are explained shortly.

Structured data is becoming more and more important. You don't need to know how to code schema markup, but you should understand these concepts so that if you see the opportunity to add them your website, you will know what they are and how they might boost your search results. In simplest form:

>> Schema markup is the computer code.

>> Structured data is the information you want to show.

>> Rich results are what is displayed on search engines.

>> Schema.org is where you get the code.

Organize your content with structured data

Structured data is just that: It is data with structure. Structured data is fields of information. At its core, structured data refers to a method of organizing and labeling content on a website in a standardized format, making it more accessible to search engines. Organizing and labeling information is key here.

When you go to the doctor, you most likely need to fill out a form about yourself. You enter your first name in the box where they want the first name. You enter your last name in the box where they want your last name. You may have to list past surgeries in another box. Then, when the doctor needs to review your information, they know exactly *where to look* to find your name and your recent surgeries. This data is structured, organized, and labeled. They don't have to read the whole page just to determine your name or date of birth.

Imagine if you had a piece of blank notepaper and you had to answer all the questions the doctor wanted you to answer randomly on this notepaper. It would be a mass of words and sentences and paragraphs, and the doctor would have a hard time finding your past surgeries on this page. This is unstructured data. Unstructured data does not have a structure — it is not organized or labeled.

The same is true for web pages. If you simply type the benefits of one of your services on the page, this is unstructured data.

With structured data, you enter it on your website into fields so that search engines understand it better. If you and I were to go to the same doctor, we would have completely different structured data: my name is different than yours and I have had different surgeries than you have had. We would put the information in the same fields on the form, but what we enter would differ. In the same way, the structured data I enter on my website will be different than the structured data you enter on your website because you and I have different data — different content — on our websites.

Rich results are the best results

Let's begin by looking at some real-life examples of structured data that appear as rich results. Have you ever looked up a recipe on Google? If you have, you most certainly have seen search results that look like Figure 4-5.

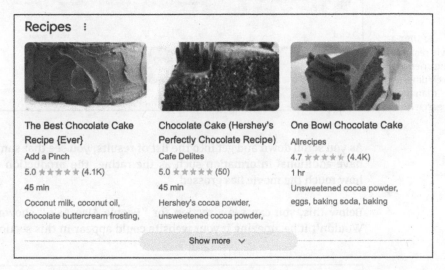

FIGURE 4-5:
When you look up a recipe on Google, sometimes the results look different.

You see that these results on the top of the page look different than the standard search results. If you scroll down past the top results, you can see a list of search results that looks typical of what a normal search would return, but you can see that there is additional information, as shown in Figure 4-6. Not only do you have the link to the web page (the URL), the title, and a description, but you also have the rating.

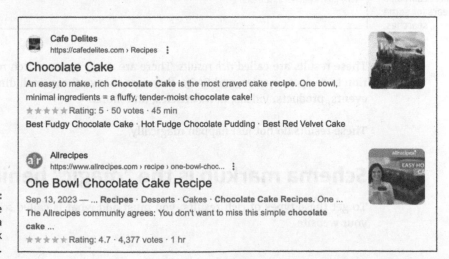

FIGURE 4-6:
Sometimes the results in a search look different.

Movie results are also returned differently. Figure 4-7 shows a search for Top Gun Maverick. This screen is definitely not your typical search results listing. You can see all kinds of information such as the rating, showtimes, cast, and more.

FIGURE 4-7:
Movie results are returned in the search differently than regular search results.

As you scroll down and get into the list of results, you see that some of the listings have additional information such as the rating, the production companies, and how much the movie has grossed.

Below this, you can see a section for "People Also Ask," shown in Figure 4-8. Wouldn't it be amazing if your website could appear in this section?

People also ask

Will Top Gun: Maverick be streaming?

Is Top Gun on Netflix or Amazon Prime?

How much was Val Kilmer paid for Top Gun: Maverick?

Why Meg Ryan not in Top Gun 2?

Feedback

FIGURE 4-8:
The People Also Ask section also appears for some searches.

These results are called *rich results.* There are many types of rich results. In addition to recipes, movies, and FAQs, there are many others, including job postings, events, products, videos, news articles, and more.

These results do not just happen magically.

Schema markup is the "magic" behind it all

To get these types of rich results, you must add what is called *schema markup* to your website.

Schema markup, a term often interchangeably used with structured data, is the actual code or tags you add to your website to provide more information about the content, such as reviews, events, products, and more.

When a search engine indexes a website and finds schema markup and structured data, it uses that information to interpret what your site is about in a better way and may return your website so that it includes more detail in the SERP, as outlined in the markup.

The way that Google presents websites with structured data is more enticing and more valuable. People are more likely to click on those "rich results" than to simply click on the title. If you are a local business, if you have events, if you are selling products, if you have a how-to or FAQ document on your site, installing structured data is a great way to help search engines understand your website and return it in the SERP.

Add schema markup to your website to get rich results

This section covers the basics of schema markup so you know it when you see it and can benefit from using it.

You can add schema markup in one of two ways:

>> By generating the code manually (using chema.org or technicalseo.com) and then adding it manually to your website

>> By using a tool

Because this book is not geared to website developers, generating schema markup manually is beyond its scope. Let's do this the easy way.

The most effective method for incorporating schema markup and structured data into your website entails using an existing platform, page builder, plugin, or modules that include structured data as a built-in feature. It's worth noting that not all web content requires schema markup; only specific content types benefit from it.

Here is a small list of content that supports schema markup:

>> Articles

>> Products

- » Events
- » Recipes
- » Reviews and ratings
- » Local business listings
- » Videos
- » FAQs
- » Books
- » Movies
- » Job postings

If you are adding any of these types of content to your website, choose software or modules that support structured data. The software comes with fields that you can fill in. When you're evaluating a module or plugin to determine if it supports structured data for your website, look for the following:

1. **Read the module description to see if it mentions structured data.**

2. **If you have modules installed, check them for schema markup features.** Look for settings related to structured data or schema markup in the module's interface. Some modules may offer a dedicated section where you can configure structured data for your content types (e.g., products, events, and articles).

3. **Contact the module developers or the support.**

4. **Look for extensions.** Some modules may not provide built-in structured data support but may have add-ons or extensions that offer this functionality.

The availability and level of structured data support can vary significantly from one module to another. If you have the option, always choose a module that aligns with your specific needs and the type of structured data you want to implement, whether it's for products, events, recipes, or other content types. Figure 4-9 shows some structured data options.

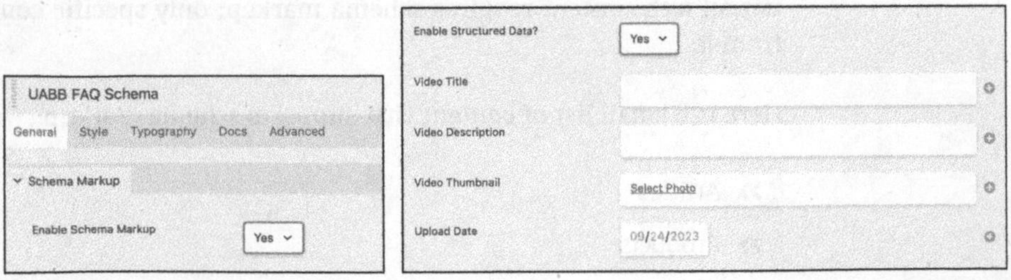

FIGURE 4-9:
Some modules come with structured data markup built in.

This is the easiest way to add structured data to your website. As time goes on, I think more software packages will include the structured data feature in their modules. Pretty cool, right? Be on the lookout for these options and then fill in the data Google is looking for.

Local business websites need local, structured data

One of the most important types of structured data revolves around your local business. If you have a brick-and-mortar store, or you serve clients in a local area as opposed to a national area, you need to have local business structured data on your website.

Local business structured data puts information that helps Google and other search engines know what your business does and where it is located, directly on your website so that your website can be returned in the map (technically called the "local pack") and when people search for services "near me."

TIP

To determine if you already have local structured data on your website, head over to Google's schema markup testing tools (search for "schema markup testing tool google"). You want to see zero errors and zero warnings. You can also verify that the information you added (such as your business' name, address, and phone number) are present and correct. If you don't have local structured data on your website, you should add it following the instructions in this section.

Your Google Business Profile also helps you show up for these types of searches and in the map or local pack. Remember though, that is a Google product. There are plenty of other search engines that do not use the information in a Google Business Profile. If you have local schema markup on your website filled with local structured data, *all* search engines will read this information and return it in searches when it matches a person's search intent.

To set up local structured data, there are required pieces of information and optional pieces of information. The required pieces of information are as follows:

>> @id (the globally unique ID of the specific business in the form of an URL)

>> The name of your business

>> The address (street, city, state, ZIP, and country)

>> An image

You should also add your business phone number, even though it is not required.

Your name, address, and phone number is known as your NAP. Along with your NAP, other information that you can add to your website that search engines will read and understand includes the following:

» Longitude and latitude

» Logo

» Service areas

» Services offered

» Hours of operation

» Menu (if you have one)

» Aggregate rating

» Department (for example, Best Buy has a department called Geek Squad, and CVS has a pharmacy department)

» Cuisine types

» Price range

» Payments accepted

Add local structured data to your website

You can add local structured data to your website by generating your own code using a tool or schema.org, but an easier way is to use the tool integrated with your platform:

» For WordPress, I recommend Yoast's Local SEO plugin. See https://yoast.com/wordpress/plugins/local-seo/.

» For Wix, you can enter this information on your page settings. See https://support.wix.com/en/article/creating-local-business-markup-for-your-sites-homepage.

» Squarespace wants you do this manually, but they provide instructions. See https://www.stylefactoryproductions.com/how-to-add-schema-markup-to-a-squarespace-site.

» If you are using another platform, contact support or search for "Local Structured Data for *platform name*" to find the instructions.

These types of tools are pretty easy to use because you are basically filling out a form that's part of your website builder. You don't need to copy or generate code; instead, the software does this for you.

Setting Up a Primary Google Account for SEO

If you plan on growing your online presence, you need a Google account in order to set up tools and services, such as your Google Business Profile (which helps you advertise your business for free), Google Analytics (which helps you measure how busy your website is), Google Search Console (which helps you determine how Google understands your website as well as understand how people are finding your site and where you rank in searches), and Google Ads (which helps you run advertisements).

TIP

Setting up an account is easy, just visit `https://accounts.google.com` and choose the option to create a new account. Use your professional email address containing your domain name. You will see an option to associate your current email address with a Google account, and you want to choose that option instead of creating a Gmail account. See Figure 4-10a. Choose the "Use my current email address instead" option. Then enter your professional email address, as shown in Figure 4-10b.

FIGURE 4-10:
Set up a Google account by associating your professional email address with a Google account.

Chapter 5

Killing It with Keywords

Keywords are one of the keys to your website's success, so let's put these nuggets of information on your keychain. This chapter explains what keywords are and then shows you how to pick the best ones so that search engines list your site appropriately when users search.

Understanding Keyword Types

Keyword is a term you hear a lot in relation to the Internet. The word "keyword" refers to words you type into a search engine to find something. Keyword is used when discussing SEO (search engine optimization; covered in depth in Chapter 4) to mean one or multiple words strung together (even though keyword is singular). You'll also see the term *keyword phrase*.

Keywords are the foundation of SEO. Search engines index all the words on the Internet and use their algorithms to determine what different websites offer based on the text on their website. Their *web crawlers* take the words on your website and put them into a database to analyze them. As you can imagine, this means that the words you use on your website are critical to search engines returning your site when people search.

There are four main types of keywords or key phrases: short-tail, long-tail, evergreen, and fresh:

>> *Short-tail keywords* are a short combination of three or fewer words. For example, "modern condo."

>> *Long-tail keywords* are a longer combination of words that are more specific, niche, and targeted. For example, "modern condo for rent in Brooklyn" or "modern condo design ideas" or "modern condo median selling price in Tampa."

>> *Evergreen keywords* are search terms that consistently maintain relevance and high search volume over an extended period.

>> *Fresh keywords* refer to recently emerging search terms or trends that are gaining popularity.

Short-tail keywords

Short-tail keywords have a huge amount of search volume (they are used most often when people search the Internet) but are also highly competitive. Internet users sometimes start with short-tail keywords when beginning a search. They will enter a few words in a search engine's search box, like "nice condo." The search engine might have a hard time figuring out the user's "search intent" when there are only a few words.

For example, if someone is looking for a contractor to build an outdoor firepit in their back yard, they may start off searching for "outdoor firepit." Search engines do not know what the person is searching for, they don't know the person's search intent. Are they searching for photos of outdoor firepits? Do they want to purchase a portable one from the Internet? Do they have a question about how much smoke comes out of them or what to look for in a good outdoor firepit Is the firepit made of stone or metal?

If you experiment and type the words "outdoor firepit" into a search engine, you will see what I am talking about. You are presented with a SERP (*search engine results page*, discussed in Chapter 4) containing links to Home Depot, Lowes, and other places where you can purchase a firepit. Going back to the original concept, which is a contractor who will install an outdoor firepit in your back yard, you can see that this list is not that helpful. It is difficult for Google to pinpoint the clear *search intent* of many short-tail keywords.

Short-tail keywords are highly competitive, meaning many, many websites are jockeying for position 1 for these simple keywords. In general, short-tail keywords do not convert well because of the difficulty in matching search intent — they're often too general and are only the first step in a user's search journey. Users will often need to add more keywords to the search phrase and create longer, more specific phrases.

This is where long-tail keywords come into play.

Long-tail keywords

If you looked at the SERP of the outdoor firepit search, and you didn't find what you were looking for, you would most likely try again. You might change your keywords around and use a longer search phrase; in other words, you'd use *long-tail keywords*. You might change your search words from outdoor firepit to "contractor build outdoor firepit" or "landscaper to install outdoor firepit" or "mason installer outdoor firepit" or even a full sentence or question like "Where can I find a contractor to install an outdoor firepit in my backyard." Plus maybe even your city or town and state.

Long-tail keywords have lower search volumes compared to short-tail keywords so you don't have a large audience, but they make up for it in value by being more targeted.

Fresh and evergreen keywords

There are also *fresh* and *evergreen keywords*. Fresh keywords are trending now. During the COVID-19 pandemic, fresh keywords included N-95 mask, hand sanitizer station, COVID symptoms, and so on. It's not that nobody had ever searched for those keywords before, but the search volume for those keywords shot up exponentially at that time, making them fresh.

Fresh keywords refer to recently emerging search terms or trends that are gaining popularity, requiring timely content and optimization to capitalize on current user interests.

Most of the time you will build your site and content around evergreen keywords, because they are relevant today and yesterday and tomorrow. Evergreen keywords are search terms that consistently maintain relevance and high search volume over an extended period, making them valuable for long-term SEO strategies. For example, you might want to use keywords like "home workout routines" or "ways to work remotely from home."

Choosing Keywords Based on Metrics

What type of keywords should you use on your site, on your pages, in your descriptions, and on your titles and headings? My recommendation is to concentrate on evergreen, long-tail keywords on your website.

Even if you add keywords in the future, (which you should), starting with those specific, lower competition, long-tail keywords will help your site be searchable by search engines and help people find you when your product or services match their search intent.

When you are choosing keywords, there are a lot of metrics you can pay attention to, but the most important for basic keyword research are:

» Search volume

» Domain authority

» Competition

Search volume

If nobody is searching for what you're writing about, you won't get traffic from Google — no matter how hard you try. For example, my son was an early talker and when he was barely 1 year old, he used to call ice cream "tannini." If I had an ice cream shop and I referred to ice cream on my website as tannini, do you think that Google and other search engines would start returning my website when people wanted to get an ice cream cone with their kids? No. They would not.

You need to know what words your target customers are actually using to search for your products or services and then look at how often those words are being searched in your service area. You may be in a niche market and the words that describe your offer are not used by many people, but that may be okay, even beneficial! You may be in a market that is saturated by websites, such as real estate and you will find that many people are searching for the words that describe what you do.

You want to figure out the words that people are actually using and then look at how competitive those words are.

The way that you describe what you do or what you offer may be different from what your customers type into the search box to find your services. If you do not figure out what words users are searching for that pertain to your offerings, you will not get traffic to your website.

EXAMPLE

For example, years ago I had a client that provided Botox, facials, and other skin care regimens to their clients. She wanted to be known as a skin care clinic. When I was helping her layout and plan her original website, she kept telling me that she did not want to be known as a "day spa." I made sure that we did not include that verbiage on her website. A few years later we were redoing her website. One day during the project she mentioned that a new woman had just moved from Texas and was searching for a day spa online and that her business did not come up in search, so the new woman from Texas originally did not make an appointment. Then the woman who just moved here met some friends and found out about her establishment and made an appointment. My client said to me (I can still remember this conversation), "So Jennifer, when we do the new website, we will come up in search when someone is searching for day spa, right? This new website will fix that, correct?"

No, no it won't "fix" this issue. This was years ago, and maybe now search engines might lump skin care clinics in with day spas and determine that they should match this website with a visitor's search intent, but you don't want to leave it up to search engines to "figure out" what you really offer.

In this case, we changed the text we included on the website's pages. This is a good example of how you want to understand your customer and what they are searching for may not necessarily be what you offer.

Domain authority

Think of the Internet as a gigantic library. In this library, *domain authority* (DA) is like the reputation of a publisher. If a publisher (the website) has a good reputation (domain authority), then the books (the web pages) it publishes are more likely to be placed where more people can see and reach them easily. In the same way, when a website has a higher domain authority, its pages are more likely to rank higher in search engine results.

When you're choosing keywords, domain authority is like a friendly reminder of how competitive the race is to the top of search engine results. If your website has a low domain authority and you decide to target keywords that the top-ranking sites with very high DAs are targeting, it's like trying to win a footrace against professional athletes — not impossible, but quite challenging! On the other hand, if you target keywords where the top-ranking sites have lower DAs, your chances of winning are much better.

Look up your domain authority using one of the many tools on the Internet so that you know what types of words you should target. Check out these sample tools to determine your Domain Authority:

>> `https://moz.com/domain-analysis`

>> `https://ahrefs.com/website-authority-checker`

>> `https://ahrefs.com/website-authority-checkerhttps://lp.semrush.com/Metrics-for-Sites-Quality-Check_en.html`

>> `https://loganix.com/domain-authority-checker-tool/`

Competition

Considering the competitiveness of keywords before choosing them is a fundamental aspect of any successful SEO strategy. This competitiveness describes how easy or difficult it is to rank on a search engine's organic search results for a specific keyword. This careful assessment is vital for several compelling reasons:

>> First, it helps you gauge the feasibility of ranking for a particular keyword. Highly competitive keywords, often dominated by established websites or businesses, can be exceptionally challenging to rank for, especially if you're just starting or have limited resources. By understanding the level of competition, you can make informed decisions about which battles to fight, focusing your efforts on keywords where you have a reasonable chance of success.

>> Second, keyword competitiveness impacts resource allocation. SEO efforts require time, labor, and financial resources. Selecting keywords that match your available resources ensures a more efficient allocation of these valuable assets. Highly competitive keywords may demand significant investments, both in terms of content creation and link-building efforts. In contrast, less competitive keywords can be targeted with a smaller budget and less extensive content, making this a more cost-effective approach.

This last point may seem counterintuitive, but it is important. Different keywords attract different audiences with varying levels of intent to convert. Highly competitive keywords may bring in more traffic, but this traffic could be less targeted, resulting in lower conversion rates. Conversely, less competitive keywords often attract a more specific audience with a higher likelihood of converting into customers or leads.

For example, I had a client that handled security class action filings for pension funds, hedge funds, and other large institutional investors. Not for individuals. Originally, they were using highly competitive keywords such as "class action" and they were finding that they were getting a ton of traffic to their website, but the traffic was from individuals who wanted to bring or jump on the latest small class action lawsuit. It was wasting their time. They changed their strategy to go for less competitive, longer-tail keywords, such as "securities class action lawsuit filing," and they found that their traffic was more targeted and would convert on a higher percentage of the time.

Assessing keyword competitiveness is not just about SEO; it's a strategic business decision that can significantly impact your online success.

Competitive keyword strategy

After you find all your keywords, you need to assign a different keyword phrase to each page of your website. My suggestion is to use the words that are part of your core offering on your most important pages, such as your homepage, features pages, service pages, or product pages, even if they are very competitive. You probably won't be able to rank for them just now. Then, find less competitive words and write a lot of content in the form of articles and blog posts. Publish it on your website around those words. Start bringing in some traffic on those lower competitive words, move up in the SERP for those words, and then as your website gains more authority, you will begin to be returned for the more competitive words that you used on your home and other core web pages.

TIP

Think of the number of pages on your website as raffle tickets. If you wanted to win the raffle, you would buy more tickets so that you had a better chance of winning. Websites are similar. If you have a one-page website, you have basically one chance to appear in the SERP. If you have a lot of pages and posts on your website, you have essentially more raffle tickets/chances to appear.

Researching Keywords

Keyword research helps you determine which keywords people are typing into search engines. You can literally "research" the keywords that people are using in searches and determine if those searches have grown or shrunk recently. These are powerful insights that will help you choose the perfect keywords and phrases to use on your website.

The goal is to build a list of keywords and keyword phrases that you want to appear in the search results. The best keywords stand on actual data — they are keywords and phrases that people are actually typing in and searching, thousands of times a month.

There are many tools you can use to do keyword research — some are paid/premium, and some are free — and there are lots of ways to do keywords research.

Find seed keywords

You'll start by making a huge list of keywords, called your *seed keywords*, and then you will cull the list down, and finally you will assign one keyword phrase to each page and post of your website.

Seed keywords are the foundational or core keywords that serve as the starting point for your keyword research. They are typically broad and general terms related to your industry, niche, or the topic you want to explore in SEO or online marketing campaigns. Seed keywords are essential because they form the basis for expanding your keyword list.

For example, if you have a website selling hiking gear, your seed keywords might include terms like "hiking," "outdoor gear," or "camping equipment." These are fundamental terms relevant to your business, and from there, you can use various keyword research tools and techniques to generate a list of related keywords, long-tail keywords, and specific phrases that potential customers might use when searching for products or information related to hiking gear.

Seed keywords help you kickstart your keyword research process, identify search trends, and discover opportunities to target the most relevant and effective key-words in your SEO and content strategies.

Follow these steps to begin building your seed keywords:

1. **Open a web browser, head over to Google, and type some search terms that you think your customers will use or have used to find your website.**

   When you see the SERP, look closely at the websites that Google returns for your search and ask: Does this look like a list that your company should appear in?

2. **If list doesn't match your business, refine your search terms and use long-tail keyword phrases. Find some specific phrases that, when searched, return a list of your competition.**

   These are the results you want to appear in, and hopefully appear on top of! These phrases are a great place to start your keyword research. Do this search for each term you can think of.

3. **Add these phrases to your initial keyword list.**

4. **For each keyword phrase you choose, scroll down the page.** You will see "Related Searches" (at the time of the publishing of this book Google is calling it Related Searches. They used to call it "People Also Search For" and "People Also Ask").

    This section can be a valuable strategy when it comes to generating search terms and enhancing your content strategy because it shows related search queries that you can use to expand your keyword list, inspire content ideas, reveal user intent, aid you in competitive analysis, and uncover long-tail keyword opportunities. Look at this list and add these words to your seed keyword list.

5. **You should now have a pretty long list of keywords. Take that list and put them into a tool of your choice to get some real data.**

    There are a ton of tools you can use, and I mention just a few here.

Use keyword tools

REMEMBER

For most of the platforms in the keyword research space, you need to set up an account on their platform in order to use their tools.

You may have heard of tools such as Moz, Ahrefs, and Semrush. These are paid platforms that have a ton of additional tools besides simple keyword research to help you optimize your website. Once you set up an account, you are prompted to enter the keywords or key phrases (the one you saved from the exercise you just did), and off you go!

There are also free options, such as Keyword Planner, which is a part of Google Ads. Figure 5-1 shows what Keyword Planner looks like.

When you set up an account on Google Ads, you need to enter payment information and set up a pretend ad, although you can pause it immediately after setting up your account because you are not ready to run the ad yet. If you do not run the ad, your credit card will not be charged. (Note: Google may test the account by authorizing $50 on your account.)

Once you enter your keyword phrases into the tool of your choice, you will be presented with a table of information of related keywords, phrases, and metrics. See Figure 5-2.

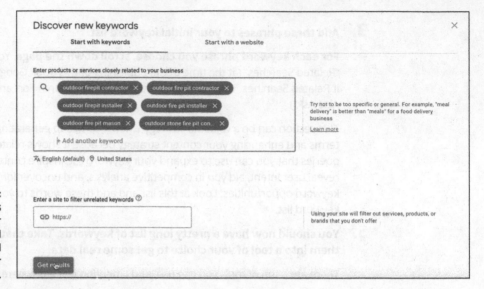

FIGURE 5-1:
Google Ads Keyword Planner is a free and good way to find keywords for your website.

FIGURE 5-2:
When you use Google Ads Keyword Planner, you can research other keywords that might be good for your website.

This table has several columns, and you can sort those columns by clicking the appropriate header cell.

>> The first column (Keyword) shows the keywords you entered plus potential keywords that Google found related to your keywords.

>> The second column (Avg. Monthly Searches) shows you the average monthly searches. You can sort this column to see what keyword phrases are getting the most use. These are great phrases to write down to use later, when you are writing your content. Record these phrases.

>> The next two columns show the number of searches performed compared to the past few months or year. These are helpful trends: You can see if more people are looking for your service. If you see a few phrases that are trending upwards, you might want to include these in your list of phrases.

>> The next column (Competition) shows you the how competitive each keyword is: High, Medium, Low, or Nonexistent. This shows you the number of advertisers running ads using those keywords.

There are other columns that help you with ads, but for keyword research, lets focus on the Average Monthly Searches, the changes through time, and the competition. You want to use keywords that people are searching for on the Internet. The terms with the highest average monthly searches need to appear on your website, but remember if the words are very competitive it will be hard to rank for those words at first. As your website grows its authority, you have a better chance of ranking for those keywords, so use those keywords on your core website pages. Document these words somewhere and keep them handy when you are writing your content.

Keep adding new keyword phrases to see Google's other suggestions.

While you are documenting your keywords, you should also make another list of "potential blog posts" from some of the keywords you find in these lists. There may be some phrases that look like great titles of blog posts, so write those down and keep them in a safe place for later in case you want to write a blog someday.

TIP

Speaking of blog post ideas, tools can also help you come up with topics to write. The tool called Answer the Public from Neil Patel, who is a guru in the SEO space, gives you nice charts with potential blog post topics. Ubersuggest is another tool from Neil Patel that helps users come up with good blog posts.

If you want to try to ride a pop culture wave, you can use Google Trends. Google Trends is free. Visit trends.google.com. If you scroll down that page you will see the most popular search terms. You can write an article or two in a timely manner using some of these search terms to see if you can ride this cultural wave, but remember those might be fresh keywords, not evergreen.

TIP

It's also important to research what your competition is doing when it comes to optimizing their websites. SpyFu (www.spyfu.com) helps you learn what your competitors are ranking for and how you are doing compared to them. Once you get going, you may want to start paying attention to your competition.

Use your giant keyword list

Once you have a keyword list, you want to sort it. Place the keywords you want to be returned in the SERP, no matter how difficult, in one list. If you have a new or low domain authority website, you may not rank for those terms just yet. That's okay if they accurately tell the story of what you offer.

Place the rest of the keywords, especially the lower competition keywords, in another list. Reserve this list for blog posts. You can write a lot of content around those lower competitive keywords and get some traction. Then, after you have some traction on those keywords and you get some backlinks, search engines will move your site up in search and your domain authority should start to increase. As your domain authority increases, your site will be returned based on your primary keywords. This may take years, but that is okay! I assume that you plan to be in business in a few years!

When it is time to write your *sitemap* (which is the list of all the pages on your website organized into menus), you will choose the most important keywords and optimize your static pages around them. Chapter 6 covers the process of writing sitemaps in detail.

You have a lot to do, but you should now understand search and the need to put your best effort forward online so that you can reap the rewards for years to come!

3

Architecting Plans for Your Website

Chapter **6**

A Place for Everything and Everything in Its Place

n this chapter you are going to plan your website. Planning your site before you start building it helps you determine the content you need to gather and gives you a high-level overview of the site's organization.

Organizing Your Sitemap

It's time to get working on building your website! In this section, you learn how to organize a sitemap, or the menu for your website.

A *sitemap* is an outline of all the pages on your website. This is sort of like the outlines you wrote in school, before you wrote your paper. If you wrote an outline before you started writing your paper, you probably found it much easier to organize your content and to ensure that you were including all the correct information. The same is true for a website. You want a place for all your information, and a sitemap helps you determine place.

As an example, Figure 6-1a shows the sitemap outline for a landscaping website, and Figure 6-1b shows how the menu looks on the actual site.

FIGURE 6-1:
A sitemap (a) outlines your pages, as shown in the end product (b) of this landscaping website.

MAIN MENU
Tree Services
   Tree Removal
   Tree Pruning
   Stump Grinding
   Lot Clearing

Landscape Construction & Stonework
   Paver and Natural Stone Walks and Patios
   Outdoor Kitchens and Fireplaces
   Lawn Installation/Renovation
   Irrigation System Installs/Service
   Natural Stone and Block Retaining Walls
   Drainage Systems
   Outdoor Lighting
   Tree and Shrub Plantings

Lawn Care and Landscaping
   Weekly Lawn Maintenance
   Spring and Fall Cleanups
   Mulch Installation
   Fertilizer and Weed Control
   Shrub and Bush Pruning
   Gutter Cleaning

I love the phrase, "A place for everything and everything in its place." It certainly applies to this section. Here's a little secret: this exercise is going to become a sort of to-do list or checklist. After you have written content lists for each page, you can begin to gather the content and organize it into folders on your computer (you'll need a good naming convention for all the files too). If you don't have access to content right now, make a list of things you need to gather and then schedule time to gather or create that content.

Determine all the pages you need

There are a few ways to create a website outline. I recommend starting by jotting down all the information you want to include. You can do this in a word processor, a spreadsheet application, or using a tool online.

These are some of the basic pages that almost all websites have:

» Home

» About

» Contact

» Privacy policy

» Terms of service

Some other popular options for pages include these:

» A page for each service you offer or product you sell

» Categories for the items you sell

» Blog

» News

» FAQs

» History

» Team

» Partners

» Events

» Success stories

» My Account

» Cart

» Features

» Pricing

Organize your service pages

If you have a business that provides services, you need to include pages that show visitors what you offer. When you create your sitemap, you most certainly should include a page or more that pertains to your service offerings. You can create your sitemap so that all your services are listed and discussed on one page, you can group your services together by theme on one page, or you can create a separate page for each service. There is no right or wrong way to lay out your services section, but you should know the pros and cons of each.

The pros of listing all your services on one page are as follows:

>> If you have just a few services but you have a lot of other pages and sections on your website, this will simplify the navigation menu.

>> If your services are not the central part of your business, you may want to list them on one page.

>> Quite frankly, it's less work. You don't need to create multiple pages and you can write less text and gather fewer images. You can always come back at a later time as part of the iterative process and break your single service page into multiple pages.

The cons of listing all your services on one page are as follows:

>> It can be more difficult for visitors to find your offerings. Since you don't have a separate menu item for each service, visitors need to scroll down the page to find out what you offer instead of seeing it in the menu.

>> Your opportunities to optimize the page for search engines are reduced. That's because the more pages you have optimized on your website, the more pages search engines will index for different keywords, and you then have a better chance of coming up high in the SERP.

How about grouping your services together by category or theme? The pros of this approach are as follows:

>> If you offer many services, this approach helps you organize your content better and helps visitors find what they are looking for quickly. For example, if your business is a health center and you offer all types of health-related services, you may want to group your services together. You could put all the services that the radiology department provides on one page: MRIs, CT Scans, Mammograms, X-Rays, and so on. Or if you provide plumbing services, HVAC

services, electrical services, and more, you may want to create a page for each of those service categories. Then on each page, you talk about how you maintain HVAC systems, how you repair HVAC systems, how you install new HVAC systems or ducts, how you have different options for HVAC such as geothermal, central, ductless, and so on.

>> If people search for the category of your offerings, you may want to use this approach. If you work for a health center and you offer cardiology services such as heart valve surgery, bypass surgery, angioplasty, and so on, you may want to put all of these on one page entitled "Cardiology Services," since that is what people will most likely search for. They will look for a cardiologist instead of the procedure. Doing this will help you optimize the page for search and make it easier for visitors to find information.

The main con of this approach is that your opportunities to optimize pages on your website for search are limited to your categories. This may be fine, but it is something to consider.

The last option is to create a page for each service you offer. The pros of this approach are as follows:

>> You can explain the features and benefits of each service thoroughly to the visitors.

>> If you have all of your services as separate pages listed in your menu, people will know what you provide right away, without having to read a single page on your website.

>> Most importantly, you have additional opportunities to optimize your pages for search. This should help your website rise in the SERP listing. I choose this option whenever feasible.

TECHNICAL STUFF

You can also list all your services in a dropdown menu, and still have only one page that houses all your services. This is done by creating *named anchor links*, which are links to a specific *spot* on a page that discusses each service. You can do this by adding a CSS ID to each specific section, but that is beyond the scope of this book. If you're curious, search for "create a link to a specific spot on a page."

The main con of this approach is that it's more work. You must write a lot more, find more images and visuals, and so on. But remember, once you do this work once, it can pay off in perpetuity.

Create the About pages

Your About section can also contain one or multiple pages. You can create a single About page or split it into multiple pages, like About, Team, and History. There's no strict format; it's based on your content volume and preference. For instance, if you have many team members crucial to your brand's appeal, consider a dedicated Team page. If your long, rich history with photos and stories is a selling point, a separate History page can be beneficial. Decide whether to consolidate or distribute your content.

Consider e-commerce pages

An e-commerce menu should *tell a story* about your products and your offerings. *The menu should show what you offer.* You want visitors to understand what type of items you sell right away. So it's good to list your categories as main menu links. Category terms are important not only for visitors to easily find items in your store, but they are also indexed by search engines to understand what you are selling. This is a great place to insert target keywords for a boost in the SERP!

You may also have subcategories. If you do, they should be included in the drop-downs menus on your main menu. For example, if you sell Children's outerwear, that would be a great top category to include on your sitemap. Subcategories might include youth gloves, youth winter coats, children's boots, children's raincoats, and so on. Again, the subcategories help the visitor find what they are looking for easily and might also suggest related items they can purchase. Just like top categories, subcategories are typically indexed by search engines.

Unless you only sell one type or category of product, I don't recommend "hiding" your product categories, such as under a Shop menu item, because this forces the visitors to go through multiple steps in order to see what you offer. That is, unless you have so many categories they won't fit as top level items in the navigation. For e-commerce, I also recommend that the main menu *not* contain links to pages like Home, About, Contact, and Blog. You won't see this on any major e-commerce site, because the goal is to get the visitors to the product they're looking for as fast as possible.

There are also some important links that customers are accustomed to finding at the bottom of the page of most online stores. These include a Customer Service menu containing links to My Account, Returns, Shipping Information, and Contact Us.

Writing Your Sitemap

Write your sitemap outline now. Start by including Home, About, Contact, Privacy Policy, and Terms of Service pages. I explain the purpose of each of these pages more in another section — for now just make sure they appear on your sitemap/outline. Then follow these basic steps:

1. Organize your content into buckets or categories. One way to organize your content is to add a top category or idea. Then, underneath that category or idea, add more specific pages — these may or may not become dropdown menus. This is called *nesting*. You have a "parent" page and a few or many "child" pages. For example, a large company's website might have a section called About and then under that section header are About the Company, Team, Board of Directors, and History menus. On a restaurant's website, you might see a top-level item called Menu and under it, you see Breakfast Menu, Lunch Menu, Happy Hour Menu, and Dinner Menu. Organize your content by creating an outline of pages.

2. Refer to the keyword research you did in Chapter 5. Most likely your keyword research will contain phrases that relate to your services or product offerings. Do these words appear in some of the page names? The page names don't need to match your keywords exactly, but make sure that there is a page for each topic related to your most important services or products.

3. Spend some time looking at your competitors' websites. Look at their menus. Look on the top of the website — the main menu — and look at the footer. What pages do they have on their websites? Did you miss any important pages? How are theirs organized compared to how you organized yours?

WARNING

You may also notice that some of your competitors have terrible menu organization or are missing huge opportunities. . . do not follow those sites. However, you can learn from them what you *don't* want to do.

On the contrary, you might find that some of your competition has thought of some ingenious ideas that they offer on their website. Go ahead and borrow these ideas if you like them. Add any to your site that you have missed and reorganize yours if you get some good ideas.

Organize your pages into separate menus

If you plan on having a "smaller" website (fewer than 20 pages), it's advisable to include all or most of your website's pages in at least one menu. There are some menu strategies that do not do this, but for smaller websites like the one you are most likely building, it's best that all your pages appear in at least one menu on your website (this does not include individual blog posts or news articles, products, galleries, or posts like that — this refers just to pages).

You don't want visitors to click a link, visit a page, and then not know how they got there or how to get back. For example, if you have links to your team page, and you link to the team page only from the homepage, visitors will have a difficult time finding the team page again. They most likely will not remember where they "found" and clicked the link to that page. This is frustrating and leads to a bad user experience, which is also called *bad UX*. You want your visitors to be able to navigate your website easily and come back to pages that they want to look at again.

That being said, let's talk about the three main types of menus, each of which has a separate purpose:

>> Main menu (sometimes referred to as the header menu)

>> Top menu

>> Footer menu

Your pages should appear in at least one of these menus. Where each page should appear depends on the type of page it is. The following sections explain each of these menus in more detail.

Your main menu

The main menu is the most prominent menu on your website and is usually located horizontally near your logo, as shown in Figure 6-2. It can also appear vertically. In that case the menu will appear down the left or right side of the screen. Sometimes, this menu is hidden behind a *hamburger menu* (the icon with three bars for a hamburger bun), like in mobile designs.

In any case, this menu appears on pretty much all websites. If you have a large website, this menu should tell a story about your company and your offerings. *This menu should show what you offer.*

If you have a much smaller site with 10 or fewer pages, the main menu can contain links to all the pages on your website, apart from the Terms of Service and Privacy Policy — even ones that do not provide information on your offerings, such as your Contact page.

FIGURE 6-2:
The main menu is
the most
important menu
on your website.
You can place
it above your
logo, next to
your logo, below
your logo,
horizontally on
the page, or
vertically.

The main menu should contain links to all the main sections and/or pages on your website. This menu can be organized with dropdown menus, or simply contain links to sections, pages, or posts with no dropdowns.

Your top menu

You may choose to use a top menu, but it's not mandatory. A top menu appears at the top of the screen, sometimes in a bar that is a different color than the header area, or it may just sit at the top of the page. It can appear on the left, right, and/or center of your website, and you can have more than one top menu, or you may not have one at all. Top menus generally do not have dropdown menus; they include links to individual pages or posts.

The font size of the top menu is generally smaller than the font size of the main menu (see Figure 6-3). That is because you want people to look at the main menu first to learn about your company. This top menu doesn't need to be noticed until the visitor needs to do something on your website. In other words, the top menu, in general, is a *utilitarian* menu. For example, you may see a menu that contains links to log in, sign up, view your cart, find a location, search, donate, or book an appointment. Other top menus contain links to social media channels, or links to call you, email you, or get directions. Most of the time, links that tell the story about your offerings do not appear here.

FIGURE 6-3:
A top menu of some websites; note that the font is smaller than the main menu.

The options in the top menu are important enough to appear at the very top of every page because these are things that you want visitors to do on your website. You don't want them to have to search for these pages or links; you want to make it easy for them to find these types of pages or links.

Your footer menu

You may also choose to use a footer menu, but this is also optional. The footer menu can appear horizontally all the way across the bottom of the page in the footer (see Figure 6-4), or it can appear on the right, left, or center. Footer menus can also appear vertically in columns on the bottom of your website.

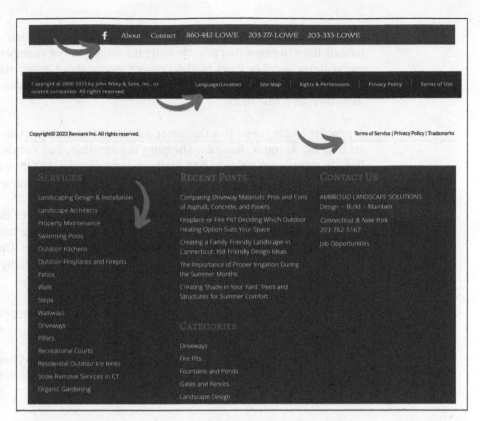

FIGURE 6-4:
You can place your footer menu horizontally or vertically on your footer. You can have one footer menu or many.

Designers generally do not include dropdown menus on footer menus (there's no space at the bottom of the page for the menu to drop down). You can include multiple footer menus if necessary, even six or more (see Figure 6-5).

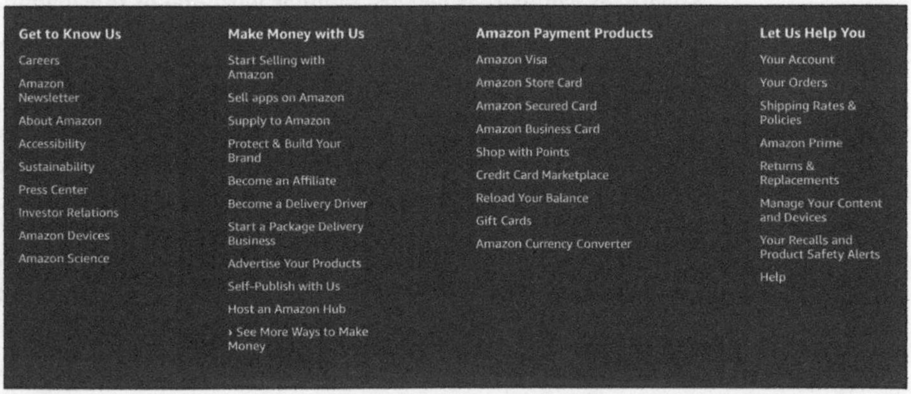

FIGURE 6-5:
Amazon is a much larger website than you are most likely building, but you can see that they have a lot of menus in their footer.

As with a top menu, footer menus are utilitarian as well, but they also often include links to pages that provide more information. For example, popular footer menu items contain links to the Contact page, About page, History, Board of Directors or Team, Employment or Careers page, Terms of Service, Privacy Policy, Returns Policy, and more.

A popular footer menu is a Customer Service menu that contains links to items such as My Account, Returns, Shipping Information, and Contact Us. These are links that you want users to find easily on your website, but they don't fit in with the main menu in that they don't usually tell a story about your offerings.

REMEMBER

Note that you can have a page appear in two or more menus. For example, designers frequently include a link to the Contact page in both the top and the footer menus. The same goes for Blog and possibly the About menu. One strategy is to repeat the main menu links as one of the footer menus, especially when you have more than one footer menu space.

TIP

Check the page list you created and make sure that each page appears in one of the three menus.

Organizing all of your pages into menus gives you focus. Then, when you're designing the content of each of these pages, you can break down the work into bite-sized chunks.

Assign keywords to your pages

This section helps you organize your site and ensures that Google can find it. Take out your keyword research from Chapter 5 and your sitemap and have them handy. I recommend performing this exercise in a spreadsheet program like Excel, Google Sheets, or Numbers if you are familiar with one of those applications. If you are not great at using spreadsheets, you can do this exercise in Word, Pages, Google Docs, Notes, or another word processing application as well.

You need to assign each of your keywords to a page of your website. Then you plan your URLs, titles, and meta descriptions for each page of the website. This helps you build a great search engine optimized foundation.

1. **First, set up your spreadsheet. In the first row, type the following column headings: Page Name, Keyword Phrase, Title, Meta Description, and URL.**
   Your sheet should look similar to Figure 6-6.

FIGURE 6-6:
Set up a
spreadsheet with
these headings.

	A	B	C	D	E
1	Page Name	Keyword Phrase	Title	Meta Description	URL
2					
3					

2. Type all of your page names into the Page Name column.

3. Match your keyword phrases with each page of your website and enter that keyword phrase into the Keyword Phrase column, next to the page it is assigned to.

Each page should get a different primary keyword phrase, based on your research. Start with the homepage and assign the most valuable, most important keyword phrase to that page. Next, work your way through the list. Use your most important keyword phrases first. Match the keywords with the pages as best you can. You can also add some secondary keywords to additional columns. That is a good idea.

TIP

Try not to reuse a keyword phrase if possible. Sometimes you may not have a good match. You may have way more keywords than you have pages, or you might have very similar keywords and very different page names. That's all normal. If you did not have issues like too many keywords or difficulty matching them up, that would be very strange. Do your best to assign one keyword phrase to each page of your website. You can use the leftovers as secondary keywords for each page or on blog posts. If you don't have enough keywords, take a few minutes and do a little more research to get some fresh ideas and phrases.

4. Save the document. You don't want to lose your hard work!

Plan your titles, meta descriptions, and URLs

The next step is to write titles and meta descriptions for each page, as well as create URLS for them. First, I show you where the titles will appear so you understanding what to write as a title.

Writing your titles

As discussed, when you search for terms in Google, the SERP is returned. Each website that relates to the search appears in the format shown in Figure 6-7: The *title* is shown as hyperlinked text, indicating that you can click it to visit that page.

When writing your titles, consider these three goals:

>> Include your keyword phrase.

>> Make it interesting and intriguing.

>> Consider the visitor's search intent.

FIGURE 6-7:
The SERP includes
the title and meta
description you
assign to each
page.

S SEI Wireless Solutions
https://seiwirelesssolutions.com ⋮

Title

Two-Way Radio Rentals And Sales | SEI Wireless Solutions

SEI Wireless is an experienced and trusted advisor to help ensure that your building projects meet the new Public Safety Signal Enhancement Guidelines. We are ...

Your title can make or break your organic SEO. Even if your site rises to a top position in the search, if your title is too generic or uninspired, no one will click it. Then, the search engines will demote your site and replace your top position with a website that does get clicks.

REMEMBER

The measurement of how many returned links are clicked is called the *clickthrough rate* (CTR), and it essentially measures the ratio of times that your website was returned for a search term versus how many times it was clicked. If a search engine returned your website in 100 searches, and people clicked your listing ten times, your clickthrough rate would be 10 percent. Your title is largely responsible for your clickthrough rate, so it has an important job.

AUTHOR
SAYS

Ten percent is a very high CTR (clickthrough rate), by the way. Most industries have a high CTR of 6-7 percent.

Because the title of your page has such a big job and you want it to be effective, you need to think of the visitors' search intent when you write the titles. Consider the following example.

EXAMPLE

I once worked with a client on his optimization efforts. He had a successful online motorcycle parts store. Every time he added a new product, he would add his titles and meta descriptions to his website. When looking at his numbers in the Google Search Console, I noticed that one of his motorcycle parts (forward foot controls) came up in position 2 in search. This was awesome! But his CTR turned out to be very low. The title he had assigned to that product explained what a forward foot control was, yet he was barely getting clicks.

Let's think about this. I am not a motorcycle person and I have no idea what a forward foot control is, so if I did a search for that term, most likely my *search intent* would be to find out what it is. I might want to see a title that starts to explain the product. His customers, though, know what a forward foot control is — their *search intent* is to shop for a forward foot control. What would make his customers click his listing? What would entice them to purchase?

Some ideas for this title include Guaranteed Satisfaction, Lowest Prices, Free Shipping, or some other feature that is above and beyond what other stores offer. His searchers are actively looking to make a purchase. They don't need to learn what a forward foot control is. Instead, the title should emphasize why someone should choose to buy a forward foot control from this site rather than another. Always consider your visitors' search intent as you write your titles.

Going back to your spreadsheet, write and assign your titles for each page and add these titles to the Title column.

Here are the rules:

>> Use the keyword phrase assigned to this page in your title, preferably at the beginning of the title. If it can't be the first few words, keep it as close to the beginning as possible. For example, if you wanted to target the keyword phrase "natural anti-aging skincare," you might create a title like "Clean, Natural Anti-Aging Skincare | Acta Beauty."

>> Be concise and short. The title of the page can only contain 50-60 characters, depending on how fat or thin the letters are. This includes spaces and periods. Try to come as close to 50 without going over 60. Do not go over 60 otherwise your title will be cut off and you will see ellipses (. . .) in the SERP.

>> Consider including the name of your company at the end of the title. Do this by adding a space to the end of the title you write, then a hyphen or a pipe (the straight line character that is above the right Enter key), and then type the name of your company. You don't need to include LLC or INC here. Just the name of your business. Using the previous example, you see "Acta Beauty" added to the "Clean, Natural Anti-Aging Skincare | Acta Beauty" title.

>> Do not use the same title for each page. Write a different one for each page. This should happen anyway if you correctly assigned a different keyword phrase to each page.

>> Make the title compelling and interesting — something that people will want to click.

Assigning your meta descriptions

After you have given each page a title, save your document again. Next you need to assign a meta description to each page.

Going back to the SERP, the meta description appears below the title. See Figure 6-8. Again, this tells visitor what they will get on this page if they click the listing. Meta descriptions give visitors a short, relevant summary of what a particular page is about. They are like a pitch — the goal is to convince the visitor that this page is worth clicking. Remember their search intent. You want to include your keyword phrase as close to the beginning as possible.

Going back to your spreadsheet, add your meta descriptions to the Meta Description column.

markjosephcreative.com
https://www.markjosephcreative.com ⋮

Mark Joseph Creative

Multi-award-winning **entertainment** booking agency. We produce live **entertainment** with access to local, national, and international talent. ◀ **Meta Description**

FIGURE 6-8: Meta descriptions appear in the SERP for each listing.

Here are the rules when writing meta descriptions:

>> Use your keyword phrase you assigned to this page.

>> Use the keyword phrase as one of the first words in the description.

>> The meta description can only contain 155-160 characters, depending on how wide the font is. Try to get as close to this number as you can, but do not go over. This includes spaces and periods. Use one space after a period and use abbreviations if appropriate and universal.

>> Make this description juicy and compelling. You want your potential customers to feel compelled to click the link.

>> Use *active* language, a call to action. Avoid passive language.

>> Write about what the visitor will get when they visit your website, instead of explaining what you are or what you offer.

>> Do not repeat a description from another page — write unique descriptions for each page.

>> Do not include the name of your company in the description.

TIP

Don't be afraid to check out competitors' meta descriptions — or check out sites that you really like. You can get inspiration from other sites. But make your selling points unique.

Save your document once you've added the meta descriptions.

Planning your URLs

The last step is to plan your URLs. This is also called a path, slug, permalink, page address, hyperlink, and more. The URL appears in the browser's address bar and looks like this:

```
https://www.wiley.com/en-us/shop/etextbooks-courseware
```

Each page has an URL. This is also called the web address, permalink, slug, and more. Creating a structures URL and logical naming convention helps your SEO.

Most of the time you can change the URL, and you want to so that search engines understand your page and the hierarchy of your website. A good URL structure helps search engines crawl your website. You also want to the URLs to look professional to visitors.

WARNING

If you already have a website and you decide to change your URLs, you must set up 301 permanent redirects; otherwise, visitors will get the dreaded 404 Page Not Found error. A *redirects* maps an old URL to the new URL so that the user's browser knows that the page has a new address and will automatically follow it to get to the content instead of hitting the 404 dead end.

If you have any pages in your sitemap that are nested under another page, you will want to indicate this in the URL. For example, say you have an Investors page that is under the About section. If so, your URL might look like this:

```
/about/investor-center
```

If you grouped your services, you might have a top category and your services organized underneath each category. I had a client who had a therapy practice for adults, families, and children. She organized her URLs like so:

```
therapy-and-counseling/adults/cognitive-behavioral-therapy/
```

```
therapy-and-counseling/adults/miscarriage-grief-loss/
```

```
therapy-and-counseling/kid-and-teens/divorce-counseling-foar-kids/
```

```
therapy-and-counseling/kid-and-teens/play-therapy-for-young-
children/

coaching-services/life-coaching/

coaching-services/career-counseling-coaching/

evaluations/dyslexia-screening/

evaluations/autism-screening-and-diagnosis/
```

Her content is very neatly organized and nested. The URLs explain what content you might find on the pages. She also uses keywords in her URLs. Search engines love this, because they can group content together as well, so they know what pages to return when someone is looking for therapy for an adult or a child, or if someone is looking for coaching or an evaluation.

Back in your spreadsheet, create your URLs using this system and add them to the URL column. Then save your document.

I hope you found this exercise beneficial. It helped you focus on keyword phrases and organize your pages so that you have a planned, focused SEO effort. You will reference this document when you are writing your page copy. In addition, you will reference this document after your pages are built and enter this information where search engines are looking for it. Bottom line: Be sure you know where this document is saved so you can find it again later.

If you completed this exercise, you are ahead of most people building a website. Most people wait until their website is built to start thinking about organization, and then they have double the amount of work to do! The process covered in this chapter will save you hours of time and frustration, and it will help to propel your site forward in the SERP.

IN THIS CHAPTER

» Building content with its purpose
in mind

» Building your service pages

» Creating support pages for nonprofits

» Creating amazing showcase pages

» Adding blog posts

» Brainstorming your homepage

» Building your homepage

Chapter 7

Content Scaffold: Supporting Your Website's Information

This chapter is all about providing your visitors with the information that matches their search intent, SEO strategies so search engines return your website in the SERP, keeping people on your website, building trust, and most of all, ensuring that you have place for everything and everything in its place.

In Chapter 6, you created your sitemap, so it's time to figure out what information you want to include on each page of your website. You don't need to write down the exact words you want to include on each page, or determine the exact images. Instead, you want to get a general picture of what each page will contain.

Each type of page requires different types of content, and the next section explains some great ideas for things you can include on each page.

Setting Up Your Service Pages

Recall that the purpose of your services pages is to present the services or products you offer to potential customers. The goal is to provide value by providing a richer experience. You want to upsell if you can, gather leads, help visitors understand more of your offerings, and keep users on your site longer.

Keep in mind that the content described in this section is not exhaustive, and you might have other options that work perfectly on your service pages. Do some searching and check out competitors' sites for inspiration.

>> **Information about your services/offering:** For sure you want to let people know what you offer. Be specific but not wordy. When it comes to lawns, do you only offer mowing and trimming? Or do you offer fertilization, sod installation, pest protection, design, or something else? See Figure 7-1.

Our Property Maintenance Services

JC Outdoors is an industry leader in the proper care and maintenance of both residential and commercial lawns and landscapes. We utilize only the best equipment, mulches, soils, plant materials, grass seeds, and practices to properly maintain your property in an efficient, cost effective and timely manner. Our property maintenance services include but are not limited to the following:

✓ Spring and Fall Clean-ups

✓ Bed edging, mulch installation, and shrub trimming

✓ Lawn renovations including aeration & over seeding and sod installation

✓ Commercial lawn mowing

✓ Brush clearing and field mowing

✓ Planting flower beds, shrubs and trees

✓ Installing and Maintaining hardscaping

FIGURE 7-1:
Including specifics about your offering is a good idea, and lists can help you do that.

>> **Pain points, features, and benefits:** When you write the copy for each service page, pull out the sheet you worked on in Chapter 3 that lists your pain points, features, and benefits. For example, you may want to talk about

how some customers face brown lawns or patches (pain point) but your customers can expect a green lawn all year long (benefit)! Then list the features of your offer, such as fertilization, weed control, seeding, and so on.

>> **Links to features:** You may have decided to create a separate page for each feature of your offer in your main menu. If so, you can list the features on the service pages in a bulleted list and then link to each feature page. Search engines love when you link to other pages on your website, because it helps them crawl your site more easily and understand your content. Lists also help visitors understand your offer.

>> **Visual elements:** Visual elements include amazing photos, illustrations, and video. Professional visuals that support your text will resonate with visitors.

>> **Portfolio or gallery:** If you have a portfolio or gallery on your sitemap, you could show the items in the gallery that pertain to this service. For example, if you are a home remodeler and you have a service page for bathroom remodels, you should show the bathroom jobs you completed on this page, with a link near the photos to view the entire gallery. It's okay if your photos appear on multiple pages. Placing images contextually like this is good site design.

>> **Testimonials:** If you have reviews and testimonials, include them on your service pages. You can have one page that shows all of your testimonials and add them to each service page, in context with the service. You have a better chance of them being viewed when they are "integrated" with a page.

INCORPORATING TESTIMONIALS

There are a few ways you can add testimonials to your service pages. You can put one or two static testimonials on each page, meaning they always appear where you put them. You could use a feed that pulls in reviews from an online source, such as Google reviews, and these will change depending on new testimonials you receive. You can also use a review module or plugin and enter all the testimonials in the backend of your website. You can categorize them by the service they pertain to and then display that category on the service page. This feature depends on the platform you are using and the modules you have.

Testimonials and reviews can also be videos. When you add a video testimonial, pull out a few words from the video and place them next to the testimonial or write a brief description so that people will know what they will be watching if the commit to clicking the Play button. The testimonial will be more effective that way.

» **Numbers/statistics:** Do you have any numbers or statistics that pertain to this service? Have you performed this service over 100 times? Did this service solve xyz problem 85 percent of the time? Numbers speak well to your credibility. See Figure 7-2.

2023 STATS ARE IN!
WEB DESIGN FOR EVERYBODY!

Toto Coaching Helped	Toto Coaching Worked With	Toto Coaching Presented
9,604	**11**	**46**
Students & Businesses	Organizations	Speaking Events

FIGURE 7-2: Numbers can be very powerful in communicating your authority.

» **FAQs:** Adding FAQs that pertain to each service is good UX. People will read your service page and will most likely have specific questions. This way, they don't have to hunt around for the answers.

» **Video:** Using video to explain your service is a great idea. Some people learn and understand concepts better when they are presented with videos. Adding a video to your page not only helps you explain your service easily, it also helps you connect with the visitor and builds trust, as they can see you in action. In addition, creating that interactivity with the visitor is helpful in building that relationship with them. People volunteering to click a Play button is a commitment, and hopefully you are bringing the visitors further down the buyer's journey.

The background video is another option. This type of video isn't "watched" from beginning to end, but instead gives an idea of the service in a fresh and exciting way. You can overlay the video with a color so that when you place supporting text on top of the video, you are able to read the text. This is a nice addition to a website.

No matter what type of video you add to the site, you most likely will need to host the video at a video streaming service such as Vimeo, YouTube, or Wistia for best results. Don't upload videos to your own website. See Chapter 8 for more about using videos effectively.

» **Relevant news or blog articles:** If you have a blog, a press page, or a news page, the individual articles or posts should be categorized. If you set up categories for each of your services and then put each post in a category, you can display the articles that pertain to the service category directly on this service page, This can drive visitors to another page on your website, thus keeping them on your website longer, which is great for SEO.

» **Relevant events:** If you have any events that pertain to this service and you are using a calendar module, add each event to a service category. Then you can simply place the code to show any events that are in this category right on your service page. This keeps users engaged and you might even get some more attendees.

» **Call to action:** A CTA on each service page is important. This can be an image, button, form to fill out, registration link, or line of text that prompts your visitors, leads, and customers to take action. Ask yourself what action would your visitors naturally want to take after looking at this page? Would they want to download a template? Would they want to fill out a form for a free demo? Would they like to subscribe to a newsletter? Include at least one CTA.

» **Forms:** Forms are a wonderful way to build your mailing list. If a person shows interest in your services, and they are willing to give you their personal information, this is a great start and gives you a warm lead. Consider different forms for the different reasons a person would fill out the form.

There are many types of forms you could have on your website:

- A simple newsletter signup form capturing emails and possibly names.

- A request for an estimate, capturing name, email, some categories of services you offer, and a message area. These can also include location, budget, photos of existing area, and days that would be good to meet.

- A request for a demo, capturing name, email, and date for the demo, as well as what should the demo focus on.

» **Case studies:** If you have case studies that pertain to a service, include them on the services page. Consider creating a category for each service area, and then tagging the studies based on the service area. Once your case studies are categorized, you can pull in only the case studies that pertain in this particular service area. Case studies can build trust and generate sales.

» **Team members who perform this service:** This is helpful when visitors need or want to choose a specific provider. Attorney and healthcare websites do this well. For example, you might have pages that pertain to each practice area, and then on that page you list the attorneys who practice that type of law. On an orthopedist's website, you may have a service page for "hip replacements" and then on that hip replacement page, you could have all of the doctors in your practice who do hip replacements. This concept applies to preschools and teachers, sports teams and coaches, photography services and photographers, and more. This also helps search engines understand your site and what content relates to what. It also helps boost your SEO because you are adding internal links to other pages on your website.

>> **Links to other services:** If someone was just learning about your company and they are reading this service page you are working on now, what other service areas do you think they might like to see? Think of this as a way to keep visitors on your website longer, and also as a chance to provide more services to one customer.

Remember that the goal is to provide value by providing a richer experience. You want to upsell if you can, gather leads, help visitors understand more of your offerings, and keep users on your site longer.

Take a few minutes to look at the list of the services you provide and make a list of all of the content that you want to provide for each service. On some pages, you might want to include a video, and on other pages you want to include a form. The pages do not need to contain the same content.

Building Support Pages for Nonprofits

If you run a nonprofit or collect donations, this may be the most important page on your website. I have worked with many nonprofit organizations, and they usually tell me that getting donations is often the goal of the entire website. Therefore, this page can be very important to the success of the organization going forward.

USING CUSTOMER RELATIONSHIP MANAGEMENT (CRM) SOFTWARE

If you run an organization that takes donations, you should probably invest in an online fundraising software application (a CRM, for customer relationship management software) to help you effectively manage your donors. CRMs can help you manage your constituents, view trends, target your marketing efforts, nurture your donors, and more. Search for "online fundraising platforms for nonprofits" to see a list of options.

Be sure to determine the options the CRM provides. You want to determine if it includes the ability to:

- Add a widget or form that will integrate with your website to collect donations

- Customize the form or widget on your website so that it uses the same fonts, colors, borders, and so on, as your website

What to include on your support pages

Keep in mind that visitors may not be ready to donate yet — in fact, the industry average conversion rate for support pages is somewhere around 21 percent. This means that 79 percent of the people who visit your support page will not fill out that donation form. The more you build this page intentionally, the better your return. You want your visitors to understand why donation is important, make it easy to give, address their key concerns, and reinforce the value of donating. Be thoughtful about this page and start with the features covered here.

A header row

Your first row on the support page, also called the header row or hero row, should contain a very strong visual and a strong message. This row needs to be engaging and contain a compelling *why*. The more it can talk to the heart of your potential donor, the better. Look back at the buyer personas you created and address your visitor's true motivation for donating. It may not have anything to do with what you offer. It may have to do with something that happened in their own life or their own guilt about something. Use a supporting image or video to back this up.

Forms

The next most important item for this page is your actual donation form. This could be a customizable widget or form from your donor database application or a form that you embed, included with your page builder or a plugin or app. When building the actual form, remember that shorter forms are better. Ask only the required information. Strip the questions down to the bare minimum. Your form might offer suggested donation amounts, tangible donations, options for recurring donations, and the ability to have visitors pay the credit card processing fees.

Mission/impact statement

If you do not have a statement yet, there are a ton or resources online to develop one. Display your mission statement in a beautiful way by using a different font, putting it in a different color, or maybe indenting it. Consider putting the mission statement in its own row with a nice background or supporting image.

A story

Share a story on this page. How has your organization helped someone specific? Bring your mission down to a personal level so that visitors can resonate with your cause. Sharing a story allows potential donors to picture themselves in this situation or to picture themselves solving this problem.

Visuals

Visuals are very powerful, and the better the photos or videos you have, the more powerful they can be. Hire a professional photographer if you can.

Dedications

Dedications can encourage visitors to act. Making the donation personal encourages potential donors to engage with your organization.

Corporate giving and matching

Promote corporate giving or matching on your donate page. Explain the process for corporate matching, then include some language that they can take to their company.

FAQs

FAQs are a great way to address additional last-minute questions or reservations that a visitor may have prior to donating. Answer those questions to create trust and confidence. See Figure 7-3.

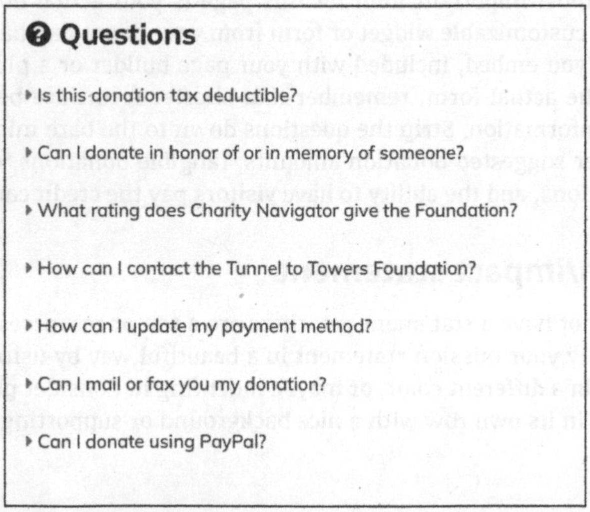

❓ Questions

▸ Is this donation tax deductible?

▸ Can I donate in honor of or in memory of someone?

▸ What rating does Charity Navigator give the Foundation?

▸ How can I contact the Tunnel to Towers Foundation?

▸ How can I update my payment method?

▸ Can I mail or fax you my donation?

▸ Can I donate using PayPal?

FIGURE 7-3:
Adding an FAQ section to your support pages encourages trust in your organization.

Social channels

If you have a strong presence on social media, include the links to your channels and encourage donors to visit your channels to learn more about your organization. If they follow you, you are strengthening your bond and you are more likely to have returning donors. If you keep yourself on your donors' minds on social media, you'll be top of mind when it is time to renew a donation, participate in a larger fundraiser, purchase gift memberships, or refer others to your organization.

Sharing links

Include sharing links on this page so visitors can share the donation page with others. You can include these links on the donation page as well as the thank you page of your donation form. Encourage your donors to share all the great work you are doing with their peers.

Other ways to support

Encourage your visitors to support your organization in other ways, such as volunteering, attending events, and receiving your newsletter. On your support page, consider adding other ways they can support your organization. When visitors see your donate page but are not ready quite yet to donate, they may dip their toes in the water by volunteering at an event. One of my clients built a separate page for each type of support and then, on the main donate page, they built a row with a CTA that drove visitors to the other pages.

Three things that every nonprofit should do

Now that you know what to add to your donation pages, you need to do three more things:

>> **Add a noticeable button to the header row:** Make sure that your donate page is easy to find on your website! Many organizations place a button in the top bar of the website. Remember that the top bar is for utilitarian menu items — things you want visitors to do on your website. Make it easy to donate by adding a background that makes this menu item look different and stand out. Figure 7-4 shows an example of a Donate button.

FIGURE 7-4:
Be sure to place a Donate or Support button at the top of every page, set off from the other links.

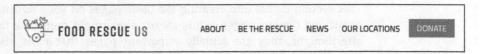

>> **Add rows to your website to drive traffic:** Include a row on the homepage and on other pages that directs people to this page. Advertise the donation page around the website contextually, so that visitors might be swayed to donate right then, as shown in Figure 7-5.

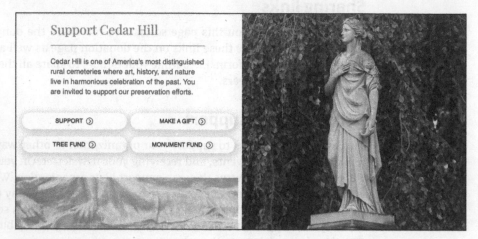

Text within the figure:

Support Cedar Hill

Cedar Hill is one of America's most distinguished rural cemeteries where art, history, and nature live in harmonious celebration of the past. You are invited to support our preservation efforts.

SUPPORT ⊙   MAKE A GIFT ⊙

TREE FUND ⊙   MONUMENT FUND ⊙

>> **Create an amazing thank you page and follow-up email:** Think about what happens after donating. Direct the donor to a beautifully laid out thank you page and send them a follow-up email. Reinforce the great feeling of giving and instill confidence that the donor has made the right decision. You don't want buyer's remorse. On this page and in this email, make sure you thank the donor with heartfelt messages. Include the donor's name if you can, explain how the donation will be used, and provide links to other relevant information as well as your contact details. This is also a great place to include any tax donation IDs and numbers.

Creating Pages that Every Website Needs

This section delves into creating the basic pages on your website, including the About and Contact pages. While these pages might seem like that would be an afterthought, they are actually important pages that most visitors will view. Include the information that people are expecting, and add a bit more if you can.

The About page

In some industries, the About page is the most important page on the entire website besides the homepage. Understanding the purpose of the About page is crucial. It showcases your expertise and builds trust. Visitors want insights into you or your company. Key questions to answer might include:

>> How long have you been in business?

>> Are you experienced or a newcomer?

>> How many products or services have you sold?

>> Are they interested in specific figures or data?

>> How many locations do you operate, or how many people do you employ?

Reflect on your target audience. What matters to them? What information would compel them to contact you or visit your location?

Ask yourself why someone would visit this page? This will guide the content you include. Write this down for each page in your About section. You will get better results if you think of this information from your customers' point of view. When you are writing this content, add a human touch to any facts.

Here are some ideas for what you can include on your About page.

What you do

Begin with a concise overview of your company's purpose or activities. This can be your mission statement or a brief description of your offerings. Make sure that it's succinct and, if you're using a mission statement, confirm that it clearly conveys what you do.

Your differentiators

What sets your company apart? Distill that uniqueness into a phrase and highlight it at the start of your About page. A compelling differentiation can resonate with visitors. If you're unsure, seek insights from colleagues, past clients, or team members. An external viewpoint can offer surprising insights into how others perceive your offerings. For example, on one of my websites, I let people know that I have written this book, which is a differentiator, as well as the length of time I have been working in this field. See Figure 7-6.

Exclusive Author

AUTHOR OF "BUILDING DIY WEBSITES FOR DUMMIES"

Jennifer is the author of "Building DIY Websites for dummies", part of the "for dummies" series by Wiley Publishing. The book will be available April 2024, and is a perfect companion to this course!

📖 Preorder Building DIY Websites for Dummies on Amazon

THREE DECADES HELPING BRANDS SUCCEED ONLINE

I was writing HTML before many of today's popular websites even existed! Since learning to code websites in 1994, I've assisted thousands of companies and entrepreneurs in establishing their digital presence.

From advising nonprofits and small businesses to coaching global agencies and web developers, I understand what truly works across industries and individual needs. Now I want to pay forward those decades of knowledge directly to you.

FIGURE 7-6:
Add your differentiators to the About page. Visitors want to be convinced that they should work with you.

Videos

You can also add a short video explaining what you do. Recently, I had hip surgery and I needed to choose a hip doctor. I looked up a lot online and read reviews, but what sold me on the doctor I chose was a video that he placed on his personal About page. He posted a video that explained the different types of surgery performed, what he is an expert in, how often he performs this surgery, and more. After watching this video, I did not have any interest in reaching out to any other doctor. He sold me on his expertise.

Your history

Consider sharing a concise history of your personal or company journey. Whether it's through a few paragraphs, a video, or a timeline, highlight key moments and reasons for your qualifications. If your personal story is integral to the company, emphasize your qualifications and background. Engage potential customers by making your history relatable and inviting. Presenting your story in an engaging manner increases the likelihood of visitors connecting with it.

A mission statement

You can include your mission statement in place of describing what you do or in addition to what you offer. If you have an important mission statement, you might want to set this aside in a different font and color than the rest of your content. If you do not have a mission statement, include your values or vision, or a corporate philosophy. The About page is a natural place to include a mission statement, values, vision, or philosophy.

Bios and headshots

Include a brief bio of yourself and possibly your team, tailored to your audience. For instance, a physician might opt for a formal tone, while a dog walker could be more casual. Consider adding a creative headshot, even exploring unconventional ideas like illustrations. Decide whether to feature just yourself or include team members, especially if they interact with clients. Always prioritize what your potential customers will find valuable when showcasing your services or products.

EXAMPLE

One of my clients, owners of a coffee shop, actively employed individuals with disabilities, providing them with workplace training to foster independence. To enhance customer engagement, they featured their team members on their website, complete with personal notes about each individual. This thoughtful approach offered visitors conversation starters, enriching interactions with the team members when they visited the shop. See Figure 7-7.

FIGURE 7-7:
Featuring your team members on your About Us page can create a more welcoming atmosphere, making customers feel at ease when interacting with your staff.

A story

Maybe you have a fun story to share that is engaging or entertaining. Do you have a moving story of how your services or products have helped others? This may be the place to add that story. Your story can be in text, video, or a photo gallery format. If you can think of a story that will help create that connection with visitors, include it.

Education, certifications, achievements, distinctions, and awards

The About page is also a natural spot on your website for your education, certifications, achievements, distinctions, and awards (see Figure 7-8). Chapter 4 discusses E-E-A-T (Experience, Expertise, Authoritativeness, and Trustworthiness). Posting your education, certifications, and awards is a great way to do this. Include links to the educational institutions if possible and to your awards online. Set yourself apart from your competition by sharing these achievements.

ANOTHER LEVEL OF SERVICE

EDUCATION

Purdue University
B.A. Communication, 1986, Brian Lamb School of Communication

Hofstra University
J.D. 1989, Maurice A. Deane School of Law

BAR ADMISSIONS

State of Connecticut
1989

United States District Court
(Connecticut)
2003

MEDIATION TRAINING & CERTIFICATION

Completed 40 Hour Training Course: Mediation Matters, Rockville, Maryland

AFFILIATIONS

Connecticut Bar Association

American Bar Association

APPOINTED SPECIAL MASTER

Stamford Superior Court

Danbury Superior Court

FIGURE 7-8: Show your E-E-A-T on your About pages by placing any certifications that illustrate your authority.

PHOTOS

Adding photos that support any of the items in this section is a great idea. Not only do they validate what you are saying, but visuals are also much more powerful than the written word. If you do not have a lot of photos, consider taking more photos when you can.

Statistics and data

Do you have numbers that back up what you do or have done? How many people you have helped, how much revenue you have raised, how many locations you have opened — these types of statistics are great for your About page.

Contact information

Providing contact information helps you appear transparent. Visitors need to be able to contact you in multiple ways — email, phone, WhatsApp, or social channels?

Social feeds and links

If your social media posts reinforce why visitors should engage with you, consider displaying recent posts. Use available software or embed codes from platforms like Facebook to showcase posts. Include any links to your channels and use their official icons on your website. To keep visitors on your site, ensure that these links open in a new tab or window.

Testimonials

You can simply copy and paste text from an email, pull in your Google reviews, or use reviews from another platform like Yelp or Facebook. Let visitors know that people love your work!

Volunteer work

If volunteering enhances your credibility or reflects your values, mention it. List and link to the organizations you support, detailing your involvement if desired. Sharing volunteer work can strengthen your narrative and differentiate you, especially in industries with less reputable individuals.

Mentions on other websites or the press

If you've been mentioned in the press or featured online, highlight this by sharing an excerpt and linking to the original article. Avoid duplicating the entire article; instead, provide a direct link that opens in a new tab or window. A therapist I worked with did this by showing the logos of the publications she was quoted in, as shown in Figure 7-9.

CTAs

The last item to include on your About page is a *call to action*. What do you want the visitor to do next? Book a demo? Request an estimate? Contact you directly? Explore your store? Whatever you want the visitor to do, add a good CTA here. Direct users to the next logical step in their journey. This can help solidify the relationship.

The Contact page

The Contact page can be a primary destination for visitors, sometimes even before the homepage. It's essential for it to be visually appealing and comprehensive. As always, think about the visitor's expectations when designing this page.

The primary role of the Contact page is to provide ways to connect with you or visit your location. Depending on your business type, this information varies. Here is a list of common Contact page elements; note which are relevant to your business:

>> Name of the business

>> Other names the business is known by

>> Owner's name

>> Names of managers or other important people

>> Main phone number

>> Department phone numbers

>> Cell phone number

>> Fax number

>> Email address

>> Department email addresses, such as sales@ or support@

- Links to other department pages that people might want to contact, such as HR, Media, and so on

- Physical address and mailing address

- A map displaying the location

- A link to directions or actual directions written out

- Hours of operation, including holiday hours

- A general Contact Us form

- Specific forms for different activities, such as a form for general contact, orders and returns, technical support, and so on

- Rules about the property when you visit (are dogs allowed, when are the grounds open, and so on)

- Scheduling appointment links

- Booking calendar or link to book an appointment

- Newsletter subscription form

- A photo of your business, especially the outside

- Social media links or feeds

Consider all the reasons that someone may want to reach out to you, or connect with you, and then make it *easy* for them to do so!

Privacy policy and Terms of Service pages

You may have not even thought of, or heard about, these two pages before, but don't skip this step. Many times, these pages are an afterthought.

Privacy policies page

A privacy policy informs visitors about data collection and usage on your website. Essentially, it details what information you collect, how it's used and stored, and how users can modify or remove their data. Given the legal implications, it's crucial to have one.

Different businesses have varied needs. Depending on your audience, laws like the EU's GDPR or California's CalOPPA might apply.

Terms of Service (ToS) page

The Terms of Service (ToS) page outlines the rules for using your website. Often overlooked, it's an agreement between the website owner and its users, detailing the rules of engagement and the consequences of not adhering to them. It's especially crucial for sites where users can post content or comments. A ToS can:

>> Protect your content and intellectual property.

>> Specify user behavior expectations.

>> Detail consequences for rule violations.

>> Limit your liability for content accuracy.

>> Define policies like cancellations, refunds, and intellectual property rights.

Regardless of your website's nature, a ToS is recommended. It can prevent content theft and clarify user rights regarding your content. For professionals, such as attorneys, it can specify that the website doesn't provide professional advice.

Crafting a privacy policy or Terms of Service

The same principles apply to creating a Terms of Service that apply to a privacy policy. There are three main ways to craft these policies:

>> **Use an online template:** These can be free but might not cater to or address your specific needs.

>> **Use an online privacy policy or ToS generator:** Budget-friendly options like Termaggedon or Termly customize policies based on your inputs. This is the preferred method for small business. This policy will not only be tailored for your situation, but you will also be given code to add the policy to your website. The code keeps the policy up-to-date automatically, which is helpful, as governments continue to change their regulations and laws.

>> **Hire an attorney:** Hiring an attorney will provide you with the most comprehensive policy, but can be costly.

AUTHOR
SAYS

You can also take a hybrid approach: Combine an online-generated policy with attorney review for accuracy and cost-effectiveness.

Once it's been crafted, include the policy on a dedicated page.

After you have created your policies, link to the policy pages in two places: from your website's footer and from any user-filled forms (including any checkout pages).

Populating Your Showcase Pages

Your website can feature pages that showcase your products, services, and expertise, allowing visitors to explore what you have to offer before making a purchase. It's crucial to build trust with potential customers, and displaying your capabilities and experiences can be an effective way to do this. Consider including portfolio pages and product description pages to highlight your offerings.

Portfolio pages

If you offer a service, consider adding a portfolio page to your website, especially if your work results in a tangible product, such as photography, landscaping, or baking. A portfolio showcases your work, helping potential clients gauge your style and quality.

While some industries debate the need for a portfolio, I believe it aids in attracting the right clients. A well-received portfolio can guide visitors further into the buying process, while those unimpressed might not engage, saving you time. The number of items in your portfolio is subjective, depending on your preference and available content.

WARNING Be sure that you have written permission to use client-related content, possibly incorporating consent into initial contracts. When in doubt, consult a legal expert.

Your portfolio can feature various elements, tailored to best represent your work and appeal to potential clients. Here are a few ideas:

- » High-quality visuals of your portfolio

- » A summary of this project, including challenges faced, solutions provided, timelines, and customer interactions

- » Links to online projects, allowing visitors to see your work firsthand

- » Testimonials from clients

- » Logos of other companies or organizations who participated in this project

- » Links to service pages

- » CTAs, such as a form for a free estimate or demo and links to webinars or events related to the showcased work

EXAMPLE For example, one of my landscaping design clients included a page for particular projects and showed before, during, and after photos with a little writeup beside each item, as shown in Figure 7-10.

FIGURE 7-10:
Get creative with
how you show
your work. You
can include a
visual with a write
up about the
project. This
helps potential
customers
envision what it
will be like to
work with you or
use your services.

Product pages

If you are setting up an ecommerce store, there are many other things you need to think besides the products, such as choosing and configuring payment processors, shipping and tracking options, taxes, and so on. Those items are beyond the scope of this book, and in this section, I focus on the products themselves, including product layouts.

The next sections cover the key information you need to include for each product.

Product titles

The product titles should describe your offer and use your keywords. While there's no strict length for product titles, they should be clear and informative. They should tell visitors (and search engines) exactly what they are getting. Product titles can differ from meta titles, which have specific guidelines such as character count. For product titles, consider the following:

» Brand name

» Model name

» Product name

» Feature

» Material

» Product type

» Size

» Color

For example, for a motorcycle site, something like "Predator 2-UP black leather double-diamond seats with forward positioning" effectively conveys brand, model, color, material, feature, and product name. Highlighting the brand is important when your consumers are brand loyal.

Brief and long descriptions

Your product should include a brief and a long (detailed) description.

>> The brief description should immediately address the pain points this product solves, mention the benefits, and describe how this is better than others on the market. Be specific and avoid general statements like "best on the market." If you can, use descriptive adjectives. Don't use superlative words unless you back them up with specifics and data.

>> The long description, located below the product, delves deeper into the product's specifics. While it can be less sales-focused than the brief description, its aim is to address any remaining customer concerns and encourage visitors to make a purchase. Figure 7-11 shows some brief and long descriptions.

Prices

You will, of course, need to add prices to your products. Most ecommerce stores will not show the product as available for purchase if there is no price.

Main photo

The featured image is the primary product photo displayed on product listings and online feeds, such as Google's shopping feed. It's crucial to select a clear image that accurately represents your product. For a cohesive look on your ecommerce site, maintain a consistent style for all featured images. For instance, if you own a clothing store, avoid mixing images of clothes worn by models with those laid out on tables, as that can appear disorganized. Aim for a uniform, clean presentation.

Additional gallery photos

Take some close-up shots so people can see how the product looks closer up. If there is special stitching or another special feature, take photos of those features and highlight them in the additional photos. Think of any question a potential consumer will have and show the answer in photos.

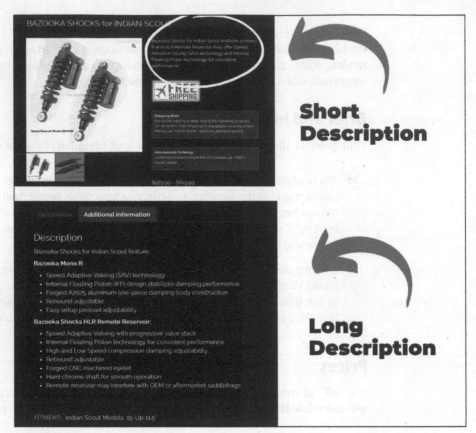

FIGURE 7-11: Include a short description for each of your products, as well as a long description, as you see on this motorcycle parts website.

SKU

You need to assign a SKU (an identifying number/letter combination) to each product. Although you can typically create your own SKU, it's wise to have a consistent method. Check if your POS system accepts your preferred SKU format. If you've been selling already, use your existing SKUs. If you are reselling a product that you did not create, you might want to use the manufacturer's SKU, as search engines index the SKU number. If a consumer is looking for this product by searching for the SKU, your product may come up in the SERP.

Box weight, length, width, height

For shipping purposes, some products require details like weight, length, width, and height. If you're using an automatic shipping calculator with carriers like FedEx, UPS, or USPS, this information is essential for accurate pricing. Shipping can get complicated very quickly and using shipping calculators can make it more complicated. You may need to enter this information for all your products.

Product type

On your website, products are categorized as either "simple" or "variable." In essence, simple products have no options. For instance, if you sell lotion in two sizes, listing each size as a separate product means you have two simple products. But if you list them under one product where the customer chooses a size, this is called a variable product. For simple products, the Add to Cart button is immediately visible, but for variable products, it's either hidden or disabled until an option is selected.

Categories

Be sure to assign you products to categories. I recommend placing each product in 1–4 categories.

TIP

Product category names are very important for SEO! Search engines index these categories, and they use them to understand your products in a better way. Make sure your categories contain your keywords when applicable.

Once your products are in categories, they will appear on the category archive or listing pages, or in other words, on the landing pages for your categories. Category archive pages will have a URL and you can create menu items that link to these pages. This makes it easy to organize your products, use helpful menus, and link to these pages from social media accounts and email marketing efforts.

Tags

Tags are like categories, but they are more descriptive. This is what the SEO plugin Yoast has to say about product categories and tags:

> "Categories help you bring hierarchy to your pages, whereas tags help you group content on the same topic."

On a skin care website that sells lotion, a *tag* might name one of the ingredients in the lotion, such as vitamin C. Then if someone wanted to look at all the products containing vitamin C, they could visit the tag archive for vitamin C, or the owner of this online store might make a page that shows those products. People coming to the store are most likely searching for the category of the product, but then may be interested in seeing what other similar products this store carries. Search engines also index tags, so this is an important consideration.

Laying out your product pages

When selecting a platform or theme for your website, consider how it allows you to design product pages. Before committing to a platform, review the theme examples to ensure you like the layout, pricing display, photo gallery, and description placements. Some platforms offer theme builders, which let you customize templates for products or specific categories. It's essential to know what you can modify. Can you hide tags or move the price?

A common product page layout has a gallery on the bottom or left, with the title, brand, rating, price, and Add to Cart button on the right, followed by a short description, social links, and navigation to other products (see Figure 7-12). Be sure you're comfortable with these elements and their placements. If you want a unique layout, ensure your platform supports that flexibility.

FIGURE 7-12: Most product pages are laid out this way by default, with photos on the left and the title, price, description, and Add to Cart button on the right. Visitors who shop online are comfortable with this layout.

Event pages

Start by choosing how you will add events to your website. There are two ways you can list your events on your website:

» Manually, by copying and pasting the event text onto a page.

» Using proper event management software (calendars) that you add to your website. This might be called an app or a widget, or in the case of WordPress, a plugin.

When considering the pros and cons of using event software for your website, several factors come into play:

» One of the primary advantages of event software is that you never have old data out there. Once the date of the event has passed, it falls off your "upcoming events" list so your website stays up to date. You don't have to remove it manually.

>> Calendar software also uses structured data. This makes it easier for search engines to understand and index your content. Without structured data, search engines might find it difficult to interpret and index your content.

>> Using a calendar software ensures consistency, as the layout remains uniform across all events, providing a seamless user experience.

>> Another benefit is the ability to categorize and tag events, which not only enhances the user experience but also boosts SEO.

The drawback is that these programs might come with a price tag. Despite the initial investment, the returns in terms of improved user experience and SEO benefits often justify the cost. Although manual input might seem cost-effective and straightforward, the benefits of using specialized event software usually far outweigh the cons. Investing in a quality event management application is a wise decision.

Displaying events

When you use a proper event calendar software, your calendar page can have different layouts (also sometimes called formats or views):

>> You can choose a grid format that looks like a calendar. Choose this option when you have a lot of events. If you do not have at least one event each month, do not use this layout. See Figure 7-13.

< > This Month March 2024 ˅

25	26	27	28	29	1	2
3	4	5	6 6:00 pm - 7:30 pm REVVING UP YOUR BUSINESS: PRACTICAL WAYS TO USE AI TOOLS IN YOUR BUSINESS TO PROMOTE YOUR ONLINE PRESENCE	7 1:00 pm - 2:00 pm HOW TO HIRE AN SEO AGENCY	8	9

FIGURE 7-13: Use a grid layout if you host events and have several events each month.

>> A list format looks like a list of events. Choose this option when you have months that do not have any events. This way, the visitor will see some upcoming events, even if they are far off in the future. See Figure 7-14.

SEP **1** 2023	September 1 @ 12:00 pm - 4:00 pm **Port Sanilac Lighthouse Tour Sept 1st, 2023** **Port Sanilac Lighthouse** 81 S Lake Street, Port Sanilac Overview of the Tower Tour: You'll climb up 50-step tower with its views out into Lake Huron and experience the unique feeling of traveling back in time like a lighthouse keeper. Up the spiral staircase and a shipman's ladder, this brick tower boasts unparalleled views from the lantern room at the tower top. View the… $5.00
AUG **25** 2023	August 25 @ 12:00 pm - 4:00 pm **Port Sanilac Lighthouse Tour August 25th, 2023** **Port Sanilac Lighthouse** 81 S Lake Street, Port Sanilac Overview of the Tower Tour: You'll climb up 50-step tower with its views out into Lake Huron and experience the unique feeling of traveling back in time like a lighthouse keeper. Up the spiral staircase and a shipman's ladder, this brick tower boasts unparalleled views from the lantern room at the tower top. View the… $5
AUG **18** 2023	August 18 @ 12:00 pm - 4:00 pm **Port Sanilac Lighthouse Tour August 18th, 2023** **Port Sanilac Lighthouse** 81 S Lake Street, Port Sanilac Overview of the Tower Tour: You'll climb up 50-step tower with its views out into Lake Huron and experience the unique feeling of traveling back in time like a lighthouse keeper. Up the spiral staircase and a shipman's ladder, this brick tower boasts unparalleled views from the lantern room at the tower top. View the… $5

>> You can show a day view with the current day's schedule — this is good for websites that have many events each day, such as a gym or school.

>> A week view is also good for those who run many events, such as a preschool.

>> A photo view shows each of your events with a large photo like a grid of photos. If your events are visual, consider this option.

>> A map view allows you to look at events on a map — great for in-person events at different locations around a city, state, or country. Allows visitors to find the event nearest to their location. See Figure 7-15.

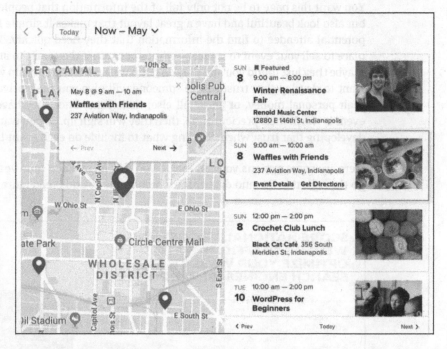

FIGURE 7-15:
This view is not used often, but if you have events in different locations and the locations matter to the attendee, show your events in this map view.

This initial page with all the events listed is called an *archive page*, and each page with an individual event is called a singular event page or *post*. In any of these archive layouts, the visitor can see events with just a few details, such as the title, day, and time. They can then click each event to get more detail, such as description, cost, duration, and more.

Where to place events

You can dedicate a single page to display all events in a calendar format. Another way to show your events is to tailor them based on the specific section or service of the website. The secret behind this tailored display lies in the use of "categories" or "tags." You can show the events in a particular category on particular service pages. This places the events contextually on your web pages — the hallmark of excellent UX.

What to include

Each event should have its own page, including a link that allows visitors to get to the page directly.

You want this page to be not only full of the information that people need to attend, but also look beautiful and have a great layout that makes it simple for the visitor or potential attendee to find the information that they need quickly. This is also your place to sell your event to someone who is not sure if they want to attend just yet, or maybe they just found you and they do not have a trust relationship with you yet. You want to develop that trust before someone will give you their private information, their personal money, or above all else: their time. Once they have trust that this event is worth their precious time, then they will sign up. So you want to think about developing that trust when deciding what to include on each event listing page.

Here are some options you can include on this page. Each time you have an event, go through this list and determine which items to add (see Figure 7-16):

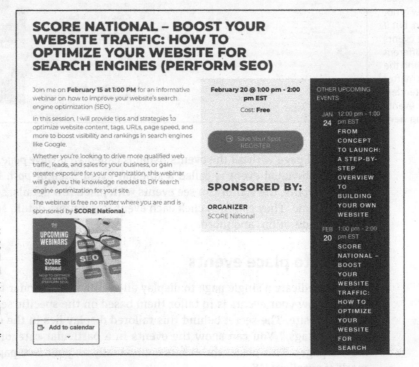

FIGURE 7-16:
Your event listing page should contain all pertinent information that someone would be looking for and answer all of their questions.

>> **Event title:** This description should be informative, accurate, and complete. If your event appears on other calendars, people might not have prior knowledge about your business.

» **Date and time:** When laying out your event page, you want to make sure this information is crystal clear! You want people to be able to know the start and end dates and times immediately so do not hide this information in a small font. Put whitespace around it and make it stand out.

» **Location/map:** If this is an in-person event, include not only the address that someone can put into their GPS to drive there, but also a map! Many calendar programs have a feature that lets you show a nice map on your event listing.

» **Event logo:** Do you have a special logo for this event? Is it an anniversary or a special project? If so, include the logo on your event page for sure!

» **Description:** Make sure you include a good description that includes all the information that attendees will need to know. Is this a benefit for someone? Do attendees need to bring certain items to the event? What is the dress? Do they need to park somewhere special? Include all information in your event description.

» **Registration form:** If you want people to sign up, include a registration form! Do not make people have to grab their phone, copy down a phone number and then make a phone call to register. Put a registration form on your event (if you need to have registration) for your sake as well as the attendee's!

» **Host:** Sometimes you may be the host of the event, other times maybe you are putting the event on at a different location and in this case the host is another organization — putting their information on the event listing is also helpful in case people have questions. If it is a great organization, this also may help promote your event and build trust!

» **Add to Calendar button:** If you have the option, include Add to Calendar buttons. This will make a calendar appointment with all the necessary information that an attendee will need to know. This way, there is more of a chance that people will remember and come to the event. Now, you may not be the type of person that uses an online calendar, and you may think that this won't be used, but trust me, it will be used! I can speak from personal experience; I use my online calendar heavily and I love to see Add to Calendar buttons so I don't miss events that I really want to attend!

» **Social media links:** Your event listing page is a great place to add your social media links, especially if you have social media accounts set up for this event. It gives people who may be on the fence about coming a chance to check the social accounts and if others are talking about the event positively, other people will be enticed to show up!

» **Speaker bios and photos:** If you have speakers, include their names, titles, a head shot and a short bio. This gives your event legitimacy and builds trust. It also will encourage your speakers and others who work with them to promote your event as it promotes themselves! If speakers are listed on your event page, you bet that they will share the event with their colleagues!

>> **Agenda:** If there is an agenda, add the agenda as well as any sessions, breakout sessions, keynote featured speakers, and activities so people know what to expect. This will give potential attendees more of an idea what will happen at the event and may encourage them to sign up!

>> **Refund or cancellation policy:** If you are taking payments you will want to list a refund or cancellation policy on this page to avoid sticky situations later. Inevitably you will have some people who will not be able to come for some reason or another. Avoid issues now by adding your cancellation policy to this page right there for people to see.

>> **Visuals:** Make sure you add some beautiful photos! They can be from the prior event if you have some. If you don't have any photos to use, consider finding some good quality stock photography, but make sure it is not super stocky. You want it to look as natural as possible!

>> **Videos:** The event listing page is a wonderful place to put a video about the event. Sometimes people will make a testimonial video or a summary video of a prior event, or maybe you want to put a video about how this event will change people's lives or add value. If you have a video or can create one, add one here.

>> **Social proof/testimonials:** If you have run events like this before, are you able to get any testimonial from prior attendees or those who Ire influenced by the prior event? If you have not run the event before, consider interviewing some people who are either organizing the event or who will be attending and put together an interesting video that talks to the heart of potential attendees. Get people excited. Video is an excellent way to do that!

>> **Sponsor logos and information:** Showcase your sponsors! Not only do they show thanks where thanks are due, but they are super important to helping you bring this event to life! Include their logo and a writeup as well as a link back to their website. Make sure you let sponsors know that you have included this information on your website and encourage them to share your event with their communities and maybe link back to your website.

>> **FAQ section:** If you think there may be additional questions that you don't want to necessarily want to include in the event description, create an FAQ area and add answers there. For example, if dogs are not allowed, an FAQ would be a great place to add that info instead of in the description.

>> **Subscribe to email newsletter:** And here is a great place to build your email list! Build your followers! If people are interested in coming to your event they may want to know more about what you offer and may want to come to more events.

Using structured data with your events

If you use software that contains structured data markup (see Chapter 4 for more information about structured data markup), be sure to add that markup to your events. Search engines can then interpret your content and will "know" that these are events. Google sometimes even pulls these events into their large calendar or into your Google Business Profile. This is free advertising! If a person is on events. google.com looking for something to do or they see your Google Business Profile and happen upon your event, you might just get a new customer out of it! Figure 7-17 shows an example. This can be invaluable. Check the event calendar software or module you plan on using to see if structured data is integrated into their product.

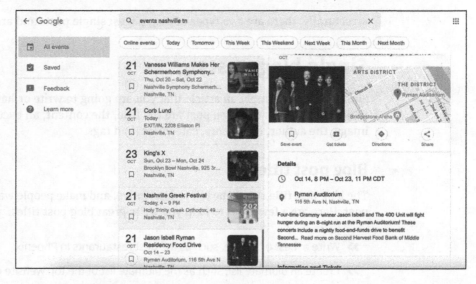

FIGURE 7-17:
If you set up your events with structured data, they might be pulled into Google events, giving you a broader reach!

There are a few required fields that you must fill in correctly for Google to pick up your event. There are also a lot of optional fields. The required fields include the event name, the start date, and the location.

TECHNICAL STUFF

For in-person event locations, you must enter in a proper, complete street address. Go to the UPS website or Google maps and copy the exact address of the event. For virtual events, you use VirtualLocation as the location. Your software should have a setting or a checkbox to indicate that the location is virtual. You must then include a URL or link. If the URL to join the event isn't available until after registering for the event, provide the registration URL.

Adding Blog Posts

A *blog* is an area of your website where you post articles and information that supports your offering in some way. Blog posts don't describe the services you offer or the products you sell. They are written articles that expand on some aspect of your business.

Blog posts are helpful for bringing people into your website when they are interested in the topic you are writing about, and they help your credibility when people want to know that you are knowledgeable.

You may have heard of a *vlog* as well. This is a video blog that expands on some aspect of your business. Vlogs can be very effective. The features covered here pertain to blogs and vlogs.

Structurally, there are two types of blog pages: single posts and archive pages.

Single blog posts

Single posts are simply an article that you are going to write or have written. The major components of a blog post are the title, the content, an excerpt, a featured image, the author, comments, categories, and tags.

Blog post titles

The blog post title should be juicy, descriptive, and make people want to read your post. Here are a few ideas to help you write great blog post titles:

>> Write a "best of" article, such as the best restaurants in Phoenix.

>> Create an ultimate list, such as the ultimate list of the top website developers.

>> Create guides to. This is a great way to start the title of your blog post.

>> Begin with a number, such as "Nine ways to clean your carpets."

There are many other options as well. Remember that the title needs to be pertinent to the article you are writing and enticing, so that people will click it.

Blog content

The actual blog post is your copy. This is where you write your article. Search engines are looking for complete and helpful content and they favor long articles that offer new information. A good rule of thumb is to make sure each article is at least 300 words, but over 1,200 is even better.

Excerpts

The excerpt of an article can be a short summary of the article or the first section. You can write your own excerpt or you can let your website pull the first lines of content from your blog post. It's typically good UX and better for SEO to customize the excerpt. I've seen countless times where the excerpt pulls in headers or HTML content, making it basically nonsense. It's better to write a custom excerpt. Tell the readers what they will learn in this article and encourage them to read it.

A featured image

The featured image is the main image that goes along with this post. The featured image is sometimes displayed on the blog article and also on the main blog listing page, also called the archive page. Using beautiful, featured images can increase readership on your blog.

Author

Each blog post will also be assigned an author. The author typically will include a name, a photo, and a short bio. You can show the author bios on the bottom or top of each article, or not include the author at all. Most of the time, I do not show the author on smaller websites, but if your industry falls under YMYL (see Chapter 4) and is in the financial or health industry, you should show the author and the bio. This develops your author profile and can increase your expertise score.

Comments

Most of the time you will see the option to allow comments on your blog posts. For smaller websites and blogs that are not heavily trafficked, I do not recommend you allow visitors to comment on your blog. The reason for this is that most of the comments you get will be spam or phishing attempts unless your blog is very active and people go there just to read it.

You can set up apps that weed out the spam comments, so if you do decide to allow comments, make sure that you have a plan in place for the spam. There is nothing worse than going to a website blog and seeing a bunch of spam and gibberish below each article. That is a good way to erode trust, so I recommend that you turn comments off.

Categories and tags

Each blog post must be in at least one category. I recommend placing each article into one to four categories. Categories are indexed by search engines, so make sure your categories contain the keywords you identified.

**AUTHOR
SAYS**

WordPress creates a category called "Uncategorized" and each of your blog posts are placed into this category by default. Do not use this category! It will do you no good and it looks unprofessional. To determine which categories you should create, consider a recipe analogy. You can categorize each recipe by meal, so you have breakfast, lunch, dinner, appetizer, dessert, and snacks. If you have a post that is a recipe for chocolate chip cookies, the categories that this article would appear in would be dessert and maybe snacks. These category names should also line up with your keywords, if possible, because search engines will index your category names to better understand your content.

You should also "tag" your blog posts. Tags are like categories but more specific. Using the recipe analogy, if categories are the meal, then tags are the ingredients. A recipe for chocolate chip cookies would be in the dessert and snacks categories, and it would have eggs, flour, butter, vanilla extract, and brown sugar tags, for example. You can add as many tags as you like to a post.

Blog archive pages

An *archive page* is simply a listing of the blog posts on your website. On your main blog archive page, you should see all the blog posts. You can also have other types of archive pages that use a filter, such as category archives that list all blog posts in a particular category.

Search engines index category archives (otherwise called *category pages*). A category archive will also have an URL so you can share or reference that link if you want to direct visitors to all the articles in a particular category. A tag archive is a listing of all the articles on your website that are tagged with a particular tag. You'll have a link to each tag archive as well. An author archive is a listing of all the articles written by a particular author.

On any archive page, you will typically see a listing of posts that contain a title, a photo, an excerpt, the date it was posted, maybe the author, and a photo. You will then most likely see a button or link that lets you read the entire article, or you might be able to click the title or the listing and go to the actual blog post.

Strategies for creating a helpful and amazing blog

To get traction to your blogs, it is not simply about posting a few articles online. You need to have a strategy and follow some important content guidelines. The best place to start is to think about these issues:

>> What is the purpose of your blog?

>> What is the tone for your blog?

>> What do you want your blog to be about?

> ➤ How often would you like to post?

> ➤ Will you include a posting schedule?

> ➤ Will you post automatically?

The purpose of your blog

It is helpful if you come up with the purpose for your blog and keep that in mind when writing articles. Why are you writing these articles? Is it to teach potential customers something? Do you want to keep people up to date on something? Is it to show your authority?

The tone of your blog

You can write a humorous blog that makes people laugh or take an informational tone and write blog articles that explain how to use your products or services. You could use a technical tone and write very technical articles for those in your industry. Many people write inspirational blogs, and this may fit your purpose. The tone is up to you. Your articles do not need to be written in only one tone, but remember if the tone switches drastically from one article to another, you may lose your visitors.

The subject of your blog articles

What subject matters would you like to cover in your blog? If you have some ideas for blog articles, you should record them now so you are ready to write later and you don't need to go back to the drawing board.

A posting schedule

Determining a regular schedule for your blog posts is helpful for many reasons. First, it ensures that you are consistently adding new content to your website. Search engines see that your site is active, and they look favorably on new content. Visitors will also see that you post on a regular basis, so they will have an idea when to be on the lookout for the next article. Consistent posting also shows that you care about your website, and you have not forgotten to update it.

A content calendar

A content calendar is simply a plan of what, where, and when you plan to post new information. This is a great framework for your business plan. You use a calendar format and plug in which days will show new content and what the content will be. There are lots of content calendar templates online that you can use, but you don't need to use anything formal. You can simply create a Word document or use your calendar on your desktop or device.

For example, if you are posting once a week on Thursdays, make sure that you have an article title that fits the purpose of your blog for each Thursday of the next few months or year. When you create a content calendar, you save time in the long run, as you don't need to come up with a new blog post article each time you sit down to write — you already know what you will be writing about in the future. You can plan your messaging over seasons and holidays. You can also write all of your articles at once if you feel creative, and then you can schedule them out over the future. This is a great practice for keeping up to date on your blog and your content calendar.

How to get visitors to your blog

You can push the articles or visitors can pull the articles:

>> When people come to your website because they have decided to type in your URL or they have done a search for something, they are doing what is called pulling the information on your website.

>> If you send out your new blog posts via an email, or post them on social media, you are pushing your information out to your audience.

You can simply post blogs to your website, but you'll then need to wait for visitors to come pull the blog posts themselves. If you can push out your article to your email list and your social media channels, you will probably have a greater readership.

If you have multiple social media channels, pushing out your articles to each one can be tedious. You have to log into each platform individually, write a teaser for your article, create the correct size image for each platform, upload the image, paste the link, and add some hashtags for each channel individually.

Instead, I suggest you sign up for a social media marketing tool such as Hello Woofy, Social Pilot, or Hootsuite (and there are tons of other options). These platforms allow you to log in to their platform and connect all of your social media accounts one time. Then you make a single post and the social media marketing platform will send it to all of your social media accounts at one time. Check out each of these social media marketing tools if you are interested and see how they can help you save time!

TIP

There are many other benefits of using a social media marketing tool. Say you feel very inspired one week and you write a ton of blog posts, but you want to post these articles over time instead of on one day. You can upload your posts to your website, add all the images, tags, and categories, get it all set, and then schedule when each is posted. You can schedule out your push notifications as well. Get everything on autopilot so that for the next few weeks or months, you can concentrate on running your business or doing something else.

Content to include on your blog articles

Now that you've established a robust strategy for your blog, it's time to consider how to enhance its visibility on search engines. Conducting keyword research, optimizing each article, selecting relevant categories and tags, maintaining consistent posts, and delivering valuable, informative content are all crucial. Moreover, there are several additional suggestions that can assist you in crafting top-notch blog posts that gain momentum.

Include more images besides your featured image to break up the content and to reinforce a concept. Screen shots are a great example of images that appear in an article but not be beautiful enough to be the featured image.

At the bottom of your blog post, you may want to include a link to related posts or articles, as shown in Figure 7-18. These are articles or posts that are in the same category or contain the same tags as the current article. Including a related posts area at the bottom of your blog posts gives visitors something else to do on your website, which in turn helps keep them on your website for a longer period. If a visitor read a post that you wrote and liked it, they may be interested in learning more about what you have to say.

READ MORE TIPS!

FIGURE 7-18:
At the bottom of each blog post, include a section that offers more blog posts for visitors to read in this category.

Include a CTA at the bottom of every article, or in the middle of each article. Your call to action could be to sign up for newsletter, fill out a form for a product demo, or get a *lead magnet* (also known as *gated content*, which is a free item like a PDF, infographic, or video access that you give away for free after someone has filled out a small form and given you their email address). There are many other types of CTAs you can put on your blog posts. Include at least one! Encourage people to engage with you after they have read this amazing post.

Many blogs add social sharing buttons, which makes it easy for someone who loves your article to share it on their social channels. These social sharing buttons offer a one-click service — the visitor clicks the button and the article is shared right to their Facebook or LinkedIn or wherever they choose.

Many times, you will see a sidebar on each blog post. The sidebar will contain things such as other recent posts, a list of categories that are used on this blog, and a list of tags that this blog uses (also called a *tag cloud* — see Figure 7-19). As you use a tag more often, the word that is tagged will become larger. This allows visitors to see the subjects you are writing about more often, and to find other articles that contain the same content. Use tag clouds so that visitors can find more articles about topics they are interested in.

TAGS

Account Access alt text Artificial Intelligence AI Brand Consistency Design Best Practices Design Strategy Footer Layouts Full-Width Column Google Ads Google Analytics Google Search Console High-Quality Imagery Internal Linking Lasting Impressions local SEM local seo Minimalistic Design Mobile Responsiveness Multi-Column Footers Online Security SEO SEO Agency SEO Strategy service area optimization Team Members on Websites title and meta description optimization Top Bar Top Menu Typography Tips User Experience User Feedback User Permissions Video Integration Visual Impact Web Design Web Design Strategy Web Design Tips Website Aesthetics Website Design Website Iteration Website Management Website Navigation Website Optimization Website Organization Website Visibility

FIGURE 7-19: A tag cloud shows all of the tags you are using on your blog posts.

This sidebar could also contain a little writeup about the business or organization, it can contain contact information, and it might contain the most popular posts on the website. You do not need to add a sidebar, and many blogs do not include one. This is up to you.

TIP

If you are using WordPress and your theme automatically adds a sidebar or you add a sidebar, *do not* keep the default content that is included in it. Look at the sidebar and make sure it looks good and all the information included is important.

You might have the option to add a search box for the blog. You only need this if you have hundreds of articles and pages on your website. If you do decide to add a search box to your website or blog, be sure to test it. See how accurate the search engine is on your website and then review the format of the results. You might need to modify how the search is returned. If you do not look at how the search behaves, you may end up with frustrated visitors who will leave your site.

Building Your Homepage Last

Your homepage could be the most important page on your website, so you want to make sure it's doing its job! The homepage has a lot of jobs, but here are the four most important:

>> **Lets visitors know they're in the right place by showing the services or products you offer and, if applicable, your location.** If you provide local services, let visitors know right away where you are located. For example, if you are a landscaper or doctor in Idaho, people in California or Arizona are probably not going to use your services. Many times, a business will have a similar name or the same name but they might be in different states. . . so you want to let visitors know right away that they are in the correct place!

>> **Makes a great first impression and encourage the visitors to stick around and engage with you.** You want the homepage to look gorgeous and bring the visitors in. You have three to five seconds to make this impression, so right up front you want to connect with the visitors.

>> **Shows that your company is up to date with a modern website.** If visitors see an outdated, old, shall I say "vintage" website, they will translate that feeling of being "out of touch" or "behind the times" to your company. You want to show through your modern website homepage that you are keeping up with modern technologies, services, and techniques.

>> **Strategically drives people to content.** You want visitors to take action toward your primary goals on your website.

On modern websites, information is typically organized in rows down the page. The first row on your homepage is crucial, as it's the initial area that visitors see. Therefore, you want to dedicate significant effort to perfecting this row.

With the idea of rows in mind, let's consider the information you need in these rows in more detail.

Row 1: A strong message

The first row should feature a compelling headline that clearly conveys your value proposition, resonating emotionally with visitors and addressing their needs. This headline, typically between 6 and 12 words, should directly speak to your target audience, answering questions such as, "What does this company offer?" and "Why should I choose them?" Crafting this message involves understanding your customer's pain points and motivations.

Links to other pages and content

Consider your homepage as a concierge, guiding visitors to key areas of interest. Just as a hotel concierge recommends dining or entertainment options, your homepage should anticipate visitors' needs and direct them to relevant content. Prioritize which actions or information are most valuable for your visitors, such as purchasing gift cards, making reservations, learning about products, or watching videos. List these priorities and design your homepage to lead visitors through them, balancing their needs with your company's objectives.

Write down all the most important things you would like visitors to do on your website and list them in order of importance. These to-do items become the rows down the page that direct the visitors to those areas of your website.

Chapter 8 shows you how to write the headings and the copy for each row, but for now, let's get this list together.

Videos

Your homepage can benefit from featuring a video, either as a background or as standalone. Videos enhance user engagement and differentiate your site. They cater to those who prefer visual and auditory learning, helping explain your business and build trust.

>> A *standalone video* has a Play button. Visitors click the Play button to learn something new.

>> *Background videos* are added to the background of a row to convey an idea. They are not watched from beginning to end, and there is no Play button; they play automatically. There should be no sound. Some page builders/software let you add a background video with sound, but there's no worse UX than when a site randomly starts playing a video somewhere and you have to go track it down. Don't add sound to background row videos. When you add background videos, the idea they convey should be influential.

No matter what type of video you add to the site, you most likely will need to host the video from a video streaming service such as Vimeo, YouTube, or Wistia for the best result, and I review those options (and the why) in Chapter 8.

Social proof

Next, add social proof to your homepage. The most recognized form of social proof is reviews with those familiar star ratings, like on Yelp or Google. The concept of social proof is simple: People are more comfortable trying something new if others have had positive experiences. By showcasing genuine reviews, you reduce potential customers' perceived risks.

Awards and accolades

Another type of social proof in addition to reviews are awards, or accolades. No matter what industry you work in, there is someone giving out awards and badges for what you do. Display them proudly on your homepage.

Specific numbers and data

Awards and accolades are impactful, but specific numbers resonate more than vague statements. For instance, instead of saying "I raise millions for advertising," say "In 2023, I raised $606 million in advertising value." This is more compelling. By showcasing precise stats and achievements on your homepage, you boost visitors' trust.

Galleries and portfolios

It's crucial to highlight what makes you unique. Showcasing a curated portfolio on your homepage can effectively convey your offerings and benefits. Whether you're an art gallery displaying sought-after artists or a product site highlighting trending items, a visual representation speaks volumes. This portfolio can be adjusted seasonally, too. A homepage portfolio not only appeals to customers but also aids their decision-making by showcasing your quality and offerings.

Features and benefits

Features and benefits are pivotal in showcasing how your product or service solves a problem. People seek solutions, and your homepage should build trust by addressing their pain points.

EXAMPLE

For example, I am frequently looking for software for my clients or myself. Before I go looking, I identify the problems that my customer has, or I identify the problems that I'm facing, and the benefits I'm looking for. If a website lists benefits that align with my specific issues, it indicates that they understand and can address those challenges.

Lead magnets

One way to increase newsletter signups is by providing a gift for signing up. This is sometimes called a lead magnet. This could be an eBook or other type of download with information or tips that are valuable to your visitors, a free consultation or demo, or maybe a mini course. You give away something for free in exchange for their email address and permission to send them emails.

News articles and blog posts

If you want people to read your blog or your news articles, tease them on the homepage by showing a few of the most recent articles. If people see what you are writing about, they might click an article that interests them. This will cause them not only to stay on your site longer but also to move to a second page, which search engines measure and care about. Search engines want to see visitors take action on your website, and if you have great blog posts, visitors will read your articles.

Upcoming events

If you have events advertised on your website, show the upcoming events right on your homepage. This shows that your company is active and thriving and encourages visitors to sign up.

BOILING IT DOWN

Yes, there is a lot to consider as you build your site. However, as you organize your pages, keep in mind these five main ideas:

- Build trust with your visitors.

- Resonate with your visitors.

- Let your visitors know your offering.

- Give your visitors the same information in multiple places — in other words, reiterate topics on each page. No one is going to read your website like a book from start to finish, so you need to "catch" them in a few places.

- Build a website where visitors don't need to think that much. If you provide the information that visitors would naturally want to know when they visit your service pages, you have done a good job. This is good UX.

Chapter **8**

Preparing Your Site's Content

You've secured your web space, identified your target audience, and have a clear strategy for guiding visitors through your site. With a plan to rank well on search engines and a well-thought-out sitemap, you're on the right track. It's time to gather and optimize your content. Ensuring your content is streamlined, clear, and aligned with your offerings simplifies the building process. By addressing this now, you'll avoid the constant shuffle between design, layout, and content creation.

Generating and Preparing Excellent Copy

You need to get a few things ready for your website, starting with the copy you add to each page. If you completed the pain points and benefits exercise in Chapter 3, reference your notes so that you can craft amazing copy that addresses pain points head on, offers the benefits and features of your solution, and talks to the heart of your visitors. If you completed the file with your page list, keyword phrase, and title and meta descriptions for your pages in Chapter 6, pull that out now for reference as well. If you have any notes or checklists from Chapter 7, get that document handy too, so you can reference it.

Create an outline and brainstorm topics

The first thing you want to do is create one outline per page. Each outline should include all the topics you want to cover on that page. If you have six services pages, for example, you'll create six outlines. I like to create a separate Google doc or Word document for each page.

Begin by choosing one page that will have a lot of information. Brainstorm a list of all the topics you want to cover on this page. You don't need to write the copy yet or put the topics in order. Just get your ideas and things you need to cover down on paper.

Next, pull out the list you created in Chapter 3 with the pain points, features, and benefits of your solution. Add anything that pertains to this service that you may have missed.

Look at the exercise you completed in Chapter 7 and make a note of the types of content you want to include on this page. Add any of those items that you have not already included to the outline where they seem to fit well. For example, you might have an intro, a few aspects of this particular service you want to focus on, a list of typical customers, a few pain points your offer addresses, a call to action, and a testimonial on this page.

Outline your copy

Break up your text into sections with headlines that use a larger, bolder, and different font. This way, visitors can skim your page and know what you are trying to say without reading every word.

Create an outline, much like the ones from school days. This helps keep things organized, ensures you cover all essential points, and arranges content logically. It can also serve as a checklist for the content you need. Structure your thoughts for this page into a clear, written outline. List the topics in order of importance and group items together that are related.

Generate your copy

After organizing your content into an outline, you can save yourself a lot of time by following these three steps:

1. **Write one to eight sentences for each of your main topics or points on your outline.**

Explain your service, go a bit deeper, explain the problem, or describe your solution.

2. **Convert your main outline items or bullet points into descriptive headlines.**

Make these headlines friendly, strong, and descriptive. When you are generating or rewriting your headings, you want to remember that most people who visit this page will skim the headings. When they see a headline they like, they will stop to read your blurbs. You want to evoke an emotional reaction from your visitors, so write some juicy, emotional, powerful headings.

3. **Review which keyword phrase you assigned to this page and ensure that you included that phrase here. If you did not, see where you can insert this phrase in a few places.**

How many times you should insert it depends on how many words you have written. Include at least 300 words. If you do not have this number, you may want to try and add a little more text. If you do have over 300 words, insert your keyword phrase so that you have a *keyword density* of 0.5 to 3 percent. This means for a 300-word page, you want your keyword phrase to appear about two to nine times.

WARNING

Don't include keyword phrases in a density that's more than 3 percent. This could be identified by the search engines as *keyword stuffing,* which is a no-no and considered a black hat technique.

Be sure to includes the phrase in at least one heading. You can add it to two headings if you like, but I would probably not add to three unless it flows naturally or you have a very long page with a lot of headings.

Complete this process for each page, even the contact page (it won't be as involved as a service page and you probably will not have 300 words on the contact page, but write out the words that you would like to appear on this page as well).

TIP

It is okay if some of the topics or concepts appear on multiple pages. Visitors are not going to read your website front to back, like a book. Feel free to overlap your content and subjects a bit. Just don't copy word for word from one page to another.

Use AI to write content

You can use Artificial Intelligence (AI) writing assistants or tools (sometimes also referred to as LLMs — Large Language Models) to help write your content, but you do not want to use these exclusively. AI writing tools can help you elevate your work and enhance creativity. They can also save you time.

There are numerous AI writing assistants available, and by the time you're reading this book, the options might have multiplied exponentially. As of this book's writing, ChatGPT is the main option. Tools like ChatGPT utilize AI to produce copy that feels as if a human penned it, rather than a machine. You provide a starting idea, statement, and some initial copy. Then, you select preferences like copy length, tone, sentence structure, readability, and intended use (e.g., headline, article, social media post). After clicking submit, the tailored copy, based on your specifications, is presented.

TIP

The more detail you provide to writing assistants like ChatGPT, the better the results.

Here are some examples of how you can use AI writing tools when writing the copy for your website:

>> **When researching and starting the writing process:** Use AI to overcome any writer's block, streamline your research process, and gather initial content ideas.

>> **For SEO:** Use AI for keyword research and SEO analysis, as well as to generate SEO titles, meta descriptions, headings, and subheadings.

>> **To improve your content:** Use AI to rewrite content in a different voice, check for grammar and spelling errors, and analyze the tone of your content for specific audiences.

>> **To write emails and social media posts:** Use AI to write small snippets of text that will not be run through an analyzer like emails and social media for content, tone, and grammar.

From these examples, it's evident that a significant advantage of using an AI writing tool is the time-saving aspect. Whether it's for crafting swift headlines or getting a head start on research, these tools can expedite the process.

While AI writers can be a helpful tool for generating website copy, it's important to use them in a way that doesn't violate Google's quality guidelines.

Google's guidelines state that websites "should provide high-quality, original content that is written for users rather than search engines. Using AI-generated content that is low-quality, spammy, or keyword-stuffed can potentially harm your website's search engine rankings and user experience."

AUTHOR SAYS

As highlighted in Chapter 4, for your content to rank well, it must be valuable, insightful, unique, and comprehensive. Relying solely on an AI writing assistant, without infusing your personal insights, might leave your website lagging in search results. If you opt to use AI, it's crucial to ensure your content stands out and surpasses what's already available online.

Consider AI writing tools as a starting point or a draft. They offer a jumpstart, but the content requires your touch. The quality of AI-generated content can fluctuate based on the underlying algorithm and its training data. Some AI tools might not be updated with the latest global events. So, for time-sensitive topics like recent news, AI might not always be the ideal choice.

AUTHOR SAYS

While AI is very good and usually very accurate at providing information, be sure to check any information that it generates. There are times in which ChatGPT provides false information. This phenomenon is becoming so common that it has a name, called *AI hallucination*.

Steer clear of duplicate content

Duplicate content refers to identical or appreciably similar information found on multiple URLs or pages. This can range from a specific section of text to an entire page. This duplication can occur in the same website or across different sites.

DUPLICATE CONTENT AND SEARCH ENGINES

When building your website, it's possible to inadvertently include duplicate content. Grasping this concept is crucial for effective SEO. Search engines intend to return the best and most relevant information. They don't want search results filled with repetitive information from various URLs. Offering identical results can frustrate users. If the original content source isn't clearly indicated, search engines must determine which URL most likely hosts the original. This poses indexing challenges, and discerning the original from the duplicate isn't straightforward. Especially in non-malicious cases, where technical glitches cause content repetition, search engines struggle to decide which version to display in search results.

In addition, original content creators (like you!) will understandably be upset if duplicates rank higher than their (or your) authentic work in search results. They expect their genuine content to be recognized and prioritized in searches.

This is how Google handles duplicate content:

>> Google *filters* duplicate content in the SERP

>> Google *demotes* copied content in SERP

>> Google *penalizes* low-quality, copied content in the SERP

Google asserts that they don't penalize websites for duplicate content unless it appears intentionally deceptive or manipulative. Instead, they filter such content in the search results. To see this in action, you can search for your company or a specific phrase on Google. Then, append &filter=0 to the end of the search results URL. This will display all the pages Google would typically show for your query, without any filtering. Google's aim is to present the most authoritative version of the content.

If you're following the best practices in this book, duplicate content shouldn't be a major concern. It's been emphasized not to copy or plagiarize content from other sources. Such actions are viewed negatively by Google, leading to the content being downgraded in search rankings. This is malicious and Google will demote this content.

TECHNICAL
STUFF

Search engines employ the concept of *canonical* content to identify the original source of an article or content online. The term canonical, means authorized and accepted content. In the eyes of search engines, every original piece of content on the worldwide web is considered canonical, signifying it's authorized, recognized, and accepted. Each page you include on your website is its own canonical source — it is the original — and you most likely have coding built-into your platform that will place a bit of code on each page that says that this page is the canonical source for all of the information (this also helps with your SEO so make sure that your canonical tags are correct). Canonical content tells search engines that this content is the original source.

HOW DOES DUPLICATE CONTENT HAPPEN?

Content can be duplicated maliciously and non-maliciously. Whether it is malicious or non-malicious comes down to intent. What was the intent of the person who created this duplicate content?

If a website displays text that was copied from another website on purpose, this could be considered malicious. Malicious duplicate content is considered plagiarism. You know that plagiarism is copying someone else's work without giving proper citation, and this is a huge no-no in almost any industry. Duplicate content is a black hat SEO technique, which search engines frown upon, as they should. You don't want someone taking your text and using it to sell their own products or services. And likewise, you don't want to use someone else's content to sell your products and services.

You can determine if your content has been plagiarized or if you are using plagiarized content by using an online tool, such as CopyScape or Grammarly's plagiarism checker.

EXAMPLE

Here are a few different examples of duplicate content I have encountered that were used purposely on websites:

>> A client once sent me a lot of Word documents with text to add to their website. As I was adding the content to the website, I noticed that there were links in the Word document, and they all pointed to a competitor's website! It turned out that my client had simply copied entire sections and pages from their competitors' website. They did not realize there a problem with this approach. I explained that this was plagiarism and their site was likely to be banned from search engine searches.

>> While at a landscapers' trade show, I encountered an interesting case of intentional duplicate content. Several landscapers approached me, seeking professional opinions on their existing websites. After reviewing a few, I realized that many of these websites looked strikingly similar. They had identical content, down to the very word! When I tested this by copying a sentence from one of these sites and pasting it into a search engine, a multitude of websites popped up, all showcasing the exact same content! Figure 8-1 shows an example.

These landscapers hired the same cheap website development company to build them a quick and easy website. They thought this was great! Well, if it looks too good to be true, it probably is. Upon further investigation, I found that this website development company displays on their website that they use prewritten content. See Figure 8-2.

Google and all other search engines do not think it is so great, so don't do this. Using text like this also doesn't set your company or products apart from the others, so it's not particularly helpful in getting new clients.

REMEMBER

If you hire someone to write your content, you *must* verify that they will be writing original copy.

SYNDICATED CONTENT

Another type of duplicate content that happens purposely is *syndicated content*. Syndicated content is text usually in the form of a blog post or blog article that is written by one person or organization and sold as a subscription to other companies so they can use that same article on their blog.

FIGURE 8-1:
When I searched
for these words
found on these
websites, I saw
that hundreds or
thousands of
websites were
using the same
words on
their sites.

FIGURE 8-2:
This company
warns potential
customers that
they will be
pasting the same
text on your
website that
they are pasting
on others.

CONTENT

Pre-written content to save you time and build
customer confidence. We make this content
available to you as an editable document so you
can modify and customize it to your preferences.

If you purchase this syndicated content, you get a blog that has articles appearing
on it on a regular basis without you needing to write them. After the last example
I gave you, you may be thinking that this is a bad idea, right? If you don't do it
right, it can be a bad idea, but it can also be okay if it's done right. To do this
correctly, place the syndicated articles on your website, and then you must provide an attribution to the original source in two ways: one for the visitor to see and
one for search engines to see. For visitors, at the bottom or top of the article, add
something like: *This article originally appeared here* and include the link to the
original article.

TECHNICAL STUFF

It's essential to give credit where it's due. If you're adding syndicated or duplicated content to your website, you should point search engines to the original source. This is done by adjusting the canonical tag on your page, which looks like this:

```
<link rel="canonical" href="https://www.example.com/link-to-
    original-source.html" />
```

If you're using WordPress with Yoast SEO, there's a handy box under the advanced settings of each article where you can paste the original URL (see Figure 8-3). You're essentially telling search engines, "I want this content to show up in searches, but I didn't write it. Here's who did." If you plan on using syndicated content, make sure you know how to set the canonical tag correctly on your platform. Do this, and you're all set!

FIGURE 8-3:
Enter the original source of the content in this box in the Yoast plugin to credit the original content creator.

Canonical URL ❓

DUPLICATE WWW SITES CAN CREATE DUPLICATE CONTENT

There are other ways that non-malicious duplicate content is created. It can happen by accident due to technical reasons mistakes made on your website.

Duplicate content can happen technically by accident if you can browse to both the www and non-www pages on your website (for example, www.amazon.com and amazon.com). Adding www. when you register your website creates a whole new site because it's a sub-domain. For example, when you log into classes at Toto Coaching, you use learn.totocoaching.com. Learn. is a sub-domain. And yes, www. is also a sub-domain, making it a separate site. So, if people visit www.yourdomainname.com, they're on a different URL than simply yourdomainname.com, duplicating your content. Not good! You want to be able to visit only one or the other.

Here's a quick test. Type your domain in a browser with and without www. Click around the website and on each page, see if you are staying on the root domain or www.yourdomain.com. If you are able to visit both www and non-www pages, there's a problem. There are two ways to fix this:

1. **Determine your primary URL.** Typically, it's the one without www. Log into your web host and find the section in your dashboard where you need to set the primary domain.

2. **Create a DNS record to redirect all www traffic to your primary URL.** If you're unsure how to do this, ask your nameserver for help.

SECURE AND UNSECURE SITES CAN CREATE DUPLICATE CONTENT

Duplicate content can also arise from using secure (https) and unsecure (http) pages on your site. Often, this happens when images are linked using http://... instead of https://.... This difference means you're serving the same content from two different URLs. The "s" in https matters! This can occur if your SSL certificate only covers one version of your URL or if you've hard-coded links with a different URL format. To resolve this, follow these steps:

1. **Ensure your SSL certificate covers both www and non-www versions.**
2. **Update all links, images, and files to use https://.**

PRODUCT DESCRIPTIONS AS DUPLICATED CONTENT

If you resell products from a manufacturer, they may provide you with all the content for each product, like the images, the SKUs, descriptions, and more. If you just plop these descriptions on your website, you will be creating duplicate content. However, in this case, Google understands and will not penalize you. Search engines can tell that your website has a different header, maybe you have different content on the page in terms of reviews, and so on. Google typically returns the website that has the item in stock or that is closest to the searcher. So, if you are using manufacturer descriptions, focus on making your product pages slightly different, perhaps with reviews, or sprinkle in your own words if you can.

There are other ways that duplicate content can happen by accident due to technical reasons, but the ones covered here are the most common.

Creating and Sourcing Your Images

Now that you have your text organized, it's time to get your images ready!

You have heard the saying, "A picture is worth a thousand words." Selecting the right images can make a significant impact on your visitors' experience, reinforcing your brand identity and enhancing the visual appeal of your site. The images on your website will either build trust or erode trust. One or the other. You want to build, not erode trust.

You have a few choices: illustrations, photos, icons, or AI-generated images. This section concentrates on illustrations and photos. Illustrations are drawings or graphics, usually digitized for online use. Photos capture real-life scenes.

Consider your company's style when choosing which kinds of images to pick. You probably have a vibe for your marketing materials. TD Bank, for instance, opts for real-life photos and icons. Mercedes Benz flaunts sleek car photos, while Red Bull rocks illustrations. The aim is instant brand recognition, even before visitors spot the logo. If you have a style, stick to it. If not, create one and stay consistent in your imagery choice.

Stock photography vs your own photos

When sourcing images for your website, you have three main routes:

» **DIY:** Create illustrations in graphic apps or snap photos with a camera or smartphone.

» **Buy stock images:** Use pre-made photos available for purchase.

» **Hire a pro:** Get someone to design illustrations or take photos tailored to your company.

Your choice hinges on these considerations:

» **Brand style and guidelines:** When your brand's style permits personal photos or custom illustrations, creating original content is ideal. It's genuine and aligns with your brand's authenticity.

» **Purpose of the image:** When showcasing specific aspects of your business, such as your lobby or product, personal images are best. For abstract concepts like peace or success, stock images, often crafted by pros, might be more fitting.

» **Business type:** If your company sells products, prioritize personal images showcasing your items. Service providers, those in sectors like banking or psychiatry where tangible products aren't the focus, can lean more on stock images to convey feelings or ideas.

» **Time:** Regular bloggers might find stock images more convenient for frequent posts. However, for main website content, investing time and money in personal images can pay off.

» **Budget:** DIY is cost-effective. Stock images vary in price, with some platforms offering monthly subscriptions or free options. Professional photographers or illustrators, while potentially pricier, can provide top-tier content.

REMEMBER

Remember, consistency is key. Whether you own a restaurant and want to show-case your ambiance or run a bank and want to convey trust, your images should resonate with your brand. If you're on a tight schedule, stock images or a monthly subscription might be your go-to. But if budget allows, hiring a professional can be a game-changer. Whatever you choose, be sure that it aligns with your brand's identity and message.

Find an illustrator

For top-tier budgets, explore portfolios on platforms like Behance.net. For more budget-friendly options, Fivver and Upwork offer illustrators with diverse styles showcased in their portfolios. See examples of other work they have done to see if they create images in your style.

Choose a photographer

If you hire a professional photographer, they need to know the purpose of the images to make the photo shoot a success. Before hiring anyone, review their portfolio and gauge their style and expertise. Remember, a portrait photographer might not excel in real-estate shots and vice versa.

When working with a photographer, keep these points in mind and mention these issues to your photographer. Do not assume that they know these things.

» **Use your sitemap as a checklist for the photos you need.** Reference it when the photographer comes. Sit down before the photographer arrives to determine some scenes to set up for each page of your website.

» **If they don't ask you beforehand, tell the photographer the style you're looking for.** Years ago, my client hired a photographer to take photos for her website. She was an endodontist. Endodontists do root canals. Most people hate getting a root canal and are very anxious when they go to their appointment. She wanted to create a website that was calming and serene to put her patients at ease. The photographer was not aware of this, and when she got all the photos back, there were pictures of a lot of pointy instruments! Pointy instruments are scary and not relaxing. You want to be very clear about the style of the photos.

» **You want the photographer to take photos where the subject is placed off center, leaving a lot of open space to the left or the right.** This way, you can use these photos in rows with your text or your copy overlaid on the left or right of the photo. In photographer terms, you can ask them to "frame wider than usual and leave lots of space for flexible cropping." Or just make sure they know that you'd like room to place text on the right or left of many of the images. Figure 8-4 shows an example.

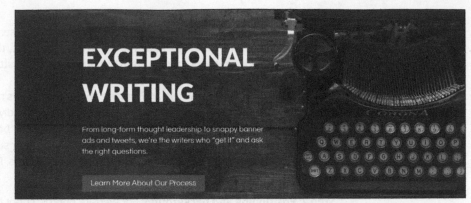

FIGURE 8-4:
Photographing
the subject to the
left or right allows
you to place
text next to the
main visual.

WARNING

As a side note, because of social media, many photographers are used to taking more vertical than wide photos, because they look better on mobile screens. On a website, you typically need more wide than vertical photos. Ask the photographer to produce more wide, or landscape/horizontal oriented images. It's usually easier to make a vertical version of an image from a wide image than the other way around.

>> **Especially when taking pictures of landscaping, architecture, offices, or portraits, make sure the photographer pays attention to the background.** I can't tell you how of my clients hired photographers and then they got the photos back and in the background were rolls of tape, garbage trucks, coffee cups, hubcaps, sweatshirts, hoses, orange cones, and other things that detracted from the message and photo. It's worth mentioning so that everyone knows the goals.

Take great photos

Modern cellphones can produce impressive images. Some even rival professional cameras in quality. Using your cellphone is cost-effective and can yield professional results. However, mastering cellphone photography requires skill. Here are some tips for taking photos on your phone.

Before you begin, check your phone's photo settings. Most, like iPhones, default to HEIF/HEIC format. While advanced, it's not yet universally web-friendly. Switch to Most Compatible or JPEG for easier website integration. If not, you might need to convert the format once you export the photos.

Before snapping, be sure you understand the photo's purpose. Whether it's a background image, showcasing work, or highlighting a product, the photo should narrate a story. This influences angles, lighting, and subject positioning.

Step 1: Angle and lighting: Angle and lighting shape the photo's narrative. For photos of people, a higher angle with soft lighting appears friendly. For photos of products, the right angle enhances appeal. Natural light is often best. Soft, diffused light, such as during the *golden hour,* is ideal (the time right after sunrise or right before sunset). Avoid direct sunlight, which casts harsh shadows. Reflectors can help bounce light, softening shadows.

Step 2: Positioning and background: For website photos, shoot horizontally, leaving space for text. Use the rule of thirds for composition. Position subjects off-center, making room for overlaid text. The background matters too; avoid clutter. For environment shots, ensure it is tidy and aligns with your brand's story. For subjects, a simple backdrop works best. Some phones offer a portrait mode, blurring the background for emphasis.

Step 3: Keeping horizon lines straight: Straight horizons exude professionalism. A tilted camera, or "Dutch angle," can induce unease. Use your phone's grid feature to align horizons. Some phones also offer a level feature, ensuring perfectly straight shots.

Find good stock photography

There is good stock photography and horrible stock photography. When you are on a website searching the photography, there are a few factors you want to keep in mind.

High-quality, relevant images can draw in visitors, create an emotional connection, and convey your brand's message effectively. On the other hand, poor quality or overused images can turn visitors away. Here are some tips for choosing good stock photography for your website:

» **Consider your audience:** When selecting stock photography for your website, it is important to consider your target audience. Ask yourself what type of images will resonate most with your audience. Choose images that help communicate your message in a meaningful way.

» **Consider your brand's tone and aesthetic:** Images should align with your brand's tone and aesthetic.

» **Choose the color palette:** Choose images with colors that complement or match your brand's color palette. This helps create a consistent and harmonious visual experience.

>> **Make sure photos are authentic:** Choose images that feel genuine and natural, as opposed to overly staged or unrealistic. Authentic images are more relatable and can help establish trust with your audience.

>> **Pick creative commons/royalty free images:** When searching for free stock photos, look for Royalty Free or Creative Commons labeled images on websites. Some software may offer different licensed images, which can become costly, so be cautious. Always read the terms of use. If you happen to use an image that you do not have the rights to, you can get fined significantly. Don't get into this situation. Purchase them, or if they are free, make sure you are allowed to use them.

WARNING

Now, let's talk about what to avoid. Overused images can make your website feel generic and forgettable. To avoid this pitfall, stay away from clichés! Common clichés include businesspeople shaking hands, smiling customer service representatives with a headset on, and people staring at computer screens. Photos like these feel fake and sterile. These images lack originality and can feel inauthentic, which as you have discussed throughout this book, erodes trust in your website and your company.

After you choose a few images, make sure they aren't overused. Did you know that you can do a reverse image search? To find out if an image is overused, you can run at reverse image search using Google Images or TinEye. You can do this easily by downloading the "test" image with watermark before you purchase it, and then uploading it to TinEye or Google Images. Once you upload the image, you are presented with all of the pages on the Internet where the image has been used and determine its uniqueness. You want your website to seem authentic, and if you are using the same image that a lot of other websites are using, people may realize this and trust in your website erodes.

Understanding Image Formats and Naming Conventions

When you are choosing, creating, saving, editing, and optimizing photos and images for your website, you want to follow a few rules.

The first rule concerns the formats of images and photos. The format is important because web browsers such as Chrome, Safari, Firefox, and Edge each recognize and understand only certain types of files.

If you stick with these four basic types of image formats, you will be safe with all browsers:

>> JPG images

>> PNG images

>> GIF images

>> WebP images

You cannot use .TIFF, .HEIC, or other types of images because many browsers don't know how to display these. Internet browsers can open JPG, PNG, GIF, and SVG files. They cannot open .TIFF and .HEIC files.

JPG images

The most popular type of image is .JPG (saved as .JPG or .JPEG). JPEG is a commonly used lossy image file format that is well-suited for photographs and images with lots of colors. When properly optimized, JPEG files are generally smaller than other image file formats. This makes them easy and fast to download and load on a website! However, because JPEG uses *lossy compression*, which permanently removes data from a file during compression. When you uncompress the file, it will not look as crisp and clear; the image quality may degrade slightly each time the image is saved.

Also, keep this in mind: JPEGs cannot show images that use transparency. This is a big deal! If you need transparency, you need to use a different format, such as .PNG or .GIF. Bottom line: Use JPEG images for most photos on your website when you don't need transparency.

PNG images

PNG (Portable Network Graphics) files are used when you need transparency on your background. For example, when you have a logo or a circle image that you want to place on a row that uses a different background color and you don't want to show a square box around the image, you want to save your logo as a transparent PNG.

See Figure 8-5 shows some examples, where you can see the box around the images on the top. The images on the bottom were created as PNG files and the background is transparent. You can see that these images look much better.

FIGURE 8-5: When using images such as logos, make sure the image is saved as a transparent PNG file so that you do not see a square box around the edges of the image.

You may be thinking that you should always use PNG files, but PNG files are generally larger than JPEG files. Use them only when you need the added functionality.

GIF images

GIF images aren't used much anymore. This is a *lossless* image file format that is often used for simple graphics and animation. When you compress and uncompress these types of files, they stay crisp and clear because they do not lose any data during compression. You certainly have heard of animated GIFs, which are images that move. There is no play button on these animated images, they simply play when the website is loaded. The animation can be in a loop, meaning that it will show the animation over and over infinitely, or it may play once and stop. GIFs also support transparent backgrounds like PNG files; however, GIFs are limited to 256 colors, which may not be sufficient for high-quality photographs or images with a wide range of colors.

WebP images

WebP images are a newer type of image format that's especially useful for website development. Created by Google, WebP offers a significant advantage in reducing image sizes while maintaining high quality, making it ideal for faster website loading times. This format is versatile, supporting both lossless and lossy compression, with the former ensuring no data loss and the latter reducing file size by eliminating some unessential data. Websites using WebP images can enjoy quicker loading pages, which not only enhances user experience but can also improve search engine rankings. These images are compatible with most modern web browsers, including Chrome, Edge, and Firefox, and their smaller size can be particularly beneficial for saving storage space.

WebP is effective for a wide range of image types, including photos with rich colors, line art, animations, and images requiring transparency. Its ability to provide high-quality compression makes it suitable for detailed photographs or line art. Additionally, WebP supports animation, making it a good choice for animated images, and it handles transparency well, which is essential for overlay images and graphic design elements.

Creating and editing WebP files is straightforward once you have the right tools. If you're using software like Adobe Photoshop, you may need to install a plugin to handle WebP files. After installation, creating a WebP image involves simply choosing the Save As option and selecting the WebP format. This process allows you to convert existing images, such as PNGs and JPEGs, into the more efficient WebP format.

WARNING

While most current browsers support WebP, older browsers like Internet Explorer do not. As an open-source format, WebP is continually evolving, with improvements and updates enhancing its functionality and usability for website development. You may see this format more often as time goes on.

SVG images

SVG (Scalable Vector Graphics) is a vector image file format that is good for logos, icons, graphics, and images that need to be resized without losing quality. SVG images are created using *vectors*, which are points of data and the mathematical calculations of the lines that connect the points. Using algorithms like this allows SVGs to be scaled to any size without losing detail, while using a very tiny file size, because the information stored are just points and math, instead of a map of millions of pixels, like a JPEG.

SVG files don't handle millions of colors and are unsuitable for photos. A picture of, say, a landscape requires millions of colors to be interpreted as a picture, and so needs to use a raster-type format. SVGs are good for company logos and icons, which are usually limited in colors and made up of flat shapes. Since it's primarily useful for print designers and artists, SVG files require special software to open and edit, such as Adobe Illustrator or Affinity Designer.

TECHNICAL STUFF

Font files are technically based on the same technology — they are vector-based rather than raster-based, and that's why you can print or size fonts on a website or in a word document sharply at any size. They just don't carry the SVG extension because fonts are installed and used as a collection of vector files. An SVG file is typically a single artwork.

Since SVG files can be scaled to any size, you might need to define in your code how large your SVG files should display. If you're using WordPress, SVG files currently cannot be uploaded by default and require a separate plugin. This is because, as an image file that is essentially made of computer code, SVG files can be modified maliciously to include code that can redirect users to another website, or can even trigger certain attacks! All SVG files therefore need to run through a scan and check process called *sanitization*, which discards any extra code in the SVG file that isn't expected or trusted. It's sort of a hassle, but it's necessary for the safety and security of your site visitors. Chances are, you may never need to use SVG images. I've built hundreds of websites without using a single one.

HEIC images

The "Live" feature on an iPhone allows you to take photos in a format that creates a short, looping video rather than a still image. These photos, which are sometimes referred to as "live photos," can be identified by the concentric circle icon that appears at the top of the screen when the feature is turned on. When you take a live photo, the iPhone captures a short video along with a still image. This video is then used to create the live photo, which animates when viewed on the phone or when shared with other devices that are compatible with live photos. Live photos are saved in the HEIC (High Efficiency Image Container) file format.

You cannot use HEIC images on websites. You might be able to upload an HEIC image on your platform, but recall that the images that can be viewable on your website depend on the browser and what images it understands and can read. Only Safari 17.0+ and Safari on iOS 17.0+, natively as of the date of this book, support HEIC images. It's best to simply convert any HEIC images to JPG files.

Here is a quick summary of the image file formats:

>> JPEG is a good choice for photographs and images with lots of colors.

>> PNG is a good choice for graphics and images with transparent backgrounds.

>> GIF is a good choice for simple graphics and animations.

>> WebP is a good choice for graphics, photographs, and animation with reduced image file sizes

>> SVG is a good choice for graphics and images that need to be resized without losing quality, but most likely you will not use these.

>> At this time, it's best to convert any HEIC images to JPG images for best results

Name your images

Now that you know how to save your images and which format to use, let's talk about the rules for naming your images!

Here are some best practices for naming your images:

>> **Use lowercase letters only.** This is a best practice.

>> **Use hyphens in place of spaces and underscores.** Instead of using underscores or spaces, use hyphens to separate words in your filenames. This helps with readability and search engine optimization. Avoid using spaces, as browsers may misinterpret them and replace spaces with %20, which looks unprofessional. Underscores can technically be used, but they look unprofessional. Hyphens are the modern and recommended choice for separating words in filenames.

>> **Use descriptive filenames and naming conventions.** Avoid using generic names like image1657.jpg or photo.png. Instead, choose filenames that accurately describe the content of the image. For example, blue-flowers.jpg or cityscape-at-dusk.png.

>> **Logos should be named logo-name-of-company.png.** This way, you can find the logo quickly and easily in your media library when you need to.

>> **Use certain words in a certain string when files are related.** For example, if I am using a lot of icons on a website, I name all the icons something like this: icon-features.png, icon-dinner-menu.png, icon-gift-card.png, and so on. This way, if I want to find an icon that I have uploaded to my media library, all I need to do is search for the word *icon* in my library and I will find all the icons I uploaded! If I am creating portfolios for certain jobs, I might name the files portfolio-landscaping-smith-front-yard.jpg, portfolio-landscaping-smith-tree-work.jpg, and portfolio-landscaping-smith-paver-walkway.jpg. This way, I can search for all of the smith projects and find a particular image or I can search for all portfolio images to find an image used in the portfolio. You also see there are some SEO keywords. This not only helps users understand what the image is, but it also helps search engines understand the content of your website, which brings me to the next point.

>> **Keep SEO in mind.** Use your keywords in your filenames. This does not have a huge impact, but it does matter.

>> **Don't include special characters.** Special characters, such as ampersands, pound signs, and dollar signs, can cause problems with some browsers. It's best to stick to letters, numbers, and hyphens in your filenames.

>> **Keep the names short.** Although it's important to use descriptive and relevant filenames, it's also important to keep them as short as possible. Long filenames can be difficult to read and may be truncated by certain systems. Aim for filenames that are no more than a few words long.

Optimize your images

Optimizing images and photos for your website is an important part of maintaining a fast and efficient website. Not only do correctly optimized images help improve the speed of your website, but they also play a part in helping your website to rank higher on search engine results. A faster website is key to a better user experience, and overall user experience is always a key factor in whether search engines recommend one site over another. The following sections discuss the factors involved in image optimization.

Proper resolution

Choose the right image resolution for optimal results. Resolution, measured in megapixels (1 million pixels), impacts image size and quality. High-resolution images can lead to large files and slower loading times, while low-resolution images may appear pixelated.

TECHNICAL STUFF

High-resolution images have more dots per inch (dpi), so the images are clearer when blown up because you still can't see the edges of each pixel or each dot. A file with a lower dpi has fewer dots per inch. As an example of images with low resolution, you might have seen the game Minecraft. The characters and images in Minecraft have hard, chunky edges. This is called *pixelation*, when you can see the edges of the dots.

When capturing images, phones and cameras use high resolution for various uses, like printing billboards. However, when saving for the web, 72dpi is suitable. For print, use 300dpi. If you're repurposing print images for the web, optimize them to 72dpi before uploading.

Color mode

There are two key modes: RGB (Red Green Blue) and CMYK (Cyan, Magenta, Yellow, Black). Web browsers use RGB when displaying images, so make sure your images are saved in RGB format. RGB uses these three colors in pixels for digital displays, similar to older TVs. CMYK uses four colors and is used for printing, as printers combine these four ink colors to produce various shades. If you use an inkjet printer, you're familiar with CMYK cartridges. Photos taken with cameras are typically in RGB mode.

Dimensions

When you take photos with your camera, they are very wide and very tall so that you can print them out or blow them up. For computers, though, you don't need them so huge! Most computer screens nowadays show images up to 1920px wide and 1080px tall, although there are some who use an 8K monitor, which will display in 7680px x 4320. In other words, the resolution is 1920 pixels horizontally times 1080 pixels vertically. Look at your images before you upload them. Are they larger than 1920 pixels wide? If they are slightly over that, say at about 2200 or so, that's okay, but if they are 4000pixels wide, you should reduce the dimensions of the images before you upload them so that they are smaller and load faster.

Also, think about where you will be using the image. If you will be using the image as a background row, you want to use a larger size in case someone is using a 27-inch, high-resolution monitor and they have their browser window as wide as the screen. If you will be using the image next to some text, the image may only need to be 600 or 800 pixels wide, as shown in Figure 8-6a, and you want to downsize it to make the file smaller. The smaller the file, the faster it will download to the visitor's browser. Don't make it too small, though. If you save the image at 200 pixels wide, but you use it in a block that enlarges it to 800 pixels wide, the image might be what is called *pixelated*, and you will see jagged edges instead of nice crisp lines, as shown in Figure 8-6b.

You want your images to be the correct size or over a bit, but not too wide or tall and not smaller than the area you're putting them in.

Compress your images

Images are usually the biggest contributor to the overall page size. The overall page size matters because when a visitor uses a browser to access a page on your website, the computer needs to download all the elements on the page to their computer. One metric that matters when a browser downloads a web page is the *page load time*, which is the time it takes to display all the content that appears on the page.

There are lots of tools you can use to measure this metric. Search engines measure and use this information as part of their algorithm when choosing which pages to return in the SERP. Faster load time is a good metric. In addition, visitors don't want to wait around for the site to load. If your website loads slowly, visitors will leave, and this reinforces to search engines that this is not a good site to return in the SERP.

Other things can affect the loading speed, such as the website host, the way the site is built, the amount of apps or plugins you have, if you have social feeds or other feeds pulling in information from other websites, and so on. But images do play a huge role in how fast your site loads, so make sure you compress your images!

Compressing images can significantly reduce their file size without affecting the quality of the image. You want to make sure the images are still crisp and clear after compression.

There are several tools that can compress your images, including TinyPNG and JPEGmini. TinyPNG will compress all of the image files you upload and when it is done, the panda will tell you how much you saved and the size of each image. Your images will be much smaller and they will still look amazing. Then you can download them one at a time or all of them at once. I compress every image I upload to a website. Every single one. Do not skip this step.

Use alt tags

Alt tags describe images to search engines and users who rely on screen readers to view sites. Originally, *alt tags,* short for "alternate," were introduced during slow dial-up Internet days when users disabled images for faster loading times. In place of images, the alt text provided context. For instance, a button image was replaced with alternative text like "Download this document."

Importantly, alt tags can't be added to images before uploading; this is done on your platform after uploading, with each platform offering a specific location for this purpose. By incorporating relevant and descriptive words in your alt tags, you not only enhance your website's SEO but also create a better user experience for those with visual impairments. This is commonly known as website accessibility or ADA compliance.

CREATING A FAVICON

Favicon is short for "favorite icon". A favicon is a small, square icon that represents a website or web page. Once you upload a favicon to your website, it will appear in various locations, such as browser tabs, bookmarks, and address bars.

A favicon helps strengthen your brand identity and distinguish your website from others. It also makes it easier for users to locate your site when multiple tabs are open or when browsing bookmarks. Having a favicon gives your website a polished and professional appearance. If you do not upload your own favicon, most likely there is a default favicon that will be displayed instead. This looks unprofessional.

These icons are typically sized at 16x16 or 32x32 pixels and saved in .ico, .png, or .svg format. You may need to upload a large favicon, such as 512px x 512px, which is downsized to a small size. It is always a square.

Normally name it favicon.png or something like that. You can use a design tool like Photoshop or an online tool such as photopea.com, favicon.io or favicon-generator.org to create a favicon.

Your platform will recommend a size for you — look at that first and then create the favicon. Your platform will also tell you the format they use. Most likely it will be .ico, .png, or .svg format.

When you create your favicon, you want to ensure the design is simple, recognizable, and legible, even at small sizes. Many companies pull out a section of their logo for the favicon. In Figure 8-7a, you see the Fairfield Capital's logo contains a sun that runs into a bar in their full logo. Figure 8-7b shows how the favicon looks in the browser tab.

After you add a favicon, test it by refreshing your website and checking the browser tabs and bookmarks.

Producing Video for Your Website

Video content has become an essential element in modern web design. Adding video content to your website can enhance user engagement and provide a dynamic, immersive experience for visitors. Videos are a great way to engage your audience and increase your conversion rates.

There are a few types of videos you can add to your website:

>> *Standalone videos* are self-contained pieces of content that tell a story or convey a message. I suggest you have at least one standalone video on your website. Create standalone videos when you want to provide detailed information, showcase a unique selling point, or connect with your audience emotionally. Ensure the video is engaging, concise, and adds value to the user experience. You can create the video yourself or you can have someone produce it for you.

>> *Background videos* are used as design elements to create visual interest and set the tone for the website. They are usually short, looped, and play automatically without sound. They are placed in the background of a row or column of your website. You can overlay the video with a color as well, so that you can place text on top of the video. Background videos create an immersive atmosphere and set the mood for your site. They also instantly capture user attention and keep users engaged. Background videos can also visually showcase your product or service without requiring users to interact. Strong messaging is relayed from the background videos. But you don't want the video to be too distracting. Ensure the video is subtle and doesn't distract from the main content or the CTA. The video should add to the experience and information on the page.

>> *Webinars*, such as ones that cover a product launch, Q&A sessions, interviews, or workshops, are also great video content. When you add a webinar

to your website, it fosters a sense of community and connection with your audience. In addition, webinars offer exclusive content that users can't find elsewhere. It shows your leadership as well, and establishes you as an authority, which is great for E-E-A-T (see Chapter 4). You want to add webinars to your website to educate your audience, generate excitement for a product launch, or establish yourself as an industry expert.

>> *Animated videos* use illustrations, motion graphics, or other forms of animation to convey information, explain complex concepts, or entertain the audience. They can be very effective to simplify complex ideas and make them more digestible. Animated videos, when done right with a good script and good illustrator, do a good job explaining a complex idea. They also add a touch of creativity to your content or can create a unique brand identity.

If you need help creating videos, you can hire online consultants at Upwork and Fivver. Also consider a video or marketing team that is local who can help you. Don't worry about being perfect at first. Start with creating some video content on your own and see how it comes out. Test and iterate.

Where to purchase videos

Just like with stock photography, there are many places online where you can purchase stock video for your website. Some sources include Shutterstock, Adobe Stock, Storyblocks, Pond 5, iStock, and VideoHive. The same rules that apply to choosing good stock photography apply to videos.

Where to host videos

If your video is going to be viewable on your website, you need to upload it somewhere. Do not upload videos to your own website. Instead, upload videos to a video hosting service.

A *video hosting service* or server is a server or computer where your video files are stored. It is a service that is built specifically for hosting videos. They have many benefits:

>> **They use powerful servers and advanced technologies to deliver videos efficiently, ensuring your website remains accessible and responsive even during peak traffic times.** These powerful servers deliver huge video files very quickly to the visitor's browser.

>> **Large video files can slow down your website's loading time, leading to a poor user experience and reduced search engine rankings.** Video hosting

services compress and optimize video files to minimize the impact on load times, resulting in faster-loading videos that improve user engagement, enhance overall website performance, and reduce *bounce rates,* which occur when people come to your website and leave immediately without going to another page or clicking anything. Some platforms even offer *adaptive streaming* to ensure smooth playback, which means the video quality is automatically adjusted based on the viewer's Internet connection.

>> **Video hosting services also automatically optimize videos for different devices.** This ensures compatibility with all types of devices, such as laptops, phones, tablets, desktops, and more. This leads to a consistent user experience. Using a video hosting service saves time and effort by handling these device-specific optimization automatically.

>> **Video hosting services simplify video management and updates. Managing and updating self-hosted videos can be time-consuming and requires technical expertise.** Video hosting services offer user-friendly interfaces and tools for managing your video library, including editing, organizing, and updating content. When you update a video on a hosting service, it automatically updates on your website, eliminating the need to manually replace files or update code.

>> **Many video hosting platforms also provide features like video analytics, customization, and sharing options, further streamlining the process of managing your video content.**

Most video streaming hosting works so well because they use *content delivery networks* (also called CDNs). A CDN is a network of servers distributed across the globe that work together to deliver content, such as videos, to users quickly and efficiently. CDNs store copies of your video on multiple servers worldwide. When your video is stored on multiple CDN servers, the CDNs allow for faster delivery to viewers in different locations. The visitor's browser grabs the video from the closest server to them. As you can imagine, this reduces *latency* and *buffering* — you have seen a video buffer before right? When you have a poor connection, the video will stop playing, usually displaying a spinner while the next segment downloads, and then will play. The video or a portion of the video downloads ahead of you watching it, then if you catch up watching it before the rest of the video is downloaded, it has to buffer again. This is why you want to use a video host! Video hosting services include this feature as part of their offering.

You upload your video to a hosting service and then you embed the video on your website. The video looks like it is playing on your website but the video player is really playing the video from the video host. It is like a window on your website that is looking at the video over there on the video hosting server. How you do this depends on your platform or your page builder. Most likely you will drag a video module onto your page where you want the video to appear. Then, the video module will ask you for either an embed code or a link to the video. Simply browse to the video where you uploaded it and grab that link or embed code (you might see a "share" or embed link somewhere) and paste it where your platform or page builder is expecting it.

Choose a video hosting service

You have a few options for hosting video on your website. Some of the most popular platforms include Vimeo, YouTube, and Wistia. Each of these services has its own advantages and disadvantages, and the one that is right for you will depend on your specific needs and requirements.

Vimeo

Vimeo is a popular video hosting platform that is often used by professionals and businesses. One of the main advantages of Vimeo is that it offers high-quality video playback, with support for 4K resolution and HDR content. This makes it a great option for businesses that want to showcase their products or services with high-quality video content. Some of the pro-level features include HD streaming, captioning and closed captions, audio leveling, and more. Another advantage of Vimeo is that it has a clean and minimalist interface, which makes it easy for users to find and watch videos.

You also have a lot of control over how the player looks (see Figure 8-8). You can choose to show the title of the video, show sharing links, show the Play button, and more. This is awesome for your website because you can make the video look clean and professional! Vimeo also has a strong emphasis on privacy, with options for setting password protection and enabling or disabling embedding for each video. This means that you can upload a video to their platform and you can control where it shows on the Internet — for example, you can control where it is embedded by telling Vimeo that it can only be displayed on YOUR website.

One of the main drawbacks of Vimeo is that it is a paid platform. Additionally, Vimeo does not have the same level of reach as YouTube, which means that it may not be as effective at driving traffic to your website. Even with these two drawbacks, I love Vimeo and recommend using it.

YouTube

YouTube is the largest video hosting platform in the world, with over 2 billion logged-in users per month. One of the main advantages of YouTube is that it is free to use, which makes it an attractive option for businesses that are just starting out or have limited resources. It is free to upload videos but you have to pay if you want to remove ads from your videos or use some of the other advanced features that YouTube offers.

You might want to use YouTube if you want a lot of people on the Internet to see your video, not just the visitors who land on your website. YouTube has a massive audience. This means that posting your video on YouTube can be an effective way to reach a wide audience and drive traffic to your website.

TIP

Another advantage of YouTube is that it is owned by Google, which means that videos on the platform are often given preferential treatment in search results. This can be a great way to improve the SEO of your website and help it rank higher in search results.

However, there are also some drawbacks to using YouTube. One of the main drawbacks is that the platform is heavily monetized, with ads being shown before, during, and after videos. This can be a distraction for users and may not provide the best viewing experience. It also doesn't look very professional. The player is also not customizable to have a clean look like Vimeo (see Figure 8-8). Additionally, YouTube might play related videos after your video and these may not be appropriate, unless you explicitly set the embed or link to show related videos from your own channel. Because of these drawbacks, you might not want to use YouTube.

FIGURE 8-8:
See the differences in these player windows. Vimeo offers a clean player while YouTube's is more cluttered.

Wistia

Wistia is another option for hosting videos and it has some advantages, such as analytics, conversion tracking, and high-quality playback. Wistia is specifically designed for businesses. One of the main advantages of Wistia is that it offers a range of features that are tailored toward businesses, including the ability to add calls to action, lead generation forms, and custom branding. These features can be a great way to engage with users and drive conversions on your website. Another advantage of Wistia is that it offers high-quality video playback, with support for 4K resolution and HDR content. The platform also has a clean and intuitive interface, which makes it easy for users to find and watch videos.

However, one of the main drawbacks of Wistia is that it is a paid platform. Also, Wistia does not have the same level of reach as YouTube, which means that it may not be as effective at driving traffic to your website.

4

Designing and Laying Out Your Website

IN THIS CHAPTER

» **Developing a cohesive website theme**

» **Using WordPress page builders**

» **Organizing your web page's rows and columns**

» **Laying out your header row**

» **Creating hero rows**

» **Building a useful footer**

Chapter **9**

Deconstructing the Anatomy of Web Pages

C reating an amazing website that resonates with your visitors requires a keen understanding of its foundational elements. From selecting the perfect theme that resonates with your vision, to opting for a user-friendly page builder, to mastering the building blocks of web layout — rows, columns, and modules — this chapter equips you with the concepts needed to create and design web pages that are functional and aesthetically pleasing.

Determining Your Website Theme

The simplest and quickest way to design a stunning website is to write your content first, then determine placement on the page. If you're following the guidelines in this book, by now you have prepared your content and are ready to position it on your pages. That means you're ready to choose a theme and possibly a page builder if you are using WordPress.

Conversely, if you start by determining a theme first and then try to fit your content into the sections that come with the demo pages, you could omit crucial details, emphasize trivial information just to fill space, or simply become overwhelmed and frustrated. At this point you should have your content written and organized into pages and your images optimized and named properly — if so, you are ready to consider the design.

One of the first design steps is choosing a theme. Almost all websites nowadays are built on themes, whether this is a free/paid theme that was chosen as a starting point, or a custom design built just for that website. A *website theme* is a pre-designed template that determines the look and feel of a website. It includes the layout, color scheme, and graphical elements. A theme is a set of files that controls the look, feel, and functionality of a website and can be customized to a certain extent to suit your needs and preferences. Choosing the right theme is an important decision. It can significantly impact the UX and the overall effectiveness of the site.

TIP

Website themes might be included for free with your platform or you might be able to purchase or find a theme in-app or from third-party marketplaces such as ThemeForest or Creative Market. Also check out theme repositories such as WordPress.org. You could also hire a designer to create a custom theme specifically for your website, but this will likely be a more expensive option and I don't recommend it. However you do it, you need to choose a theme to begin to build your website.

Choose a good theme

There are many factors to consider when choosing a theme for your website. The following sections cover many of them.

Features and functionality

Check out the features and functionality of the theme. Functionality refers to the various options and tools your website requires to perform its intended purpose. Different industries might be looking for different features in a website theme. For example, a restaurant might prioritize a theme with a built-in menu and reservation system, while a photography portfolio might need a theme that showcases high-quality images with a sleek, modern layout. An online store will need a shopping cart and payment processing option, while a news or blog site might need a commenting system. It's important to have a clear understanding of the features you need before choosing a theme. Be sure to choose a theme that is either designed for your industry or can be easily customized to fit your needs.

The visual design of your website

Once you have determined the functionality you need, the next step is to consider the visual design of your website. You want the design to be visually appealing and consistent with your brand's identity. This includes colors, fonts, and overall style. Most likely you have looked at themes at some point and considered the user experience. You want the website to look good and match the look and feel you are going for, which brings me to my next point: *branding*.

The theme you choose should align with the branding of your other materials and support the overall messaging and goals of your site. Does the theme use similar lines and design ideas that align with your brand? If so, this may be a good option.

How customizable the theme is

Next, you want to determine how customizable your theme is. A good theme should be customizable to a certain extent, allowing you to tailor the look and feel of the site to your specific needs and preferences. This may include options for changing the color scheme, font, and layout of the site. Maybe you want to put the logo in the center with the main menu below it. If so, you want to make sure you find a theme that has this option. Maybe you want the blog to have a sidebar that you can customize with certain information. If so, you want to make sure you find a theme that you can customize in this way.

Sometimes it is difficult to tell how customizable a theme is. If there is a section that allows you to see demos of the theme or if there is a portfolio of websites built on this theme, look at those to see how much the websites have been customized. A theme with easy-to-use customization options will allow you to make your website unique and tailor it to your preferences without needing extensive technical knowledge like coding things with *shortcodes* or CSS. The less you need to do to modify the theme to make it "yours," the better.

TECHNICAL STUFF

Shortcodes, sometimes found in WordPress themes, are code snippets enclosed in square brackets ([and]) that enable content to display on a web page. While they were once widely used, their popularity has declined due to their non-WYSIWYG nature — the editing screen doesn't represent the final page appearance. Additionally, shortcodes are tailored to specific themes, leading to potential content loss or cluttered code display when switching themes. For these reasons, I suggest you avoid using themes that rely on shortcodes to display content.

How performant the theme is

An important consideration for choosing a theme is performance. This means you want a fast-loading theme that uses resources efficiently. This is especially important for sites with a large amount of traffic or those that rely on search engine optimization (SEO), which means your site! Most likely you are not a developer, so this may hard to judge. Read the reviews that others have left. This can give you a sense of the theme's quality and performance.

Is the theme supported by the developer?

A big consideration, especially for third-party themes, is support. It's important to choose a theme that is regularly updated and supported by the developer. This ensures that any bugs or security issues are addressed in a timely manner and that the theme stays current with the latest web standards. Head over to the support area before you purchase the theme. Can you see frequent updates? When was the last update released for this theme; was it within the last month or two? Next, look at the questions that people are asking. How long does it take for support techs to answer questions? Are users complaining? How does support address their issues? This is a great way to judge a theme.

Does the theme have good documentation?

Hand in hand with support is documentation. A well-documented theme with a dedicated support team can save you time and frustration if you encounter any issues or need assistance with customization. So, look for themes that have positive reviews, a history of regular updates, easy-to-read and comprehensive documentation, and an active community to ensure that you have access to help when needed.

TIP

When purchasing a WordPress theme, it's also wise to check the associated page builder (see the next section for more on page builders, which help you lay out your content). Some WordPress themes include a page builder with their theme files and you use that to create your page layouts. Check this before you purchase a theme. Page builders vary tremendously, and if you get locked into a page builder you are not crazy about, you will not want to edit your website going forward as it will be too annoying, and you should be editing your website on a regular basis.

Change your theme

If you begin building and then realize the theme you chose is not working well, you can change themes. This is not the end of the world, but you will have a bit of cleanup to do, so you want to settle on a good theme as early as possible in the process. To change your theme, you might be able to replace one set of files with another without having to change any other part of your site's code, which saves time. However, depending on the version of your website and your platform, you will most likely have to make many other changes to your website so that things don't look all out of place and moved around. This can be a huge project.

I remember years ago, in 2009 or so, I had a client who had purchased a theme from ThemeForest for his WordPress website. We built the site and then something broke on the website that involved the theme. When we finally got in touch with the developer, they said they were not supporting the theme anymore. We had to change the theme to something else. When we did that, most of the site became broken because the modules we were using were integrated with the theme. For the most part, the themes today don't control so much of the layout — page builders do that — but there are settings and features that will most likely disappear when you change themes, so you may have a ton of cleanup to do. If you need to change your theme, build a staging or test site and test the install of the new theme on it so you can see if you have a huge mess or project on your hands.

When searching for a paid theme, see if there's a free, or "lite" version so you can test it before making a decision to purchase. This can give you a better idea of whether the theme will work for your site before you commit to purchasing it. Also, check the refund policy. If you discover you need to change the theme early on after purchasing it (usually within 30 days), you may be able to work with them to receive a refund if it does not work for your website.

Types of themes

There are many different types of themes available, ranging from simple, minimalistic designs to more complex, feature-rich themes.

» **Blog themes:** These themes are designed specifically for blogging platforms such as WordPress. The homepage may look like a newspaper or news outlet. Instead of a graphically rich homepage with sections that lead you to other pages of the website, you might see categories and excerpts of blog posts and articles. If you are creating a blogging website or a news website, choose one of these themes. Magazine themes are similar to blog themes. Magazine themes are designed for news and magazine-style websites and typically include features such as customizable category layouts, featured content sliders, and social media integration.

» **E-commerce themes:** These are designed for online stores and include features such as product listings, shopping cart functionality, and integration with payment gateways. If you are building an e-commerce website, choose an e-commerce theme if possible!

» **Portfolio themes:** Geared toward creative professionals such as photographers, designers, and artists, and include features such as customizable galleries and portfolios to showcase work. This type of theme will be image heavy. You might have lots of different options to display your gallery of work.

>> **Business themes:** Geared toward small- to medium-sized businesses and include features such as customizable homepage layouts, contact forms, and integration with Google Maps. Most likely you will choose this type of theme for your website.

Using WordPress Page Builders

If you are building your website on the WordPress platform and want to make sure your website looks modern, in addition to installing a theme, you need to employ a page builder. A page builder for WordPress is a simple tool that helps you create and design web pages easily. It's kind of like a set of building blocks that you can arrange to make a web page look the way you want, without needing to write complicated code. You can drag and drop different elements, such as text, pictures, and buttons, to build your page, making it a user-friendly way to create a website.

Upon setting up WordPress, you'll discover it comes equipped with its own page builder called the *Block Editor* (also called *Gutenberg*). While it's entirely feasible to utilize the Block Editor without involving another page builder, some users feel constrained by its capabilities. It's worth noting that the Block Editor is only a few years old, and it's still in a state of evolution. Furthermore, some find it slightly less user-friendly compared to other options. If the Block Editor doesn't sit well with you, there's a Classic plugin you can install, which transports you back to WordPress's initial, simpler page builder. This classic approach doesn't include the row-building capability but might be more manageable for drafting posts. I have been building websites so long, I like the classic builder when writing blog posts! It is easier for me to use.

If you're serious about maximizing WordPress's potential, you'll likely want a premium page builder with more functionality than the Block Editor. You might have heard of the market's top picks, namely Beaver Builder, Elementor, Divi, and WPBakery. The following sections discuss each of these.

WPBakery

Let's begin with WPBakery. It is a widely used page builder for WordPress, known for its user-friendly drag-and-drop interface and dual frontend and backend editing capabilities. It offers a wide array of elements and templates, enabling users to create intricate page layouts without needing to write code. A significant advantage is its compatibility with many themes and plugins, alongside a large add-on repository developed by the community.

WPBakery is not without its criticisms and it's not my top pick. The use of short-codes can make transitioning to another page builder or theme a challenge, as that code will be present on all pages if you change to a new page builder. Additionally, compared to some newer page builders, its interface feels slightly less intuitive, and there can be occasional bloat affecting page load times.

Divi

Divi is a robust and versatile page builder for WordPress, renowned for its visual editor that allows real-time design and previews. Users appreciate its array of pre-made layouts and the freedom to customize every detail, making it suitable for beginners and seasoned web designers. Divi's robust ecosystem includes a vast user community, offering additional modules and child themes.

However, the flip side to its flexibility is a steeper learning curve for newcomers compared to some other builders. Additionally, because Divi embeds shortcodes, migrating to another theme or builder in the future can be cumbersome, leaving behind a messy residue that requires cleanup, like with WPBakery.

Elementor

Next is Elementor, a rapidly rising star in the page builder world, rivaling Beaver Builder in popularity. It even offers a hosted version, streamlining website creation. Elementor's WYSIWYG (What You See is What You Get) nature means real-time editing, a game-changer for rapid design. It's packed with features, including modules that can be dragged, dropped, and instantly previewed. With a plethora of third-party sites providing additional modules, there's potential for truly unique designs.

Beaver Builder

Beaver Builder, which I'm quite fond of, is on par with Elementor in many ways. Beaver Builder is a renowned page builder for WordPress, celebrated for its smooth and intuitive drag-and-drop interface that seamlessly integrates with most WordPress themes. It boasts a real-time frontend editing experience, allowing users to see changes as they're made. Figure 9-1 shows the Beaver Builder page-editing interface. One of its standout features is its clean code output, which ensures that if you ever choose to deactivate the plugin, your content remains largely intact, which is not the case with some other builders. Some builders, especially ones that use shortcodes, will leave you an absolute mess if you choose to change the page builder.

On the flip side, while Beaver Builder provides a solid range of modules, to unlock its full potential, you might find you need to invest in the premium version or third-party add-ons like PowerPack or Ultimate Addons. I admit I am partial to Beaver Builder. It is super easy to use, and you can build a stunning website with it. It's my go-to theme and page builder.

REMEMBER

If your chosen theme doesn't come pre-packaged with these builders, they're available for purchase. Free versions provide a taste, and the pro versions undoubtedly offer richer capabilities. They're reasonably priced, often with lifetime license deals. It's wise to keep your license updated so you receive crucial software updates, which are vital for compatibility, security, and making sure your site always looks good!

Organizing Your Web Page Structure: Rows, Columns, and Modules

Understanding web page structure and thoughtfully organizing each row, column, and content section is key to designing attractive websites for any device. Knowing the layout of modern web pages helps you place content effectively. This includes recognizing the role and importance of rows and columns, and their impact on how your site looks on different devices.

Rows

Simply put, most web pages are built using rows, much like shelves on a bookcase. Each of these rows holds your content. When you look at contemporary websites, you can see that they are composed of these rows stacked vertically down the page. Sometimes these rows have distinct backgrounds, while at other times, they blend seamlessly. Whether you choose to have a single row or a hundred rows on your page, remember this: Every piece of content sits comfortably within its own row. Understanding this ensures your site looks great on all devices.

Think about how each row will look on your website and how to design each row so that the content inside of it is easy to understand.

Rows can be full width, extending from the left to the right of the browser window, or boxed (also referred to as *fixed*), with a defined maximum width. Sometimes you might want to use full-width rows and other times you might want to use fixed or boxed rows depending on the content included in the row and how you want it to look.

You have three options:

>> Rows can be full width and the content can be full width as well.

>> Rows can be full width and the content can be fixed or boxed.

>> Rows can be fixed or boxed and therefore the content will also be fixed or boxed. Fixed or boxed rows are a fixed number of pixels wide, regardless of the size of the browser window and therefore, the content inside must be fixed as well. See Figure 9-2.

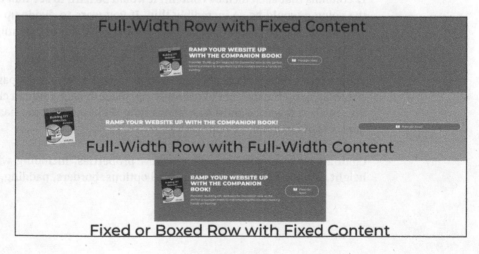

FIGURE 9-2: Full-width rows stretch all the way across the browser and the content inside these rows can be full-width, which fills up the entire row to the edge of the browser, or fixed/boxed, which is constrained within the row.

Many times I use full-width rows when I want to put a background image or color on the row, because the page looks nice when there is a noticeable background that stretches all the way across the browser window.

If the background of the row will be the same color as the rest of the rows down the page, I might specify that the row is fixed or full width, depending on the content inside the row. If I am putting four columns and each column shows a recent blog post, I might want the blog posts to stretch all the way across the screen or I might want them to appear a bit more constrained in a box inside the row. You need to think about the content that you are going to place in the row first, and then decide if you want a full-width row with full-width content, a full-width row with fixed content, or a fixed row with fixed content. There is no right or wrong here, and feel free to experiment with different options.

TIP Keep in mind that certain content types may not work well at full width, such as text modules. Consider optimal readability. Also, be mindful of background images in full-width rows, as they may appear differently on different devices.

Rows have various settings in addition to width, such as height, vertical alignment, text properties, background options, borders, margins, padding, and more. Your platform may also offer other settings, such as animation or visibility options, based on the device or conditions.

Columns

Inside each row is at least one column. Columns are nested within rows, and each row can contain multiple columns. You can actually have 12 columns, as most website themes are built on a 12-column grid, but if you create a row with 12 columns that each include content, it would be hard to see that content because the column would be so incredibly thin. If you were to divide up the screen into 12 columns and put the words in this book in each column, you might not even be able to fit an entire word across on one line.

You can use a different number of columns in each row on each page of your website. Mixing up the number of columns you place in each row can create an engaging, modern layout. Figure 9-3 shows how Williams Sonoma has used different numbers of columns very effectively.

Columns have properties similar to row properties, including width, minimum height, vertical alignment, background options, borders, padding, and margin.

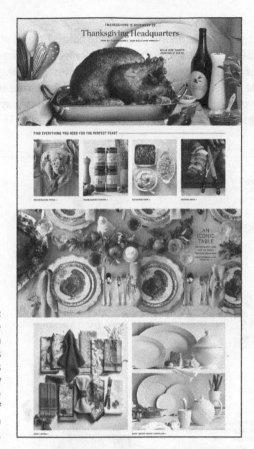

In mobile view, columns will typically stack, meaning they'll appear on top of the other. This means if you have a row with three columns, when you look at the web page on a mobile device, the columns become their own rows, one on top of the other. This is important to consider when designing your website. If you want columns to display side-by-side on mobile devices, you need to specify that in your software. Additionally, consider how alternating content layouts may affect mobile appearance and adjust accordingly for consistency.

For example, a nice look is to design your web page so that you have several rows, each having two 50 percent wide columns. Figure 9-4 shows an example. In the first row, you place text in the left column and a photo in the right column, and then in the next row you place a photo in the left column and text in the right column, and you alternate the text and image down your page.

When you look at this page on a mobile device, the columns will stack as they are supposed to. But, because they stack so that the left column is always on top of the right column, you get text, image, image, text, text, image, image, text. This is inconsistent in mobile devices. You need to tell your software that in mobile, every other row should reverse the stacking of the columns, That way, you get text, image, text, image, text, image, and so on.

FIGURE 9-4:
A very nice look is to create rows down the page with 50 percent columns and alternate text and images.

Modules and content

Inside each column you put modules that allow you to display your content. There are various types of modules to choose from, including text, photos, accordions, videos, galleries, buttons, forms, and more. This is where you place your actual words, images, links, and more.

The more modules you have to choose from in your page builder or theme, the more interesting your website. Experiment with different module types to create captivating web pages. Try using a lot of different types of modules on your pages.

AUTHOR SAYS

To design a web page that's both visually appealing and user-friendly, it's super helpful to familiarize yourself with the modules provided by your platform, theme, or page builder. Think of these modules as tools in your toolkit. Dedicate some time, maybe 30 minutes to an hour, to exploring how the different modules present content. It's like window shopping; you see what's available and get inspired. This time will pay off over and over, so don't skip this step.

In addition to the default modules, you might have the opportunity to purchase additional modules from a third party, which I highly recommend. For instance, if you're using WordPress and Beaver Builder, you can purchase add-ons like Ultimate Add-ons for Beaver Builder or PowerPack, which offer more creative ways to showcase content. Other builders, such as Elementor and WPBakery, have similar third-party modules. If you're building on an closed web-building platform, there's often the option to buy additional modules, either from third parties or as in-app purchases. Investing in these can elevate your website's potential.

Decide how to lay out your content in rows, columns, and modules

Once you are familiar with the modules you are going to have at your fingertips and you have purchased any third-party modules you like, you are ready to lay out your content.

When I'm arranging content on a page, I follow a particular thought process. If you've segmented your content as explained in Chapter 8, that's a great start. Picture each of those sections as a separate row on your website, like distinct segments or blocks.

Often, a single section will naturally translate to one row on your web page. However, on occasion, you might find two sections that are closely related in theme or content; in such cases, they can comfortably share a row.

Now think about each section separately, one at a time. Examine one section and ask yourself: how many unique ideas does it convey? For instance, if a paragraph touches on three separate points, you might consider dividing this section into three columns, with each column dedicated to one specific idea. Figure 9-5 shows an example.

FIGURE 9-5:
When you have three ideas in a section, consider dividing your content into three columns, one for each point.

Or maybe you have a list made up of words separated by commas. Such details can be neatly presented using list modules, whether they be bulleted, numbered, or another format. Figure 9-6 shows an example.

FIGURE 9-6:
Using list modules with a catchy icon can make staid content look interesting and fun to read.

When sections of content have multiple ideas that could be in a list, but you need more description instead of just a simple line, you can arrange them as shown in Figure 9-7.

Or maybe you want some content stand out on its own with a headline, like you see in Figure 9-8.

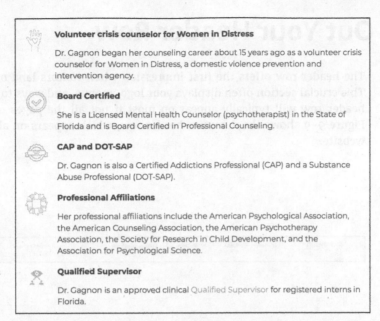

FIGURE 9-8:
Pulling out one
important phrase
and placing it in a
row all by itself,
supported with
an image, can
have a big impact.

The aim is to make the content digestible and organized. This approach not only makes your content visually appealing but also aids in user navigation and comprehension.

Once you decide which module you will use for each piece of content on your web page, add the modules to the page and then add your content. The next step is to style the modules for visual appeal and consistency, which you learn about in Chapter 10.

Laying Out Your Header Row

The header row offers the first impression when visitors land on your website. This crucial section often displays your logo, menus, and ways to reach out. Your header row will typically appear on most if not all the pages of your website. Figure 9-9 shows the dummies header row, which appears on all pages of their website.

FIGURE 9-9:
This is the header row from the dummies website. This is the first thing you see and displays the logo, menu options, search box, and a login button.

The header row should offer guidance, but not overpower the page. You can do this by making it as short (not tall) as possible. Your header row should take up less than 30 percent of the vertical space of the screen. Take a look at `apple.com`, `tesla.com`, `dummies.com`, or `microsoft.com`. Their header rows are pretty narrow.

The logo

One item that can make your website header too tall is a giant logo. Of course it's crucial to display your logo, typically on the left side of the screen (sometimes in the center of the screen), as it serves as a key branding element. When you add your logo to your website, make sure that it is not too tall. When it comes to the web world, image dimensions are measured in pixels, not inches or centimeters. Size the logo with a maximum of 150 pixels (written 150px) tall. Most of the time, I like to use a logo that's between 25px and 75px tall.

AUTHOR SAYS

The reason to display your logo on the top-left side of the screen is because we in the United States read left to right and top to bottom. Web developers years ago decided that a person visiting your website should read the logo first.

TECHNICAL STUFF

Did you know that if a website is coded properly, you can click the logo to get to the homepage? This way, you don't need to waste space on your menu bar and include a home link! Simply make sure that your logo is linked to your homepage.

The main menu

After you place the logo on your header row, you want to add the main menu. The main navigation menu should be easy to find and use, guiding visitors to the pages on your site. You can include the menu below the logo, next to the logo, or on either side. Decide on the layout you like best and one that's available in your platform.

TIP

Make sure you keep the menu confined to one line. If your menu starts to wrap to two lines, this looks unprofessional and is hard to read. You might need to take some items off the main menu and place them in the footer or combine some items into a dropdown menu.

The top bar

You might have a spot for a top bar, and you might have chosen a few items to include on the top bar when you wrote your sitemap. Remember, the top bar is a place for utilitarian items — they are for things that people need to do on your website such as contact you, look at their cart, read the blog, and so on. No drop-downs here, as discussed. If you are going to include a top bar, consider making the background a different color. Some have one section for menu items, others have two. You can center the items or move them left and right.

TECHNICAL
STUFF

Regarding search boxes — I am not a big fan of search boxes on a website unless it is a very large site or a research site. Most of the time, especially in WordPress, the search results come back in a horribly unintuitive format, although there are plugins that can provide a more accurate and better search experience. If you do have a site where people need to search the content, be sure to review the search results. Sometimes pages come back in the search results that you do not want shown, like thank you pages. You'll need to manually exclude these from the search results depending on the platform you've chosen. Just be careful with a search box and always test your search results.

Avoid placing ads or unrelated content in the header, as this can be distracting and make your website look unprofessional. Remember, the header row should be clean, visually appealing, and focused on your brand and website navigation. Be sure to prioritize the most important elements.

One thing you may see when you are building your header row is an option to make it "sticky." Sticky menus are always visible on the page, even when the user is scrolling down. The menu can shrink up or stay the same size, but either way, it appears on the page at all times. Nowadays, you see both. There is no wrong or right answer on this. Just make sure that if you do keep it sticky and the user scrolls down, that it does not take up too much of the browser window, because you're essentially losing that screen real estate for any content.

Creating Hero Rows for Home and Interior Pages

In the second row on the pages of your website, it's smart to add a *hero row* (remember the first row contains the header). The hero row includes your site's core message or value proposition. On the homepage, it's the initial touchpoint that informs visitors about what your business offers. You want it to resonate immediately with your visitor and you want to let the visitor know that they are in the right place and that you can solve their problems. The background of this row can contain an image, a video, and a color.

A well-constructed hero row can make or break a visitor's first impression, thus it's paramount to invest ample time in its design. When designing this row, think about how you want this section to look in terms of height, width, background, and messaging.

TECHNICAL STUFF

Many years ago we used to put sliders in the homepage hero row. A *slider* is a slideshow of different images or videos that changes by itself. Developers don't use sliders much now. People don't like waiting to watch a series of images or videos. If you put important information on these sliders, many visitors might not wait around to see them. Instead, it's better to have separate sections on the page for each message. Modern website design calls for one main message at the top of the page, with a picture, video, form, button, or something else that adds to this main message. This way, visitors see the most important information right away.

In addition to the value proposition or the name of the page, hero rows can contain a form, especially if your website is transactional and people are coming there to sign up for something or to get more information about something. For example, a website dedicated to providing dumpsters might feature a form at the top that offers visitors the option to schedule a dumpster to be delivered to their home or office.

You can also add a standalone video to the hero row. This is a great option when you anticipate visitors who are curious about what you have to offer but don't understand your offer yet. A video that explains your offer, or a testimonial, can help visitors understand your offer better.

Hero sections on internal or subsidiary pages typically don't dominate the screen space like the homepage hero row. Given that visitors are usually seeking more detailed information or aiming to perform specific actions, these hero sections are often more concise. They might feature the page title, possibly accompanied by *breadcrumbs*, which are those small links you see on websites that allow you to navigate around the site — something like Home > Services > Teeth Whitening, and other supplementary elements like images, forms, or videos, depending on the page's intent. On interior pages, this row can be tall or short and the background can be simple or contain images or video.

TIP

A useful guideline for these internal heroes is consistency. Opt for a standardized design across all pages — perhaps a recurring background theme coupled with the page title. The primary purpose of these pages is to convey more in-depth information.

Building a Helpful Footer

The *footer* is the row that appears at the bottom of every page on your website. You can have no footer, a very small footer, or a big footer. Some page builders allow you to place your footer appear on certain pages and not on others or have different footer on different pages.

The footer is a good place for any copyright notices. Add the copyright symbol, the year, the text "All rights reserved," and the name of your company. This gives you some protection as far as the material that appears on your website.

You can include lots of other information in your footer as well. You can include links to pages that you don't want to put in your main menu or in your top menu.

Examples of this are links to your privacy policy, to your terms of service, to the About page, or to your blog. You worked on your footer menu in Chapter 6, so you probably have a good idea what you want to place there. Figure 9-10 shows you the footer of dummies.com.

FIGURE 9-10: A footer is a great place for logos, social links, and menu items.

If your industry demands specific licenses, it could be advantageous to display your licenses and/or numbers in the footer. Similarly, showcasing logos of recognitions, sponsorships, or affiliations can be beneficial. Reflect on any commendations, partnerships, or honors you've achieved; the footer offers a splendid space to highlight them. Some websites opt to include a short newsletter subscription form in the footer.

Often, businesses include their logo, contact information, or even links to social platforms in the footer. Consider adding a map so visitors can find you easily. E-commerce businesses might even find it advantageous to display recently viewed products in this space. Essentially, the footer is a subtle arena to place elements that might not headline your site, but remain valuable for your visitors.

TIP

Look at your competitors' websites to see what they have in their footers. Also, don't be afraid to try something new. Remember that the footer, just like rows, can contain one or multiple columns.

Many sites set their footers apart with a different color. This way people know that they've each reached the end of the page and that the footer starts here. You don't have to do this, but it can be a nice effect.

Chapter **10**

Unfurling the Canvas of Design Options

Design is sometimes the hardest part of building a website. If you don't have formal graphic arts training, you might begin to style your content and realize that your site just looks busy and unprofessional. I can relate to this! Early in my web building career, I sometimes struggled with building beautiful websites. I could set up the web space, gather my images, and write my content, but when it came to design, I struggled. If this resonates with you, you are not alone.

This chapter gives you concrete ideas that will help you style your content and design your web pages, so you have a great looking website that you are proud of.

TIP

If you get stuck as you design, bookmark websites that you love, go back and study those websites, and "borrow" any ideas that fit your aesthetic.

Designing Your Logo

Before you begin designing your website, you should have a company logo. Logos are an essential aspect of any brand's visual identity. The logo is often the first impression that people have of your brand, so it's crucial to create a logo that is visually appealing and communicates your brand's values effectively. Logos also contribute to brand recognition and serve as a visual representation of your company's identity. If you are planning to build a great company, you don't want to skimp on the logo. Invest in your logo! Put some money behind developing one, as it is important!

Some of your design ideas and elements should come directly from your logo. This creates brand consistency. For example, if your logo is circular, you might want to use a lot of circular items on your website. If you have two thick bars in your logo, you might want to add two thick bars to each heading. In addition, the colors you use on your website should come directly from your logo or complement it, as I explain later in this chapter.

How much does a logo cost?

There's no one-size-fits-all answer to how much it costs to design a logo, as it depends on various factors, such as the complexity of the design, the experience of the designer, and the time spent on the project. You can hire a professional designer, use an online platform, or even create one yourself using DIY tools. That means a logo can be free if you make it, or it can cost you thousands of dollars. However, remember that a well-designed logo is an investment that can yield long-term returns by contributing to your brand's success.

A professionally designed logo can also help create a cohesive brand image across various marketing materials, ensuring consistency in all your visual communications.

Horizontal or vertical layout?

While you are developing your logo, think about how the logo will look on your website. Most of the time, you will need to size the logo down. In other words, it will be small and short. Your logo should be large enough to be easily recognized, but not so big that it overwhelms other content on the page or pushes your web content down the limited viewable space. Horizontal logos work better than vertical logos for this reason.

Where will your logo appear?

Most logos appear in the top-left corner Typically, this is because people read left to right in most of the modern languages of Europe, North and South America, India and Southeast Asia. The web world has decided that they want visitors to read the logo first, so they know what website they are visiting. This is a good idea, and people expect to see the logo in the upper-left corner. Picture the logo there and make sure your logo will look good, even if it's small.

Should you include a tag line on your logo?

Your logo may have a tagline embedded on the logo. A *tagline* is a brief, memorable phrase that conveys your brand's message or value proposition. While including a tagline on your logo can help communicate your brand's essence, it is not good to keep the tag line on the logo that appears on your website. For print, that is okay, but for your website, remove it from the main logo image file. When you make the logo as small as it needs to be for your website, you won't be able to read the tagline. It will look unprofessional.

AUTHOR SAYS

If a professional is designing your logo and you're embedding a tag line, ask your designer for two logos: one with the tag line you can use on billboards and t-shirts and one without the tagline for your website. The website version should also have a transparent background. You want your logo to be in in a transparent PNG format.

One other note: name the file `logo-your-business-name.png`. This is standard practice. This way, you can find the file easily when you need it.

How I Approach Design

When I am designing a website, I work on one page at a time. I get that one page perfect before I start on another page. I do the things I teach you in this chapter over and over, on one page. I set some options on each row and module, and then I leave the website for an hour or two or maybe even a day or two. Then I come back to the website, and I start tinkering again with design elements. I will probably tinker around with one page about seven to ten times before I start designing another page. This may be over a period of a day or two, or a few weeks. In between working on my design, I look at other things to give me inspiration.

EXAMPLE

Recently, I was working on a website for a high-end travel agency that needed to be super modern and luxurious. I worked on designing one page and went for a walk with my dog. I saw a modern home that was being built. I wanted this website to feel like this house. The customers we were trying to attract would build a home like this. What about this home made it feel luxurious and modern and cutting edge? The lines were horizontal and very clean. The roof was flat. The windows were large, with no mullions. There were large spaces of flat space. Hard angles. Some of the exterior walls were painted in large, clearly defined squares. This gave me the idea to use a very slender and angular font for the headings, left bottom justify the headings in each row, and then add a 2px solid white border to the left and bottom of the headings to give it a clean, modern feel. I put the headings on a tall row with a luxurious photo that filled up the entire screen. There was lots of space with nothing in it, similar to some of the exterior areas of this home. The heading rows felt like this beautiful, modern home that I saw. It turned out great.

In 2017 ago, my endodontist client wanted me to redesign her website. She asked me to design her website so that it had the same feel as a spread she found in a magazine (see Figure 10-1).

FIGURE 10-1: Design inspiration can come from anywhere. Years ago a client sent me this photo as inspiration for her website redesign.

People are often anxious when they visit an endodontist, so she wanted to convey her website (and office) as a serene place where patients could relax. The monochromatic photo of the woman in Figure 10-1 is displaying basically two colors: white and light brown. Then the opposing page has some text on it with plenty of whitespace. The heading is written in script. There are no bright colors or sharp angles, no heavy text or anything that jumps out at you and seems exciting. The page spread looks serene and relaxing.

I used that magazine spread as inspiration to design her website in 2017, as shown in Figure 10-2. I used a lot of gray, light designs to complement her text. I chose a monochromatic color palette and the title of each page is in script. At the bottom of each page, I included a whimsical squiggle icon. I used hand-drawn icons to support the text instead of photos. The website looked very soft and relaxing.

our technology

DIGITAL DENTAL RADIOGRAPHY

This technology enables us to take radiographs with about 80% less radiation when compared with traditional methods.

THE SURGICAL OPERATING MICROSCOPE

With it's integrated fiber optic light source, the surgical operating microscope allows for improved visualization which in turn enables us to treat and diagnose the situation better for you.

NICKEL TITANIUM ROTARY INSTRUMENTATION

This premier instrument can make us more efficient during your root canal. These instruments can shorten your appointment time and make the final root canal result better.

CONE BEAM COMPUTED TOMOGRAPHY (OR CBCT ALSO REFERRED TO AS CONE BEAM VOLUME CT)

This digital radiographic computer aided technology is used to guide the endodontist to locate difficult to find canals, complex anatomy and pathology.

FIGURE 10-2: In 2017 I designed this website based on the magazine spread my client sent to me.

TIP

Another good way to get inspired is to look at other websites and start bookmarking the ones you like. The websites do not need to be in the same industry as yours — they can be any type of website. You might find a website that you like only the top row; that's fine, bookmark that for inspiration. You might like only the homepage; bookmark that website. You might like only the footer; bookmark that website. This gives you a starting point. It is easier to start with design ideas instead of from the blank page. Find these design ideas online or in your daily life and make note of them.

Determining the General Settings

Now that you have some inspiration and a logo, you can begin styling your content. When I am building a website, I start with general settings that affect the entire website and then move to each page and style each module and each page individually. General or global settings include things such as:

>> Background color for website pages

>> Font properties for headings

>> Font properties for text

>> Accent, button, and background colors

>> Heading layout and styles

>> Menu layout and style

>> Footer layout and style

Depending on the platform or page builder you are using, you will find these general settings in different places. If you are building in WordPress, the place to find these settings is in Appearance --> Customize. If your theme has not updated to the new standards, you might find these settings on the left menu in your dashboard under the name of the theme or somewhere else. If you are building on a closed platform such as Wix or Squarespace, you will find these site settings in your dashboard.

Find the area in your platform where you make these types of global settings and make all the changes you can make first. Some themes might have more options than others. Choose as many options in the general settings area as you can. Read sections in this chapter to help you choose fonts and colors, then set them in the site settings.

TIP

Don't go to every page and adjust the fonts and colors there. Instead, set these options up in one main spot for your whole website (in the general settings). This way, everything looks the same across your site. Plus, if you want to change something, you can change it in that one spot, rather than having to make the same change on each page. It's easier and keeps everything consistent.

Choosing Fonts for a Cohesive Feel

I love choosing my fonts first. It's fun and can have a huge impact!

Fonts play an important role in how a person feels or reacts to a website. Fonts create a feeling, whether it be strong, soft, romantic, funny, serious, conservative, playful, happy, or one of many other emotions. When you are working on your website, pay particular attention to the fonts you choose to create the emotional reaction you desire from your visitors. It's smart to choose your fonts first.

When you are choosing a font, keep in mind the following factors:

>> **Readability:** Make sure your chosen font is easy to read, especially the body text.

>> **Consistency:** Use a consistent font family throughout your website to create a cohesive look and feel.

>> **Tone:** Match the font to the tone and purpose of your website. For example, a professional website should use a more formal font, while a creative website may benefit from a unique or playful font (as long as it's legible).

>> **Compatibility:** Choose a web-safe font or use a service like Google Fonts to ensure your font displays correctly across different browsers and devices.

When you are choosing a font, you need to know about the "categories" of fonts. There are four main types of fonts: serif, sans-serif, handwriting, and display. Choose the category that best represents your brand look and feel. Figure 10-3 shows these four main font types.

>> **Serif fonts:** These fonts have small lines or strokes attached to the ends of the characters. Some examples are Libre Baskerville or Garamond. Serif fonts can give your website a more traditional or formal appearance.

>> **Sans-serif fonts:** These do not have the small strokes at the ends of the characters. Examples include Open Sans and Helvetica. Sans-serif fonts are generally considered more modern and are typically easier to read on screens, making them a popular choice for web design.

>> **Handwriting fonts:** These mimic the appearance of handwritten text. These fonts can add a personal touch to your website but may not be suitable for large amounts of text or professional websites. I love using them as an accent on websites where the brand is a bit playful.

>> **Display fonts:** These are decorative and should be used sparingly, usually for headlines or titles. They can help create a unique aesthetic but can be difficult to read when used excessively. Again, depending on the brand's aesthetic, you can use these as an accent font here and there for emphasis.

Serif Font

Sans Serif Font

Handwriting Font

Display Font

FIGURE 10-3:
There are four
main font types.

Font properties

Fonts vary in sizes, weights, and how they're styled in terms of capitalization. Keep this in mind as you pick and set your fonts!

For the main text on your site, aim for a medium to large size so your audience can read it. A font size of 18px or 20px sometimes even 22px usually works well. This goes for mobile views too! Always check that your text is clear on mobile devices. If you're targeting an older audience, consider larger size. Make sure they can read your content without any hassle.

Tiny fonts were once trendy, but now they just make a site feel old and can be hard to read. So, for a modern look and feel, go with larger body text.

**AUTHOR
SAYS**

Style your headings bigger than your body text and organize them in a clear hierarchy. Your primary heading, heading 1 or <h1>, should be the boldest and largest. Next, your subheadings for each section of the outlined sections of text on your page. The heading 2s or <h2>s are smaller than <h1>s but bigger than <h3>s and certainly larger than your body text. The exact sizes aren't set in stone; focus on ensuring they're readable and distinguishable from each other. Their size and weight should convey a hierarchical order.

Font weights can range from very light to super bold. Sometimes these weights are numbered, with 100 being the lightest and 900 the boldest. "Normal" weight translates to 400, and "bold" weight translates to 700. When picking a weight, make sure you look at the available options. If a font only has one weight and you're aiming for variety, skip that one. I love using extra bold weights (like 800 or 900, also sometimes referred to as Extra Bold and Ultra Bold or Black) for some headlines because they can really make a statement. They can be striking!

Playing with font sizes, weights, and even colors can help differentiate sections and emphasize key points. This layering of fonts not only makes your content visually appealing but also organizes it in a way that feels intuitive and accessible to readers.

You also have the option to use normal case, all lowercase, title case, or all uppercase. Normal case (also called sentence case) is how the paragraphs in this book are written: The first letter in each sentence is capitalized and the rest of the words are lowercase unless they are a proper noun or some other reason. You can use this case for your headings and body text.

Lowercase is all lowercase, and for professional websites you probably do not want to use all lowercase letters.

Title case, often referred to as "headline style" or "capital case," is a capitalization style in which the first letter of most words in a title or headline is capitalized. Typically, smaller words such as "and," "or," "the," "a," and "an," as well as certain prepositions and conjunctions, are left in lowercase unless they begin or end the title. You might like this style for your headings.

Finally, all uppercase can be used for headlines and menus and look very nice. I frequently use all uppercase for my menu items, button text, and sometimes my headings.

Oversized typography

You might want to use super big fonts on your website for headings — this is called oversized typography. Using oversized typography on your website can be an impactful design choice. They capture the attention of your visitors and emphasize key messages. I love using oversized typography!

Oversized typography turns words into art. One of the most significant advantages of oversized typography is that it transforms ordinary text into a visual statement. Large, bold letters can become a focal point of your design, engaging visitors and encouraging them to explore your content further. This approach can be particularly effective in headers, banners, and hero images where you want to make a strong first impression. Figure 10-4 shows the Distillery Row website as an example.

Oversized typography can help establish a clear visual hierarchy on your web pages. By using uber large text for essential information, you can draw attention to the most crucial elements and guide your visitors through your content in a more organized and intuitive manner.

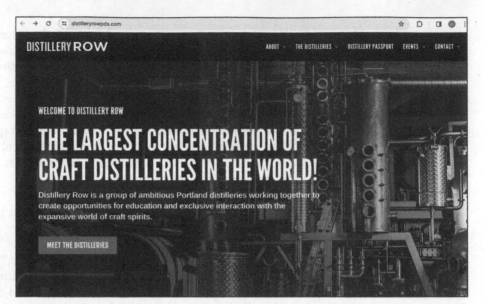

Incorporating oversized typography often goes hand in hand with a minimalist design approach. By focusing on large, bold text and reducing other design elements, you create a clean, uncluttered layout that allows your content to take center stage. Sometimes you don't need to include images when you use oversized typography, which helps you create a simpler design!

Choose fonts for your website

When it comes to obtaining fonts for your website, you have three main options:

>> You can use one of the older, web-safe fonts that most computers have installed on their device (not recommended).

>> You can upload your own special font to your website (not recommended if you can avoid this). What if you have a proprietary font that you want to use on your website? I have worked on franchise websites like the YMCA, and they have proprietary fonts that they must use on their websites. If you have a situation like this, you need to upload the fonts to your website and the visitor will need to download the proprietary or special font each time they visit your website. Each font file adds to the total size of your site, which can increase the time it takes for a visitor's browser to download it. In addition, uploading the font is not as simple as copying the font to your website host. You have to convert the font file into web-friendly formats like WOFF2 — with WOFF as a fallback for legacy browsers — or purchase those file formats. Then you must upload them to your website's server and use coding (the @font-face rule in

your CSS to link the font files and apply them to your website). As you can imagine, that is a technical process. Although it can be done, it's not ideal.

» You can use Google Fonts (recommended and free) or Adobe Fonts (formerly Typekit, a paid subscription). Most likely, your platform or page builder is integrated into Google Fonts so you have many or all the Google Fonts available for choosing. You can visit the area where you define your fonts and choose the one you like from the dropdown. Super easy! Sometimes you can see how the font looks in the dropdown (see Figure 10-5) and sometimes you cannot (see Figure 10-6). If you cannot see the font, visit https://fonts.google.com and browse the repository there. After you choose a few possibilities, go back to your web building software and see if that font is available.

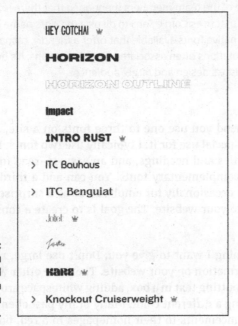

FIGURE 10-5:
Sometimes you can see the actual font when choosing it from the program.

FIGURE 10-6:
Sometimes you can't see the font in action. In that case, visit fonts.google.com to see what these fonts look like.

IT'S NOT COMICAL

I do want to mention one particular font, just in case you were thinking of using this font on your website — Comic Sans.

Comic Sans is a casual, playful, and often controversial font designed by Vincent Connare in 1994. It was initially created for Microsoft's Comic Chat application and has since gained both popularity and notoriety as a widely used and misused font. Over the years, it has garnered a significant amount of criticism, has become polarizing, and some people have developed a strong dislike for it. This aversion has led to the creation of websites and online communities dedicated to expressing their disdain for Comic Sans. Search online for Comic Sans if you want to take a break from reading this book and have a good laugh. (When meeting with the Wiley team about this book, we chatted about Comic Sans and one of the team members mentioned that there is a large water tower in the northern U.S. that uses Comic Sans to display the city's name in giant letters!) There are many alternative fonts available that offer a friendly, casual appearance without the negative connotations often associated with Comic Sans. It's best to find a different font for your website's design and target audience.

REMEMBER

Web designers recommend you use one to three fonts on a site, and sometimes one more if you have a special use for it. I typically use two fonts. I like to use one dramatic font for the titles and headings, and an easy-to-read font for the body text. Focus on finding complementary fonts. You can add a third font such as a script font that you use occasionally for emphasis or as a surprise, but don't add more than three fonts to your website. The goal is to create a consistent, simple, modern website.

WARNING

There is one more warning I want to give you. Don't use large, red, bold text to indicate important information on your website. There are other ways to get people's attention, such as putting text in a box, adding whitespace around it, increasing the font size, or using a different color. Many of my past clients would ask us to add important announcements to their homepages in a red, bold font. Then a week later, they would ask us to add more information, and that needed to be in a red, bigger, bolder font. This went on and on.

Guess what — the page gets super messy and ugly right away.

Choosing Colors Effectively

If you have a company logo, choose a few colors from the logo to integrate into your site. This creates brand consistency. If your logo is a black and white logo and then in that case, you can use a color of your choice.

Regardless of how many colors there are in your logo, pull out just a few (two to four) that you really like and use those.

When you use color effectively to highlight links and design elements, you guide users through your website more intuitively, enhance the user experience, and increase the likelihood of users taking desired actions, such as clicking links or interacting with important design features.

What color does is say, "Hey, look at me! I'm over here!"

REMEMBER

The number of colors you use on your website and how you use them is up to you, but remember that less is more. Simple looks more modern.

AUTHOR SAYS

I use roughly two to four colors besides white and black for a website. Use color strategically to highlight specific elements, such as links and design features. When you use too many colors, every color is saying, "Hey, look at me! I'm over here!" and your website visitors won't know where to look. Choosing and implementing your colors is important to creating an amazing design.

Pick a color palette

First choose a color palette for your website. There are a few different methods you can use:

>> *Monochromatic color schemes* use a single color, with variations in brightness and saturation. You can pull one color out of your logo and use that color, along with lighter and/or darker versions of that color.

>> *Analogous color schemes* use colors that are next to each other on the color wheel. For example, red, orange, and yellow.

>> *Complementary color schemes* use colors that are opposite each other on the color wheel. This creates high contrast and can make certain elements stand out but be cautious when using complementary colors to avoid creating visual tension. For example, blue and yellow or red and green.

Rules for using color

Once you choose your colors, follow these rules to create a gorgeous website:

>> **Consider creating a strong contrast between the background and the element you want to highlight.** This makes the text or element stand out and captures the user's attention. For example, if your website has a light

background, use a darker or bolder color for links and important design elements.

>> **Establish a consistent color for specific elements, such as links, call-to-action buttons, and headings.** This helps users easily recognize and interact with these elements throughout your website. For example, you might use a specific shade of blue for all your links, making them instantly recognizable as clickable elements. Inconsistent color use can create confusion when visitors attempt to navigate the site, as they may struggle to identify important elements.

>> **Use color to establish a visual hierarchy on your website.** Prioritize the most important elements by using bolder and brighter colors, while using more subtle colors for secondary or tertiary elements. This guides visitors' attention to the most critical parts of your website first.

>> **Leverage color psychology and common color associations to reinforce the function or importance of specific elements.** For example, green is often associated with positive actions or success, making it a popular choice for Submit or Confirm buttons. Red, on the other hand, is frequently used for Delete or Cancel buttons due to its association with warnings or danger.

>> **Use the colors that are appropriate for your business.** For example, a website for a law firm using bright, playful colors may not convey the professionalism and trustworthiness clients expect. Similarly, a website targeting a younger audience that uses dull or overly conservative colors might not resonate with young viewers. Inappropriate color choices can result in a disconnect between the website's content and its target audience, potentially leading to a loss of credibility and user engagement.

>> **Consider changing the color of links or buttons when users hover over them.** This not only highlights the element but also provides visual feedback that the element is interactive. For example, you change the color of a link from blue to a darker shade of blue or underline it when the user hovers over it.

Color no-nos

There are some things to avoid doing on your website when it comes to color.

>> **Most important: Don't overuse color!** If you use too much different color on your website, it could look chaotic, unprofessional, and confusing. While bright colors can create a sense of energy and vibrancy, overusing them can result in a visually overwhelming and cluttered appearance. Additionally, bright colors often do not provide enough contrast, making it challenging for visitors to read the content.

>> **A website that employs poor color contrast — such as using light text on a light background or dark text on a dark background — can be problematic for users with visual impairments or color blindness.** There are some laws on the books around creating a website that is ADA compliant, and lack of contrast makes the content difficult to read and may lead to a frustrating user experience. Additionally, poor color contrast may cause the website to appear unprofessional or poorly designed.

HEX and RGBA colors

You can use HEX and RGBA to define colors on your website. It's important to understand these simple concepts so you can choose colors easily. Understanding these will not impact the optimization or size of your images, but it's essential for defining the colors you use.

Your brand's HEX colors

If you have branding visuals in the form of a logo or otherwise, you need to know your HEX colors. If you don't know your HEX colors, reach out to the person who developed your logo and ask them for the official colors, or "palette." If you can't reach that person for whatever reason, you can determine your HEX colors by using an online tool. If you don't have photo editing software installed on your computer, simply search for one online. You can also put your logo or other assets into a photo editing software and grabbing the colors from there.

Note your HEX color codes and then save them where you can find them all the time while you build and design. I have mine on a sticky note on my monitor and I also keep them documented in a note on my computer that I reference on a daily basis. After you use the HEX colors a lot, you will probably memorize them. Establish your HEX color palette and use only these for brand consistency and recognition.

HEX colors explained

HEX colors are a defined by a string of six letters or numbers called RGB triplets (sometimes shortened to three characters called shorthand). They go from 0-9 and A-F in three sets of two and they are preceded by a # symbol.

>> The first two numbers are the value of red in that color.

>> The second two numbers are the value of green in that color.

>> The last two numbers are the value of blue in that color.

You can think of them like this: `#RRGGBB`.

The numbers go in order from lowest or least amount to highest amount from `0-f` in this order: `0 1 2 3 4 5 6 7 8 9 a b c d e f`

They represent RGB (red, green, and blue) values and look like this:

`#efefef`

`#ffffff`

`#ec008c` . . . and so on.

The lowest value is 0. This means that there is none of that color in the image. The absence of color is black, so black is the lowest number: `#000000` (all zeros).

The highest value is F. This means that there is the maximum amount of that color in the image. White is the result of all colors mixed together, so white is the highest number: `#ffffff` (all fs).

Then there are all sorts of color combinations; there are 16,777,216 color combinations you can create for the web.

Shorthand HEX colors

TECHNICAL STUFF

Generally, you will not use shorthand HEX, but you should know what it is in case you see it. If you do see it, most likely it will be either black or white referenced using shorthand. You can write some colors in shorthand HEX if each of the three pairs contains identical numbers. For example, if you have `#00 ff ff`, you have three sets that are all pairs and you can shorten this hex color to `#0ff`. In other words, you can abbreviate each color channel using one character instead of two identical characters. To be web safe, each set of numbers needs to be 00, 33, 66, 99, cc, or ff.

Here are some examples of shorthand HEX colors:

`#ffffff` → `#fff`

`#000000` → `#000`

`#666699` → `#669` . . . and so forth.

Semi-transparency with RGBA

You can also add a color that is semi-transparent. As you can see, HEX colors are solid and do not have the ability to show as transparent, as there is no value in the three sets of characters where you can define the amount of transparency.

Semi-transparent colors are perfect when you're using a photo on a background row, overlaying a color on top of the image that either darkens or lightens the image, and then adding text on top of the image. Adding the semi-transparent color allows you to view the image but also soften or mute the image a bit so that visitors can read text on top of the image. Figure 10-7 shows an example. You can put any color over an image. When you add darker text over an image, make the overlay lighter and when you add lighter text over an image, make the overlay darker. You can play around with the colors of the overlay, the level of the overlay, the colors of the text and the sizes of the text to create some really nice effects. Get creative!

FIGURE 10-7: Adding a semi-transparent overlay to your rows allows you to soften the image and add legible text on top.

The easiest way to create a semi-transparent color is to reference the red, green, and blue values (RGB) and then the level of transparency (A) by using RGBA instead of HEX. The values in RGB are different from HEX values. In RGB, the values go from 0–255, with 0 being the lowest and 255 being the highest. They are written in three sets, separated by commas.

Black is written like this: `0,0,0`

White is written like this: `255, 255, 255`

If you want to put black over an image and use transparency, you reference the transparency with a fourth value from 0–1. So you would have something that looks like this:

`0,0,0,0.7`

`0,0,0,0.85`

And so on. The higher the last number, the more opaque the color will be. When you add this color on top of an image, it's called an *overlay*. Many online platforms and page builders provide the ability to specify the transparency using a visual slider, as shown in Figure 10-8. You can move around to see the different transparency levels; the first three numbers represent the RGB values and the last number is the level of transparency.

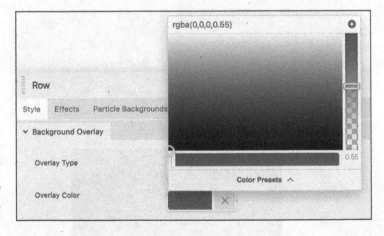

FIGURE 10-8:
When you are
using RGBA, a
slider might allow
you to set the
transparency of
your color (the A
in RGBA).

Written properly for HTML, this is `rgba(237,123,191,0.74)`.

Styling Rows, Columns, and Modules

In the previous chapter, you added modules to the columns nested inside rows on your pages, and then populated those modules with your content. The rows and modules probably look pretty generic or plain. It's time to make them your own now. You can style those modules so that they follow your brand and the style of the website.

Start by thinking about the overall page, then how the rows will look, then how the columns will look, and finally, think about how the modules should look. The following sections discuss a few ideas and things to think about to spark your creativity.

Style your rows

Think about your rows first and how you want them to look. Do you want the content in that row to be vertically aligned? Do you want the content in that row aligned to the top, middle, or bottom of the row?

You can also set properties of the text that appears in that row. For example, you can set all the text in this row to be white, or black, or another color.

You can also set the background. You can display a video in the background, set a color for the background, or choose an image that fills up the entire background.

If you choose to set an image as the background, you have more options:

>> How do you want that image to appear? Do you want it to fill up the entire row? Do you want it to appear at the size that it is when you upload it?

>> Would you like to overlay the image with another color so that you darken or lighten the image?

>> How do you want the background image to behave? Do you want it to scroll like the rest of the page or be revealed when people scroll down the page, which is called fixed.

You might want to put a thick, solid border on the bottom of the row or left side of the row. There are lots of row options to make each row look fantastic. Look through all your settings and use them thoughtfully as you refine your page's design.

Then think about how each row looks after the next. You can choose to have most or all rows have the same background color. One really nice look involves applying a very light background color to every other row on the page. I like using a light gray color such as #eaeaea, #f4f4f4, or #f7f7f7 as the background color for every other row. See Figure 10-9.

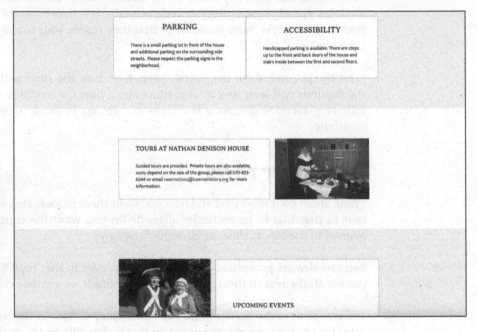

Look at different websites to see how they use different background colors for their rows. You may want to implement this treatment on your website.

Padding rows with whitespace

Once you add alternating colors to the background of your rows, you'll start noticing the amount of padding you have set on each row a lot more! Ensure that each row or section has adequate spacing and padding to separate the content from the background color.

The most effective way to define whitespace is directly in your rows (see the section later in this chapter entitled "Using Whitespace" for lots more about whitespace). Although it might be tempting to add it to individual modules, doing so can lead to unpredictable outcomes. Instead, focus on the margin and padding settings of your rows.

Margins provide space to the outside of a row, column, or module, while padding provides space to the inside. When you apply a larger margin to a row, especially with a colored background, you'll notice it creates space outside the background, which is not creating whitespace inside the row.

On the other hand, apply whitespace in the colored background by using padding. I typically add anywhere from 50px-150px as both top and bottom paddings on each row. Try different variations and see what feels best to you, looks good on the page, and matches your brand. Then standardize on one setting for all the rows on your website. If you like 80px as the top and bottom padding on each row, use that same setting for almost all rows on your entire website. Once in a while you might use more or less, but for the most part: Be consistent.

If you add padding to your rows, make sure you check your site on mobile devices to see if it also looks good there! You also should be checking each page of your website before going live, but if you have a chance to check mobile devices before the entire site is built, it can save you some time.

Fixed content and full-width content considerations

A full-width row is an impactful and modern design choice, and you can have a full-width row with full-width content, but this comes with its own considerations, especially regarding the type of content you are placing inside.

Take text, for instance. Wide stretches of text are challenging for visitors to read, especially on larger screens. If you place a full-width row on your website with a full-width text module, on larger screens, visitors will need to move their heads left and right to read the text. This is bad practice.

Think carefully about which background row images to use in full-width rows. Although you have a smaller screen, others might have a 27-inch or larger monitor or screen that causes the content to stretch. An image, particularly of a person's face, might appear flawless on a laptop or mobile display. However, on larger screens, viewers might be greeted with an extreme close-up of just the person's nose or eye. As you crop and add your images to background rows or columns, bear in mind that what looks amazing on your device might not translate as well on another. The takeaway? Always be vigilant and test your designs across various displays, including mobile devices.

Style your columns

If your website displays all the content in one column, it probably looks dated. Using one column once in a while on a page looks very nice, but if you use one column only on all of your pages, it can make your website look older. Mix up the design by changing the number of columns each row contains. There are not hard and fast rules about this, as long as your content looks interesting and intriguing and is easy for the visitors to read and understand. Figure 10-10 shows Beaver Builder's website; note how they mix the number of columns between two, three, and four.

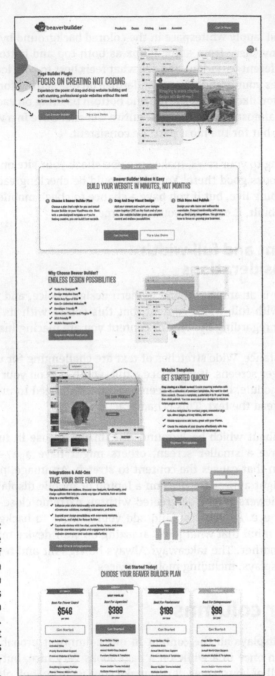

FIGURE 10-10:
Alternating the number of columns each row displays on your pages helps create a modern looking website. It creates interest and helps visitors digest your information.

Just like with rows, you can choose to vertically align the content in each column to the top, middle, or bottom of each row. You can place background colors or photos on individual columns, and you can set a minimum height so that all columns look equal. Sometimes I like to add a left or right border to create a divider between my columns. There are some great options when it comes to styling columns. Most likely you will not do too much styling on your columns: You will style the row and the module more often.

Style your modules

After placing your modules in the columns and adding content to them, the next step is to style them. The styling options available to you will vary based on the module type and the software you're using. I prefer modules that offer extensive customization.

Module options encompass features like backgrounds, borders, drop shadows, and text properties. When styling your modules, aim for a consistent look, especially for similar modules throughout your site. For example, consider forms on website pages. I might decide to style the form this way: light gray background, something like #f4f4f4; rounded corners at 30px radius, each box where visitors enter information might have a white background (#ffffff;) and maybe have a gray border #eaeaea; with rounded corners as well — 20px radius, the font size for the labels might be bold and all uppercase. If I set up one form like this, I might use this same design for all forms on my website so they look consistent. Figure 10-11 shows an example.

I like to style my headings in an interesting way. I might make the headings all 40px tall, ultra-bold, capitalized text, with a 30 percent border above each one that happens to be 5px tall, double line, in one of the colors from my logo, as you see in Figure 10-12.

Try different options. As you style your modules, always prioritize consistency and stay true to your brand.

FIGURE 10-11:
Get creative with styling your modules including your form modules. A shows what a form might look like out of the box. When you add your own styling in the form of colors, fonts, and corners, you can make your modules and forms align with your brand (b).

FIGURE 10-12:
Style all of your
modules so that
they look
interesting and
display the
content in a
readable way that
creates hierarchy.

LET'S HAVE A CHAT

Using Whitespace

Using whitespace effectively is crucial for designing an attractive, user-friendly website. Whitespace is also known as *negative space*. It refers to the empty space between different elements and it can also be the space between text, images, buttons, and other elements. Whitespace does not need to be white, either — it can be a color.

Because it is so important, I dedicate an entire section to explaining the design principles behind it. If you don't use enough whitespace, you risk the following problems:

>> **Poor readability:** When your content is too close together, it becomes difficult for visitors to read and understand the information.

>> **Cognitive overload:** Without enough whitespace, visitors can become overwhelmed and may struggle to locate the information they're looking for.

>> **Unprofessional design:** A cluttered design can make your website appear unprofessional and untrustworthy, potentially driving away potential customers.

The following sections explain the benefits of using whitespace in more detail.

Whitespace helps readability

Whitespace makes content easier to read and digest, by separating different sections, paragraphs, and lines of text. It gives your content some breathing room. Whitespace allows your visitors to digest your material in bite-sized chunks.

Figure 10-13 shows a before and after example. The left column is the before example. Do you have any idea what this content is about? What is the subject? What are the key points? What are your takeaways? It's hard to come up with an answer to any of those questions, right? Now, look at the right column of text in Figure 10-13. This is the same text as before, just broken into smaller chunks.

I gave each section a headline and of course, lots of whitespace. When you look at this text quickly, it is much easier to understand the key points. Adding whitespace reduces cognitive overload and helps visitors focus on the content. It makes your content more readable and understandable.

Whitespace exudes professionalism and clean design

Whitespace contributes to a clean, uncluttered design, which gives your website a professional look and feel, which is why you are reading this book! When visitors see a clean, professional look, they will translate that positive feeling to your company or organization.

Whitespace leads to increased comprehension

Proper use of whitespace can increase user comprehension. Not only is the content easier to read, but it also is easier to understand! Remember, you have three to five seconds to explain to visitors what your website is about, and whitespace can help you bridge that gap.

Whitespace helps reduce bounce rate and increase engagement rate

Bounce rate is the rate at which someone visits a page on your website and then leaves without visiting another page. Google is doing away with measuring bounce rate for many reasons and is moving to measuring *engagement rate,* which measures how many links a person clicks, such as when they press a play button on a video or fill out a form on the same page without leaving. Engagement rate is also affected by whitespace. Effective use of whitespace can keep visitors engaged and reduce bounce rate, as visitors are more likely to stay and explore your site.

You will also most likely end up with a better UX. Recall that UX refers to how a person feels and interacts with a website. It encompasses all aspects of a user's interaction with a website, including its interface design, visual aesthetics, usability, and the user's emotional response. The goal of UX design is to create a positive and seamless experience for the user. Good UX design often leads to increased user engagement, customer satisfaction, and business success. Properly used whitespace contributes to good UX, and therefore creates a positive user experience, increasing the likelihood that visitors will return to your website or recommend it to others.

Add the right amount of whitespace

To introduce more whitespace to your website, adjust the padding or margins of your rows, not your modules. When you add whitespace to individual modules, you can end up getting inconsistent layouts. Always start by adding padding to the rows first.

If you can't add padding to your rows, try adding a "spacer" module to your layouts. In your page builder, you can use a spacer to create whitespace by dragging a spacer module to the place where you want the whitespace and then setting the height of the spacer. These are also called *whitespace breaks.* Adding whitespace in this way is not ideal, because you are asking the browser to download a little image and then resize it itself, which creates work for the browser and could slow the page down, but it's okay if you have no other options.

A last and super easy way to add whitespace is to add carriage returns to your content. This is definitely not the correct or best way to add whitespace, but if you do not have an option to add padding to a row or use a spacer module, this is your last resort and you should use it.

There's no one-size-fits-all answer to how much whitespace you should add, as the amount of whitespace you need depends on your website's design and content. However, a good rule of thumb is to ensure that your website is easy to read and navigate while maintaining a professional appearance. Don't be afraid to experiment with different amounts of whitespace to find the balance that works best for your website.

I sometimes use 40px top and bottom padding on rows, and use 150px on the top and bottom, and all in between. Try a lot of options and see what looks and feels best to you.

TIP

If you remember only one thing from this chapter, remember to always strive for simplicity and consistency:

>> Use the same fonts in the same places.

>> Use less color to begin and add tiny elements as you go along.

>> Use the same types of borders across your site.

>> Make sure all your buttons are consistent.

>> Employ lots of whitespace.

>> Choose crisp, clear images that support your content and do not look staged.

Chapter **11**

Generating Leads from Your Website

'm willing to bet that your website's main goal is to generate leads or to make direct sales. So far, you've set the foundation for your site, nailed down your message, integrated keywords, and incorporated SEO basics. You've organized your content, determined what goes on each page, and followed the basics of web design. After all this preparation to attract and retain visitors, the next step is to prompt visitors to seek your solution to their challenges. This chapter guides you through strategies to capture and engage with potential leads effectively, using your amazing new tool, your website!

Understanding and Using Forms

You may be wondering if you even need a form on your site and whether visitors will fill them out. I am here to tell you from years of experience that, yes, you need forms on your website and people will absolutely fill them out.

CONVERSION RATE

Forms help you with your conversion rate. The term "conversion" in digital marketing refers to the action of converting a casual website visitor into a more committed user or customer. In essence, a "conversion" happens when a visitor completes a desired action, such as signing up for a newsletter, making a purchase, or filling out a form. When visitors fill out a form, they're transitioning (or "converting") from a passive role of just browsing to an active role of engagement or intent.

If you don't add forms to your website, you are missing a huge opportunity to engage with potential customers. Forms serve as guestbooks or feedback slips that potential customers fill out. Forms allow you to gather leads.

This is how this happens. Imagine that you run a home remodeling company, and you don't have a form on your website. A couple who recently purchased a home decides one Wednesday night to get some quotes to add an addition onto the home. They go online and check out some remodeler websites. Your website is the best one out there, since you are reading this book, so that's perfect. They check out all of the services provide on your website, and they decide they want a quote from you.

If your site doesn't have a form, the couple will have to write down your phone number and remember to call you during their busy workday. Then they go to work, and they are all excited and they tell their coworkers that they might add on to their house. Their coworkers say, "That's so great! You should use the guys we used they were awesome!" or, "Oh, I think that Kevin had an addition done you should reach out to the people he hired."

Then what happens to this warm lead? They don't call you. You had them right there. And you lost them.

When you have forms on your website, you won't lose the lead! This is the value forms bring to your website. Bottom line — add forms to your website.

How many forms should you include?

Most likely you will want to add more than one form to your website. Consider these scenarios:

> **» The first form is for your contact page.** This is a generic, all-purpose Contact Us form that asks visitors for their name and email address, and includes a spot for a message. This form can be filled out by anyone for any purpose.

CHOOSE A FORM BUILDER THAT SAVES ENTRIES

When picking software to create your forms, always make sure it can save the form responses. Not every form maker keeps a record of the responses. It's important to save these responses, in case there's a tech problem and you don't get the proper email. Saving the entries in the backend of your website is a safer bet and gives you a backup and peace of mind.

>> **You might also want to add a form for a free consultation.** This form should include qualifying questions that will help you understand what the visitor is looking for prior to meeting with them. For example, if you are a home remodeling company, you might want to ask the visitor the type of remodel they are looking to do so that you can determine if this is a big job or a tiny job and if this job is in your wheelhouse. You might want to ask where they are located so you can see if this is in your service area.

TIP

To help you build a quality and useful form, think of past calls you have received from leads who were not qualified. What made those customers not a good fit for you? Then ask those questions on your form. Let your website and your forms do some of the prequalification and weeding out for you.

>> **Create a separate form for each reason you need to collect information.** You might want to create a form for billing issues. On this form you ask billing-related questions. You might have a form that requests a demo of your product. That form might ask what days and times are good or what features the visitor is most interested in. You might want a form that will help you schedule an event such as a wedding or a conference. In that case, you ask the date of the event, the number of attendees, what they need such as tables and chairs, and so on.

Any time you get calls to your office requesting information, note those requests and make a form that will gather prequalification information for you.

Types of form fields

When you add a form to your website, you can ask unlimited questions. The number of questions you ask and the types of fields you include on your website forms depend on the goal you are trying to achieve. In general, shorter forms are more effective. Find a balance between keeping forms short and gathering important information. Once you decide how many and what questions to ask, it's time to build your form with fields.

There are many types of fields you can include in your forms. Here are a few of the most popular:

>> **Simple text:** Allows users to type in a short response, typically in a single line.

>> **Paragraph:** Known as the text area, this allows users to type a more detailed message, as the box is larger.

>> **Dropdown:** Users can select an option from a list. These are predefined options, which is helpful when you want to control or categorize the answers.

>> **Radio button:** Users can select only one option from a list. This is like a dropdown, but the visitor can see all of the options on the screen because they are not hidden behind a dropdown. You can choose between dropdown and radio button.

>> **Checkbox:** Users can select multiple options.

>> **File upload:** Users can attach files to their submission. This is helpful when you want someone to upload a photo or PDF file as part of their submission. For example, a form for employment might ask for a resume upload, whereas an online store might ask for a photo of a damaged item to be uploaded before the return is processed.

You can also choose from many other types of fields, such as date pickers, sorting fields, and more.

Required fields

Fields can be required or not. You can decide which fields you want to require. The only field you *should* require is the email field. (If you do not ask for an email, you might have problems with your forms.) I always require the email field and then decide which other fields I want to be required. If visitors don't fill out a required field, the form will prompt them to do so before the form is submitted. They cannot submit a form unless the required fields are filled out.

Do *not* require payment fields. If you do this, you most likely will have problems with your form. I have had that issue before and found this out by trial and error, so save your time because and do not require payment fields.

Tab order

Fields have a tab order, also known as the tab index. When some people fill out a form they will use the Tab key to move to the next field. If your tab order is mixed up, they might go to the bottom of the form before they finish filling out the top.

With newer forms, the tab order is set properly and you don't need to think about this, unless you have two or more forms on one page.

If you place two forms on one page, and each has a tab order that starts with 1 and moves up as they should naturally, you will end of having two inputs on one page with a tab order of 1, two inputs with a tab order of 2, and so on. In this case, the person filling out the first form could press tab to go to field 4, and instead might be taken to field 4 on the second form. This is horrible UX!

You fix this issue simply by setting your second form to start at the tab number that is greater than the number of inputs in the first form. This way, users can tab through all the inputs sequentially. Figure 11-1 shows an example of setting tab order.

FIGURE 11-1:
Forms have a tab order. If you have more than one form on a page, you need to set the tab orders sequentially. In this case, the forms on this page have a total number of 20 inputs.

Conditional fields

Conditional fields appear based on the visitor's response to previous fields. For example, if you are a home remodeler and you ask what type of remodel the visitor wants and they choose bathroom, the form can then provide a follow-up question, such as whether the current bathroom is a half bath or a full bath. Or you might want to ask if it's the main bathroom, a jack and jill bathroom, a basement bathroom, or other qualifying questions that will help you understand the job before you call them back.

Set up notifications

Notifications are emails sent to you, your team, or the individual who filled out the form when a visitor submits a form. Notifications contain the information that the visitor submitted in the form.

Sometimes you might want to set up an *autoresponder*, which is an email that goes to the person who filled out the form. This is usually a summary of the email they sent, or a note telling the visitor that you will contact them soon, or maybe an intro to your company or some instructions or tasks that the visitor should do before you talk.

For example, a form that requests a free estimate might go to a particular estimator's inbox, as well as the sales area manager, so that the area manager can keep up to date on the leads that their salespeople are getting. A form that requests renting space might go to the head chef, the sales department, and the facilities manager. Think of all the people who need to receive the form to do their job and set up a notification for each.

Configure confirmations

Confirmations are sent after a visitor clicks the button to submit the form. Confirmations can come in a few forms — you can send the person to a separate Thank You page or you can display a message on the screen.

Sending visitors to a Thank You page is better for two main reasons:

>> **If you plan on tracking form submissions to conversions from social media channels or other ads, you need a Thank You page.** In order to track where visitors came from when they fill out a form, you need to place a bit of code on the page. When that code runs, that means the visitor converted. (The only way that code runs is when someone visits the Thank You page and the only way they visit that page is by filling out the form.) This is a great way to track conversions!

>> **If you want to offer the visitor something else to do on your website.** You can keep them on your site and provide more value. For example, if a person filled out a form to regarding an addition to their house, you could place a testimonial video or case study on the Thank You page, which could move the visitor along the buyer's journey. Or you could include a checklist of things that they should do prior to meeting with you so that your meeting goes more smoothly. The visitor is captive at that moment, so use this Thank You page to your advantage. Provide a bit more!

TIP

If you do set up Thank You pages for your forms, make sure you tell search engines not to index this page by setting the page to `noindex`. Doing so tells search engines to skip this page when they are crawling your website and putting all of your information into their database. This way, your Thank You page will not be returned in the SERP when someone is doing a search.

If you choose not to add a Thank You page and instead want to provide a message, make sure the message makes sense. If a default message is displayed, change it to something personal and specific to your business. Let the visitor know when you will be in touch with them. Maybe tell them how you will be in touch. If the purpose of the form is to request an estimate, make sure the language confirms the request for the estimate and includes a timeframe for next steps.

Test your forms

To verify that you have set up your form correctly, you need to test it. To do this, you need to choose every option on the form and verify the following:

>> The visitor can submit the form.

>> The visitor gets the correct confirmation.

>> You get the notification.

EXAMPLE

One of my landscaping and pool contractor clients did not test their forms at the beginning of the COVID-19 pandemic. We tested the forms when their site went live and they received the notifications, but then something happened to their email system, and they did not test their forms again.

During the Spring and Summer of 2020, many people decided to upgrade their homes instead of spending money on travel. One day the client called us when they realized that they had not received any forms in a few months. We logged in saw that they had over 50 good, solid leads for new pools, stone walls, walkways, and more in their form submissions, but the emails never made into to their inbox. These warm leads worth hundreds of thousands of dollars were in jeopardy and many were lost.

The moral of this story is that you need to test your forms, especially after every change to the website, no matter how small it might seem. Test them and then test them again. Test them every month or so. Put a note on your calendar to test your forms. You can't test them too much.

Combatting Submission Spam

Over time, you might start getting a lot of spam on your forms. There are a few ways to minimize the amount of spam you get, as follows:

>> First, if you have *honeypot protection* as an option in your settings, turn it on. If you use Gravity Forms for WordPress, you have honeypot as an option. A

honeypot places a hidden field on your form that is invisible to real users, but computers and bots will see it, and they will fill it out. If a form is submitted and this field is populated, the form submission will be discarded as spam.

>> If you are still getting spam, place a math problem on the form and add *conditional logic* to the Submit button. Something simple like 1+4=. Then if anything is entered in that field is not 5, the Submit button will not appear, so the form cannot be submitted. This can prevent bots from submitting forms.

>> If spam is still coming in, you can set up *Google reCAPTCHA,* which is a protective measure that shields websites from spam and malicious activity. Its main function is to discern genuine human users from automated bots when interacting with online forms. The technology has changed over the years. originally, you might remember, it presented users with distorted text they The most recent version, reCAPTCHA v3, operates subtly in the background, analyzing user behavior on a website to decide if they are a human or a bot, and then assigns a score based on this analysis without requiring direct user interaction. reCAPTCHA is free but has a bit of a setup process. How you implement reCAPTCHA depends on the form software you are using. If you need it, look up how to integrate into your platform.

>> Finally, there are options to scan all the submissions that come in using a third party such as *Akismet.* Akismet is a paid service. You set up an account and connect Akismet with your form. Then, all submissions are sent to their servers first and are scored on all types of factors that may indicate that the submission is spam. If the submission is spam, the email is either discarded or placed in a spam folder, or maybe is sent to you with {SPAM} in the subject line. (You choose the option you want when you set it up.) A third-party scanner like Akismet can be very effective and worth the price of the subscription.

Integrating Forms with Other Platforms

Integrating your forms with other platforms can streamline your workflow and automate repetitive tasks. Email marketing platforms like Mailchimp, Active-Campaign, ConvertKit, and more can be integrated with your forms.

You most likely need to tell your form to integrate with your email marketing provider and then "connect" the two accounts. This allows you to automatically add new subscribers to your email lists and send targeted email campaigns based on the information collected through your forms. For example, if you are visited my website and wanted to watch a gated webinar (*gated* means you must fill out a form first before you watch the webinar), your email address will be added to my email list automatically and I will tag your contact record with something like "gated webinar." Then I can send an email with a special coupon to all the people who are tagged with gated webinar. This is called a *funnel*, and it can be a very powerful technique for lead nurturing. I suggest that you connect your forms to your email marketing platform, and you can find instructions online for your form software.

TECHNICAL STUFF

Say you want to connect a form to another application and you find that there is not a direct way to do this because the form software and the additional application do not have an integration out of the box. Zapier is a powerful tool that connects your forms to hundreds of other apps, allowing you to create automated workflows. For example, you can automatically add new form submissions to a Google Sheet or create a task in Trello. Zapier operates based on triggers and actions. When a specific event (the *trigger*) happens in one application, it prompts a particular outcome (the *action*) in another application, all without any manual intervention. Essentially, the trigger sets the process in motion, and the action is the result of that process. The form submission is the trigger and the action may be "add this email address to my list in my email marketing program."

Setting Up Calls to Action (CTAs)

A CTA, or *call to action*, is a request or prompt that asks the visitor to take some specific action. This can be in the form of a button, link, or banner that directs the visitor to a specific page or prompts them to sign up for a newsletter or make a purchase. You want to include a CTA on most of your website pages.

On any given page, you might choose to feature a single CTA or show several — the choice is yours. There's no fixed rule. Recall how your homepage is essentially a series of CTAs strung together? It's vital to pepper your homepage, and most other pages, with CTAs to prompt your visitors to act. After populating a page with content, try to view it through a first-time visitor's lens. Ask yourself: If this is someone's maiden interaction with my website, what would they naturally want to explore next? The answer to that question is the CTA you should include on this page.

Build a good CTA

To be effective, a CTA should be clear and specific, with a sense of urgency and a strong benefit to the visitor. It should also be placed in a prominent location and use actionable language that encourages the visitor to take the desired action.

There are at least three main parts of a CTA: A headline, a subheading, and a button or link. Some CTAs also include a form on the CTA as well as a visual. For example, Wiley.com, the publisher of this book, has many CTAs on its website. Figure 11-2 shows one such CTA that encourages visitors to make a purchase.

FIGURE 11-2: CTAs encourage website visitors to take action. They follow a pretty standard format in most cases: A headline, subheading or text, and a button.

Start your CTA with a powerful headline that is short and to the point, but most of all contains your value proposition — this is what the visitors get when they click the button or link or fill out the form. The headline should be compelling and presented in a very clear and enticing way.

Next, you can include a sentence or two below the headline to add more context or provide visitors with specifics. Using phrases that indicate saving money, piquing curiosity, and making things easy can be very effective. Your subheading should also be short, and it should add value or prompt the user a bit more to take that action. Being specific is a good idea.

Finally, you want to add some sort of prominent link or button to visit another page to receive the offer. The language should be specific and actionable! Include a verb on the button.

Some examples include:

>> Sign up for our newsletter

>> Download our app

>> Buy now

>> Learn more about XYZ

>> Contact us

Style your CTAs

CTAs can come in many forms, and you will most likely create a CTA in an entire row or column. Figure 11-3 shows some examples of nicely styled CTAs.

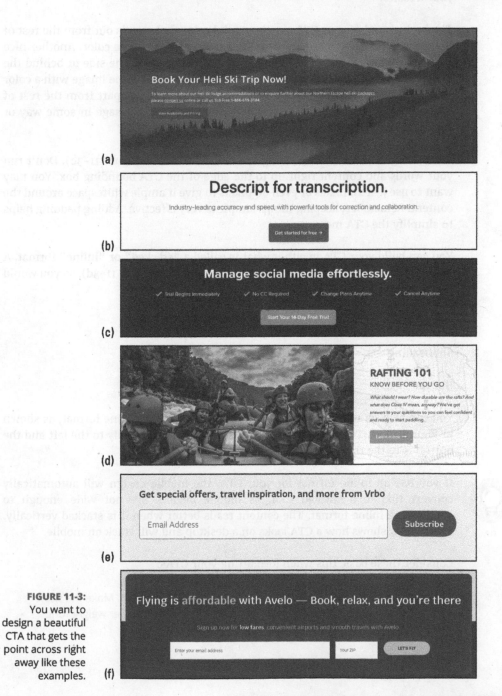

The row containing your CTA can take up all of the screen, can be in one column, or can be set inside a "boxed" layout. You can also put a CTA in a popup box. There is no right or wrong how you design your CTAs; it depends on the look and feel of your website.

The background of your CTA may be a solid color that stands out from the rest of the website (as shown in Figure 11-3) or it may be the same color. Another nice effect is adding an image in the background, either off to the side or behind the entire CTA, as shown in Figure 11-3a. You can then overlay the image with a color so that you can read the words. This can set this content apart from the rest of your website. The image you use should support your message in some way or contain a design that does not distract from the message.

Include a good amount of padding around the CTA (see Figure 11-3b). Don't run your words and content right up to the edge of the CTA bounding box. You may want to use just 20 pixels or even 80 pixels to give it ample whitespace around the content. Remember, keeping things simple is very effective. Adding padding helps to simplify the CTA message.

You can build your CTA in either what is called a "stacked" or "inline" format. A stacked CTA typically lists the elements vertically (see Figure 11-3d), so you would have:

Headline

Subheading

Button

You can also set up your CTA so that it is displayed in an inline format, as shown in Figure 11-3e. The headline and the subheading are typically to the left and the button is to the right — the pieces are next to each other.

TIP

If you use an inline format for your CTA, the mobile design will automatically convert this to a stacked CTA, as mobile devices are not wide enough to support the inline format. The content reads better when it is stacked vertically. Figure 11-4 shows how a CTA looks on a desktop and will stack on mobile.

Consider these basic tips when formatting your CTAs:

>> The headline font should be larger than the description text. Make the short headline stand out! Use a contrasting color font and a heavier weight font.

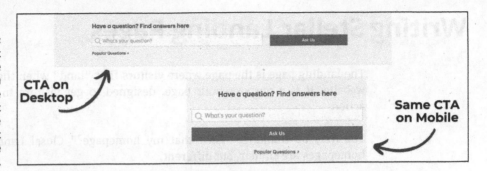

FIGURE 11-4:
CTAs can be built
so they are inline
or stacked. If you
create an inline
CTA, it will most
likely use the
stacked format
on mobile
devices.

» The subheading font can be the same as the paragraph or body copy on the rest of your website or can be larger or smaller; the choice is yours.

» The style of the button is super important! Style it so that it stands out. You can create a flat button, which means that it is filled in with one color, or you can create a transparent button that contains a border around the edge. Figure 11-5 shows you both styles of buttons.

» If you have the option, you can also control the colors of the background and the text, as well as the *hover state* colors. Choose colors that not only match your branding but also stand out with high contrast. Buttons also generally come with some styling as far as radius and drop shadow are concerned. The radius for your CTA buttons should be uniform across your entire website, so come up with a standard approach.

FIGURE 11-5:
Buttons can
be designed so
they are flat or
transparent.
Match the style
of your website
and brand.

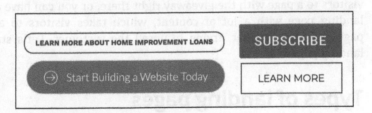

» Sometimes you can include an icon on the button, either before or after the text. I like to use these when I have an icon that supports the message of the CTA. For example, if you are creating a newsletter signup form, you may want to include an email icon on the button. I like to include arrows on buttons that point to the button text or point forward, indicating that the visitors will move forward when they click the button.

Writing Stellar Landing Pages

The landing page is the page where visitors first "land" when they come to your website. It is a purpose-built page, designed to get visitors to take a specific action.

You may be thinking, "Isn't that my homepage?" Close! Landing pages and homepages are similar, but different.

A *homepage* is primarily built to promote exploration. It provides links and access to many other pages on your website. When a visitor comes to the homepage, you want that page to encourage them to visit many other pages or complete a number of tasks, such as purchasing a gift card, attending an event, learning about a service, and so on. The homepage is like the virtual "front door" of your business online.

A *landing page* is more like a virtual "lobby" with one virtual "door" into *one* room of your business. It's kind of like IKEA, where you are forced to walk the store in one direction; you don't have a choice which direction to go. A landing page usually has a single goal for visitors, indicated by a CTA, such as a sign-up form, a video to watch, a download, or a button to click. You can, and should, have multiple landing pages for different goals!

Landing pages are part of what is called a *funnel*. Your funnel can be simple: you can have a landing page with a form or a button that, after submission, takes visitors to a page with the giveaway right there, or you can have a more complex landing page with a lot of content, which takes visitors to another landing page and then another, trying to upsell the customer. Let's start with simple landing pages.

Types of landing pages

There are two main types of landing pages:

>> **The lead generation page:** This is a "give to get." You're offering some download or piece of amazing content, product, or item in exchange for their email address. It's a type of trade. The piece of content that the visitor gets is called a *lead magnet*.

On a lead generation landing page, the CTA is a form that visitors fill out to get the lead magnet. The form builds your list of prospects. Once you have their email addresses, you add them to your CRM or your contact database and can nurture these leads. You can send them emails and encourage them to engage with your organization. You are trying to generate more leads for your business. That is the singular goal of the lead generation page.

>> **The clickthrough page:** The goal of this page is to sell something to the visitors. There's usually no form here, rather, a button that encourages visitors to take the next step. They can try something for free or purchase something now.

If you were selling a subscription service, for example, the landing page may talk about what's included and the CTA button would let the customer "Sign Up for a 7-Day Trial." The goal is to convince visitors that land on this page to click through to another page or action by enticing them with clever text. The visitors are sent to a sales funnel or to a product, service, or other to purchase or try.

Where to build your landing page

You can build your landing page on your own website or use a platform to do so. If you have a tight budget, you can build your landing page right on your website.

You may be asking yourself, "Wait, I can build a landing page somewhere else?" Yes! There are many landing page paid platforms, including ClickFunnels, Unbounce, HubSpot, Swipe Pages, Leadpages, Instapage, and others. You can create a landing page quickly using one of these platforms, but most likely the URL will contain the platform's domain name — something like totocoaching. unbounce.com or you will need to set up a subdomain that points to the landing page platform's hosting server if that is even possible.

WARNING

Here's the drawback: In Google's view, your domain does not get credit for any traffic to this page. You are sending your precious web traffic to another domain name! This does not help your SEO ratings. You want the traffic on your domain, not on a marketing platform's URL or a subdomain.

There are times when using a landing page or funnel platform is a good idea. If you are going to create a complicated funnel or you want to measure results very carefully, one of these platforms is a better choice. If you are creating your first landing page and it is simply a page with a form or button and then a Thank You page, you can use the tools you already have.

Parts of a landing page

A landing page can contain the following:

>> **A header, which can be simply your logo.** Some landing pages include their full top menu, but that's up to you. See the examples in Figure 11-6. These

landing pages have a very small header with very few or no links. The logo is always included, and the logo links to the main website. That's good for visitors who might not want to commit to your offer just yet, because they can click the logo and go to your full website to check you out. Hiding the menu encourages visitors to take action on one single goal and not get distracted.

FIGURE 11-6: Landing pages typically have very few links or no links at the top of the page.

>> **A strong, concise headline with your selling proposition.** If you're building a landing page to go along with ads, you want the headline to match your ad. This is your hook. The "why." The pain point you are solving. Sell your benefit or agitate the pain points. The headline is probably the most crucial element on your page, so spend time coming up with a great, concise headline.

>> **A small blurb that supports the headline with benefits of your offering (and matches the ad).** This should be a small paragraph or a few sentences that match your headline and your goal. Explain who you are or what the visitors will get if they convert. Use this area not only to support your main headline or your hook but also to build trust.

>> **A main hero image, animation, or video.** Remember that images and visuals are critical to conveying your message, building trust, and moving visitors toward converting or taking action.

>> **Your CTA.** Either a form for lead generation landing pages or a button for clickthrough landing pages. This is the whole reason you are building this landing page! You want to put this form or button right up top so people see it right away. Remember you need to test this page and form in mobile too. Make sure the fields are not too small and that a finger can click each field easily. Make this form as short as possible, as shorter forms have a higher conversion rate.

>> **Social proof.** This can come in the form of Internet reviews from Google Business, Yelp, Facebook, Trustpilot, and so on. You can also create a testimonial video if you have customer videos available. Stars are a nice visual cue, especially when they are yellow and close to 5!

>> **More supporting content.** You also may want to include more content down the page that supports your main goal. Although you don't want to distract from the main goal, but sometimes it is helpful to have some supplemental content on the page. Maybe an award you recently won, or a conference you attended on this topic.

Create an effective landing page

Landing pages have just one goal — they should contain only one or very few links. More links and buttons are just distractions. You can configure your landing page to omit your regular top menu or footer menu — perhaps just leaving your logo at the top, so that there are fewer links, and therefore, fewer distractions.

Pull out your buyer personas along with the table you created in Chapter 3. Read over your buyer personas again and put yourself in their shoes. Then read the problems people have, the benefits of your solution, and features columns in your problems and benefits table.

Pick *one* problem people have and address that one issue head on. Don't solve multiple problems on this landing page, just solve and address one.

After choosing your one problem, develop a strong headline and blurb around this pain point. Either agitate that pain point or sell your benefit to connect with the visitors. Choose a strong visual that supports your message. Add a form that gathers the information you need or add a button that drives visitors to the product or page you want them to convert on. Have empathy for your visitors. Get into their heads and understand what is motivating them to take action to fix their issues.

TIP

Create one landing page and lay it out beautifully and test it. If the page converts, then duplicate that landing page and change the headline, blurb, and the visuals to match the next pain point and solution.

Remember that people skim pages, so make sure that the most important pieces of information stand out. Get feedback from others — can they tell what the main point of the page is by looking at it very quickly?

Get people to your landing page

Just because you build an amazing landing page does not mean that people will come! Because this page has a singular goal, you want to build a campaign around it. Here are a few ideas of how to get people to visit your landing pages:

>> Paid social ads

>> Paid search ads

>> Email campaigns

>> Organic search

>> Affiliate marketing

>> From your main website

Whether you're creating an ad, sending out emails, or driving people to your landing page from your own website, you want to keep the wording consistent.

WARNING

If you decide to run ads to bring people to your landing page, make sure your ad has similar language as the landing page. Google might disable your ad if it promotes one thing and the landing page promotes something else! It looks like a bait and switch, where you're trying to deceive people into clicking your link. This mismatch can even get your ads account suspended, which takes a while to fix. I've seen this happen!

Since it does take quite a bit of work to configure and launch ad campaigns, you might decide to use an ad agency. If you decide to go that route, and a third-party is running your ads, just be sure to double-check the ads! Don't assume that they are doing it all correctly. Verify all the ads and check the links to make sure everything is aligned to your message and goals. I have seen many instances where an ad agency runs ads that use the wrong language or provides broken links.

Putting It All Together: Sales and Marketing Funnels

When you put forms, CTAs, and landing pages all together, you get what is called a sales or marketing funnel, or *funnel* for short. When a visitor arrives at your landing page and sees the amazing content you're offering, they're intrigued. They see the CTA and fill out the form to get their hands on that content. Voilà, they've given you their email address. The form will automatically take them to another page with the giveaway. Now, they're not just a visitor; they're a lead — a potential customer you can reach out to in the future.

A *website funnel* is like having a friendly guide at a festival who ensures visitors don't just walk past the games but stop, play, and leave with a prize. It means you don't just get traffic, you get engaged visitors who might turn into customers. And that's the magic of a funnel — it turns passing foot traffic into a parade of potential customers.

REMEMBER

Think of a landing page as a welcoming entrance to your site. It's designed to be inviting and tell visitors exactly what they can expect. It's tailored to grab attention and show off something valuable that you're offering, like an e-book, a discount, or an exclusive video.

The number of landing pages in a funnel can vary based on the specific goals and structure of that funnel. Some funnels have just one landing page, while others have several. A basic funnel has at least one primary landing page designed to capture leads or make sales.

However, for more complex funnels or multi-step processes, there might be multiple landing pages, each tailored to different stages or offers. For example, you might have an initial landing page to capture email addresses, followed by another page offering a special discount, and yet another page presenting an upsell or additional offer. The key is to design the funnel in a way that effectively guides potential customers toward a desired action or outcome.

5

Going Live and Measuring Results

IN THIS CHAPTER

» Adding keywords to maximize your SEO efforts

» Using alt tags strategically

» Adding meta titles and meta descriptions

» Keeping people engaged on your website

» Optimizing for conversions

Chapter **12**

Optimizing Each Page for Search (On-Page Optimization)

C hapter 4 introduced the basics of SEO, including understanding how search engines rate content and providing content that gets you good results. This chapter explains how to optimize each page of your website for search engines. Recall that *search engine optimization* (SEO) involves placing certain content in specific places on your web pages.

You don't *have* to optimize your web pages. In fact, most DIY websites are not optimized for search because many people don't know what to do when it comes to SEO. However, if you do not optimize your pages and your competition does, they will get your leads.

The great thing about taking the time to optimize your site is that you don't need to repeat this process unless you want to change your strategy. The main setup process only needs to be done once for each page (although you will need to continue to fine-tune and update your site as times change).

The Goal of SEO

The goals with regards to SEO include the following:

>> **Having your website returned in one of the top three search positions.** Search engines must understand your offer and return it when someone's search matches your offer.

>> **Getting as many clicks as possible to your website.** To get as many clicks as possible, your SERP listing should be persuasive and create a sense of urgency.

>> **Keeping visitors engaged on your website as long as possible.** To keep visitors engaged on your website, you need compelling content that visitors want to read, watch, or download.

The process of optimizing your pages starts with your keywords.

The role of keywords

In Chapter 5 you chose some keywords for your website and in Chapter 6 you assigned each keyword phrase to a page on your website. You'll use that list during the exercise in this chapter.

People search the Internet by typing words into a search box to find an answer to their question or problem. The words that people type into search engines are called *keywords*. Because this is how many online searches begin, they are the foundation of SEO.

AUTHOR SAYS

The process of performing an online search is changing to a certain extent. You can now perform a search based on a photo using tools like Google Lens. As time goes on, these types of searches will become more prevalent, but right now most searches are done using words.

From your keyword list, you should have assigned one keyword phrase to each page, post, or product of your website. Chapter 5 explains how to choose keywords based on their competitiveness, their volume, your domain authority, as well as their relevance to your offering.

The next step is to place those crucial keywords on your website where search engines will look for them. When search engines find particular keywords in particular places, they index your website for those words. This chapter shows you the most important places to put those words.

Optimize your URLs

Begin by placing your keywords in each URL of each page. If you did the exercise in Chapter 6, you should already know what your URLs will be. Go ahead and set your URLs according to the list we created. In case you skipped that section, here is a recap:

The URL of each page is also called its *link*. This is also called a permalink, slug, or path. Using a good URL structure can help search engines understand your content because it helps them read your website like an outline. Because search engines are understanding and indexing the words in the URL of each page, you want to include your keyword assigned to each page in the URL of each page.

When you place your keywords in the URL of each page, keep the following in mind:

>> Use your keywords in order.

>> All words should be lowercase.

>> Substitute hyphens for spaces between the words (do not run all of your words together, as search engines and people cannot read that).

>> Make your URLs short and sweet.

>> Nest your pages or products under category headings.

>> Remove *stop words* (short words such as a, an, and, are, as, at, be, but, by, for, if, in, into, is, it, me, mine, my, no, not, of, on, or, our, such, that, the, their, then, there, these, they, this, to, was, will, with, and your).

TIP

Some studies show longer URLs do not rise as high as shorter ones, so keep this in mind when writing your URLs. Removing the stop words will help.

When you created your sitemap, you might have placed some pages underneath topic headings or other pages. For example, if you run a landscaping business, you might call a page "Services" and then under Services, you would create a separate page for each service you offer. Your URLs might look like this:

mydomainname.com/services/lawn-mowing-leaf-blowing

mydomainname.com/services/lawn-fertilizing-green-healthy-grass

mydomainname.com/services/tree-trimming-removal

Search engines understand that they can find all your services in one neat, tidy spot under Services!

If you have a lot of pages that talk about your services and they are organized by type of services, another effective way of writing your URLs is as follows:

`mydomainname.com/lawn-services/mowing-leaf-blowing`

`mydomainname.com/lawn-services/fertilizing-green-healthy-grass`

`mydomainname.com/tree-services/trimming-removal`

WARNING

If you change the URLs on an established website, make sure that you set up a redirect; otherwise, if visitors with the old URL will get a *404 page not found* error message. To counteract this, you can set up what are called *redirects*, which are explained in Chapter 13.

Use heading tags

Next, add each page's keyword phrase to the heading of the page. In Chapter 8 you broke up your body copy into small sections and placed a headline on each section. When you placed the content on your pages, you indicated the headings for each section of text by making the font larger, bolder, underlined, or you delineated each heading by styling it. You should have highlighted the text in each subheading and styled it by changing the style from body, normal, or paragraph to H1, H2, and so on. Figure 12-1 shows a typical dropdown where you can choose to apply a heading style.

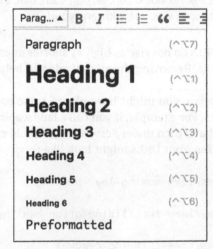

FIGURE 12-1:
When formatting
your text, ensure
you select a
heading style for
your headings.
This can be done
by choosing the
heading. A
selection box will
then appear.

REMEMBER

Heading tags tell search engines what content they can find on your pages. The words that are contained inside the heading tags are considered more important than the words that appear in the body copy, and therefore, you want to make sure you are using these tags to your benefit. They should include keywords as much as possible.

Start with your heading 1s. Each page of your website should include *one* heading 1 tag (h1). Not zero. Not more than one. Place one H1 tag on each page, and only one at the top of your page, before any other heading tags. In your H1, include the keyword phrase that is assigned to this page. Search engines read the H1 assigned to each page, determine what your page is about, and match a visitor's search intent with it.

REMEMBER

This is why breaking up your services into more than one page is important. A page with an H1 that contains the word "Services" does not help a search engine understand the content on that page. An H1 that contains "Lawn Mowing and Leaf Blowing" is much more descriptive and a search engine can determine what that page is about.

Then, down your page you can use multiple heading 2 tags (H2), and possibly heading 3 (H3), heading 4 (H4), heading 5 (H5), and heading 6 (H6) tags. The same principle regarding the importance of including keywords in your heading 1 tags applies to the H2-H6 tags. Place your keyword phrase in one or a few of the H2 tags as well. Don't put the keyword phrase in every heading tag, which is considered *keyword stuffing,* and is bad practice.

You don't have to use all heading tags from H1 To H6. I use H1s, H2s, H3s, and sometimes H4 tags, and I rarely use H5-H6 tags. If you have a lot of hierarchy on your pages and posts, and you might find it helpful to use all six tags. You don't need to use all the heading tags, but you can if you want.

TIP

When you are placing heading tags on your pages, don't skip levels. Make sure that if you want to include in H4 on your page that you also have included an H1, and at least one H2 and H3. In addition to being proper outline structuring, it also helps people who use a screen reader as assistive technology.

Consider keyword density

Make sure your keywords appear in the copy of this page. Read over your text to verify that the keywords have been added where they make sense. Include the keyword phrase toward the beginning of the page and then a few additional times, where it flows naturally. For example, if you wanted to rank for Bakuchiol, which is a natural alternative to retinol, you would add that word to the body copy and some headlines. Figure 12-2 shows how the page has included "Bakuchiol" multiple places, and that the phrase is used in logical ways so that it doesn't seem forced, which can be interpreted by Google as keyword stuffing.

Bakuchiol is a promising alternative to retinol for achieving younger-looking skin, especially around the eyes. It can hydrate the skin, improve elasticity, and soothe wrinkles.

TL;DR: Bakuchiol eye cream is designed for the sensitive eye area, offering targeted treatment for concerns like dark circles and puffiness while reducing wrinkles. A small amount of Bakuchiol eye cream is enough for the eye area. It should be applied gently with the ring finger.

Introduction to Bakuchiol

Bakuchiol is a plant-based ingredient that has anti-aging benefits and is considered a gentle alternative to retinol for mature skin. It's derived from the seeds of the Psoralea corylifolia plant and has been shown to reduce the look of fine lines and wrinkles, improve skin firmness, and boost collagen without harsh side effects often associated with retinol. This plant-based retinol alternative helps to protect your skin without irritation.

What is the Difference Between a Bakuchiol Eye Cream and a Bakuchiol Serum?

Bakuchiol eye cream is specifically formulated for the delicate skin around the eyes. It's typically thicker than a serum and includes additional ingredients to target concerns like dark circles and puffiness. A good firming eye cream with Bakuchiol, such as Acta Beauty's Luxe Moisture Eye Cream with Bakuchiol not only addresses fine lines and pigmentation, but also enhances overall skin tone and firmness.

Should You Put More Bakuchiol Around Your Eyes or Apply the Same Amount Around Your Whole Face?

"You don't need to apply more around the eyes; a small amount is sufficient," Jillian advises. "Use your ring finger and gently tap the cream around the orbital bone. The skin here is thin and doesn't require a large amount of product to see results and nourish this area." It's like a spot treatment for your gorgeous face.

The Benefits of Bakuchiol for Wrinkles

Bakuchiol's ability to stimulate collagen production and promote cell turnover makes it an ideal ingredient for tackling fine lines and wrinkles around the eyes. Within just 12 weeks of consistent use, many users see a noticeable improvement in skin firmness and a reduction in the appearance of wrinkles.

Unlike retinol, Bakuchiol doesn't increase sensitivity to sunlight, making it suitable for use during the day. However, Jillian emphasizes the importance of a good sunscreen to protect the skin from other aging factors.

Incorporating Bakuchiol Eye Cream into Your Routine

When adding a Bakuchiol eye cream to your routine, it's essential to understand how to use it effectively. After cleansing, apply the eye cream before your regular moisturizer or serum. This ensures that the active ingredients directly target the skin around the eyes.

FIGURE 12-2:
Add your keyword phrase to your headings and body copy where it makes sense, but don't overdo it.

You might find that you need to reword certain sections of your website or maybe add an entire new sentence or paragraph. That's all normal when it comes to optimizing your text on your page.

TIP

You might wonder how many times to include your keywords on each page. That's a great question. This is called *keyword density*. One general standard suggests including one to two keywords for every 100 words of copy, which is a keyword density of 1–2 percent.

Name images using keywords

You should also add your keyword phrases to your images. There are a few places to do this. Let's start with the image names.

You should name each image using keywords from your keyword list. These names should accurately describe the photo. Instead of generic names like img875465.

jpg, use descriptive keywords. This helps search engines understand what the photo contains. Changing the names of your images to words that search engines and visitors can understand is helpful.

Use alt tags strategically

Alternate tags, or alt tags, allow search engines to understand what an image contains and represent it in image search results. Without alt tags, images are invisible to text-based search. You should define an alt tag for each image that appears on your website. In your platform where you edit each image, you will find a spot to add the alt text. In Wix, you add it in a section called "What's in the image. Tell Google," and in WordPress, you enter it in the Alt text area. Look through the support documents to determine where to add the alt text on your platform.

Alt tags have a few other purposes as well:

>> **Accessibility:** Alt tags tell visually impaired users using screen readers what each image represents, because a screen reader cannot read an image, but it can read the alternate text that is assigned to the image. This makes your site more inclusive.

>> **Fallback text:** Alt tags also serve as fallback text if an image fails to load for any reason. The alt tag description is shown instead, so a visitor will know what they are missing.

Add internal and external links

On each page or post, add at least one internal link, and if you can, one external link.

>> An *internal link* is a link to another page on this same website.

>> An *external link* is a link to another website.

The text that is linked on the page is called the *anchor text*, which is covered in Chapter 4.

REMEMBER

When you include links to other pages on your own website, it helps search engines understand your website better. Search engines follow each link you place on your website to find and index more content. This is also called *crawling* your website. A search engine reads the page, finds the links on the page, and then reads the anchor text to understand the "relevance" of the linked page to this content. This helps search engines better understand your offer. Internal links help create a mini-web on your own domain with links from one page to others.

Links can come in the form of a button, an image, or simply text that is linked to another page. You can add a link to a paragraph of text and you can also add a button that links to another page. You might have an image that is linked to another page as well. Think about adding links to your page that will help your visitors navigate your website. When they are reading one piece of content, think about what information would be helpful to see next. You can even add a section on your posts that contain "related posts," or on product pages you could add other products that relate to this one, upsells, or others in this same category or tag.

Next, the number of links you include to each page tells search engines how important each page is. If a particular page or post on your website has many links that point to it, that page is considered "more important" by a search engine. This helps create hierarchy on your website. If you have 50 links on your website and 30 of them point to a particular product, search engines assume that this product is very important.

REMEMBER

On some pages or blog posts, you might want to include an *external link* (links to other websites besides your own). External links are important for SEO and can improve your search engine ranking (position in the SERP). High-quality sites that are relevant to your content make logical sites to link to. Having external links that search engines value can in turn add more value to your own pages and help improve your search rankings.

External links also show authority and trust: They demonstrate that your site provides value by connecting users to useful information on authority sites. It shows you're willing to link to quality resources, which search engines see as a sign of trust and authority. The key is choosing reputable, topically relevant sites.

TIP

A good tip is to check the domain authority of sites you plan to link to — linking to authoritative, trustworthy sites reflects well. But over-optimization with excessive links can seem spammy, so quality and moderation is important. Add an external link only when it makes sense to do so.

Getting as Many Clicks as Possible

Once search engines start returning your website in the SERP, that means you have made some progress. The next step is to entice searchers who see your listing in the SERP to click on it. You do this by making your listing relevant and exciting.

Search engine results listings

You want your listing to look its best when it's returned in the SERP, as this affects the likelihood of your website being returned in search. It also affects the CTR (*clickthrough rate*). The clickthrough rate is the percentage of times that your website has been clicked after it's been shown to visitors in the SERP. You want the highest clickthrough rate as possible and one way to increase your CTR is to make sure that your SERP listing looks the best that it can. Search engines measure the CTR rate. If your website returns high in the SERP but no one clicks it, your site may drop in position.

A typical listing in the SERP is shown in Figure 12-3. There are five important pieces of information here.

You see that the favicon (1) of the website appears next to the name of the website (the Open Graph Site Name) in small letters (2) followed by the URL of the page (3). In big blue letters, the meta title of the page appears (4), followed by the meta description (5). Below the meta description you might see some other links. You can control all these items except for the additional links. The following subsections cover each of these items.

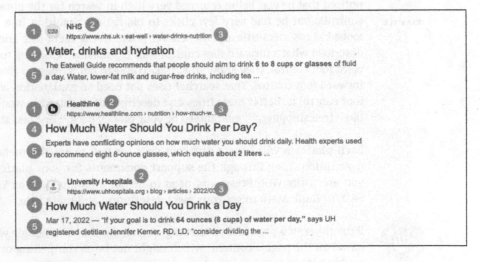

FIGURE 12-3:
Most listings come back in the SERP containing a favicon (1), site name (2), URL (3), meta title (4), and meta description (5).

Favicons

If you have read Chapter 8, you may have already uploaded your favicon to your website. Remember, you want to set a favicon for your website so that the SERP listing looks professional and is branded. If you do not set a favicon, the search engine will set one for you, which may look generic or it may pull an image from the platform or host you are using. Do a second check now and look in the settings of your platform or theme. Then, make sure you set a professional, branded favicon that looks great. This does not necessarily help your on-page optimization, but it helps your website listing in the SERP look branded.

Write titles and meta descriptions

Now it is time to set a meta title and meta description. In Chapter 6, you planned your meta titles and meta descriptions. Review these; if they still look good, copy and paste them into your pages now.

A good title and meta description improve the likelihood that your listing will be clicked, therefore increasing your CTR. Titles and descriptions that create a sense of urgency or address search intent are most effective. Think about the customers that you want to visit your website and what do you want them to do, and then write your titles and your meta descriptions that will encourage clicks based on their search intent.

EXAMPLE

I had a client that sold motorcycle parts on his website. One of the items he sold was called "forward foot controls." When looking through his search result data, I noticed that he was being returned very high in search for the phrase, forward foot controls, but he had very few clicks to his listing, resulting in a very low CTR. I looked at his meta title and meta description. In the meta title and description, he described what a forward foot control was. If someone is looking to purchase a forward foot control, they know what it is. The searcher's intent is likely to purchase a forward foot control. That searcher does not need an explanation of what a forward foot control is. Better meta titles and descriptions in this case would be something like "free shipping," "guaranteed or your money back," or "fast shipping."

Each platform will have a different spot for you to set the meta title and meta description. Look through the support documents for your platform to find it. If you are using WordPress, you need to install a plugin such as Yoast, All in One SEO, or Rank Math to set your meta description and meta title.

REMEMBER

Remember, if a page lacks a title tag, search engines like Google will generate one based on the page's content, which might not be as compelling or relevant as you could write.

Keep people engaged on your website

If your site rises to the top of the SERP, and if visitors see a great title and description and are intrigued, and if they click your listing, you have gotten them all the way to your website! Congratulations! This is excellent! This is "traffic" to your website, and many people look at these numbers to determine how effective their SEO efforts are.

Getting traffic to your website is just one of the first steps. You want to keep this flow of traffic coming to your website, and unfortunately, this can change. You might look at your numbers and see an increase in traffic and then a dip, which can happen due to a change in the search engine's algorithm, because you lost some good backlinks, or you got a lot of toxic backlinks and your domain authority might have dropped. In addition, seasonality can affect your rating, or things like economic, political, or global events can influence consumer behavior and cause general shifts in traffic across many sites.

Some of these things you cannot control, but you can influence the length of time that someone stays on your website and how much they engage with your site by making your website engaging and providing valuable content.

Search engines measure the time visitors spend on a site as well as their engagement as positive ranking signals, so it's worth investing in content that persuades visitors to stick around and explore your site.

>> *Time on site* is measured by the number of minutes and seconds visitors stay on your website before leaving it. The longer visitors stay on your site, the more search engines get the signal that this site is amazing and provides valuable content.

>> *Engagement* includes time on site, and is also measured by factors such as how far visitors scroll down a page, when they click links and buttons, play icons, and perform other mouse interactions, the number of pages they visit on a website, and any repeat visits.

If people stay on your website for a long time (three minutes or more) and engage with it, this is a signal to search engines that your site is a good one and they should keep your site in a top position in the SERP. Providing valuable, engaging content is the key to keeping visitors on your website longer and interacting more deeply with each page.

TIP

Go through each page of your website to determine if there is content that you can add to each page to make it more engaging. Can you add a video? Can you add a download? Would it be helpful to add a section with blog posts that pertain to the subject and encourage visitors to jump to another page on your website and explore further? Include intriguing headlines, high-quality images, embedded video, share buttons, clear CTAs, and other elements that appeal to your audience and encourage deeper engagement. The more compelling your content is, the more likely visitors will take the time to consume it fully, browse additional pages, and engage with your site beyond a quick visit.

Conversions: The Grand Finale of a Visitor's Journey and Your SEO Efforts

You have done a ton of work on your website. You have optimized it for SEO and you are getting returned in the SERP and getting traffic. You have one more goal to attain: *conversions.* You want to convert strangers or cold leads into warm leads and/or customers. Chapter 11 discusses how to use forms to get conversions. Recall that a *conversion* is the action of converting a casual website visitor into a more committed user or customer.

Ultimately, your SEO efforts can essentially be measured by your conversion rate. The more you are able to convert strangers into customers, the better your website is doing what it's supposed to be doing.

You want to continually work on your conversion rate. Ask these questions:

>> How can I improve my conversion rate?

>> Can I add more forms over time?

>> Do I have additional, valuable content to add?

>> Can I write more articles?

>> Can I create more videos, PDFs, or case studies?

>> Can I add more testimonials to my website?

View your website as a living document — do not build it and forget it. Your website can be your most powerful marketing tool — helping you to grow your business, make more money, and flourish. I constantly change my website, adding new content, removing older content, moving content around, and updating it with the latest design trends. If you look at all of the well-used websites online, you will notice they change their websites often, mainly to increase their conversion rates.

I hope that you will continue to do the same.

IN THIS CHAPTER

» Building redirects for old URLs

» Going live from your temporary URL

» Going live from a staging site

» Installing an SSL Certificate

» Testing your links, forms, and mobile sites

Chapter **13**

Ribbon-Cutting in Cyberspace: Your Website's Grand Opening

Congratulations! It's time to go live with your website! At this point you have learned why you should include specific information on specific pages for specific users to obtain a specific purpose. Hopefully you've built something that you're proud of and that moves your business forward. This chapter walks you through the process of going live. Some of the steps pertain to every website that goes live, and some steps depend on where you have been building your website thus far.

Depending on where you have been working, whether it be a temporary URL, a staging site, or building live, you go through different steps. After reading the overview section and considering if you need to create redirects, find the section that pertains to how you built your website and follow the instructions you find there. Then be sure to check out the section on testing your site, near the end of the chapter, before you broadcast it.

Overview of the Process

Going live with the website is not simply turning on a switch like you turn on a light switch in your house. Here is a high-level overview of the basic steps:

1. **Preserve any current URLs.**

2. **Tell your hosting service what domain name should be assigned to the hosting files.**

3. **Point your domain name to this set of files on this specific server.**

4. **Install and configure an SSL Certificate so that your website loads securely on visitors' browsers.**

5. **Test everything to make sure things work as they should.**

6. **Cancel your old hosting method.**

Creating Redirects and Preserving Current URLs

If you had a previous website and have changed the URLs for your new site, you have to create *redirects*. However, if either of the following cases applies to you, you can skip this section:

>> You do not have a current website on this domain.

>> Your new site uses the same URLs as your old site.

Redirects ensure that visitors are seamlessly redirected from old URLs to your new pages.

Say your old website (or even your current site) has a page named yourcompany. com/about-us. There are probably external links and backlinks pointing to that page on your current site. On your new website, you have simplified the URL to /about. When someone tries visiting that old /about-us URL after you launch your new site, they'll get a frustrating *Page Not Found* 404 error. Not good! Also, because search engines index URLs in their systems, they will also get 404 responses when your old URLs start leading to dead ends.

How you implement redirects depends on the platform your site is built on:

>> *If you built your site using WordPress,* you have a couple options. If you installed a redirect plugin such as Redirection or Yoast SEO Premium prior to changing the URLs, it will automatically create the redirects as you update your URLs. If you have already changed your URLs, you need to manually enter in the old URL and the new URL into the software. It is a fairly simple process, as shown in Figure 13-1.

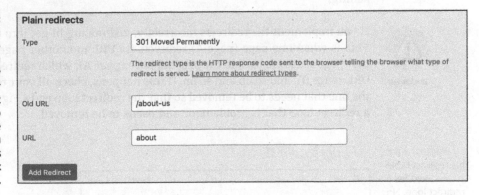

Plain redirects

Type: 301 Moved Permanently

The redirect type is the HTTP response code sent to the browser telling the browser what type of redirect is served. Learn more about redirect types.

Old URL: /about-us

URL: about

Add Redirect

>> *If you built your site using Wix,* visit the area under the SEO Dashboard to set up redirects.

>> *If you built your site using Squarespace,* it uses the Developer Tools section to set up redirects.

Don't go live until you've made a master list of all your old URLs and their new destinations. For a small site, no biggie — you could just copy them into a spreadsheet or a word document. However, if you have hundreds of pages, manually recording all your URLs would take a really long time and invariably you're going to miss one or two of them. It's better to use an online tool such as an XML sitemap generator.

TIP

Search for "XML Sitemap Generator" online — find a tool that allows you to try it for free for a limited time. Run your website through that tool; you'll receive a list of all your original URLs. Use this list to compare against your new URLs names. If you have not changed the URL, remove it from the list. You want to create a list that includes only the URLs that have changed. With this list, you can neatly match up all your old URLs with the new ones side-by-side.

You have a couple ways to input them:

>> You can input them directly into your redirect plugin or platform.

>> Your hosting platform may have a redirect tool — ask the support team.

>> If your host needs code snippets, they can insert them for you.

The key is getting that master list first, so you don't leave visitors lost on 404 errors. With a little redirect preparation, your URL transition will be smooth sailing!

WARNING

If you implement the redirects incorrectly, visitors might get into a redirect loop. This is when one page (page A) redirects its URL to another page (page B), and that page redirects back to the original page (page A), which redirects to the other URL (page B), and so on and so on. If this happens, check all your redirects to find the one that needs to be removed so that the redirect loop ends. Figure 13-2 shows a redirect loop that is problematic and needs to be removed.

FIGURE 13-2:
This redirect table includes a redirect loop. No one will be able to visit /about-us or /about, as they will be sent in a never-ending loop!

Old URL ⇕	New URL ⇕
/about/	/about-us/
/about-us/	/about/

Going Live from a Temporary URL

If you have been building your site on a temporary URL, you need to take two steps to go live:

>> You need to give your website host the domain name that should be assigned to your website files.

>> You need to tell your nameserver where to find those files.

Give your website host the domain name

To give your website host the domain name that should be assigned to your website files, log into your hosting site. Somewhere in your settings you will see the domain names that are assigned to this hosting. Because you're on a temporary URL, you'll see your temporary URL's name in this section. It might look like this:

```
battcas.wpenginepowered.com
```

```
wordpress-291391-4042118.cloudwaysapps.com
```

```
4jet9.flywheelsites.com
```

```
box###.temp.domains/~username/
```

You need to add two entries here:

» One with just your root domain name, such as etsy.com

» One with the www. before your domain name, such as www.etsy.com

Once you have added these two domain names, or possibly during the process of adding these domain names, you will see a place to make one of these domain names the primary URL assigned to your website files. Choose the non-www version of your domain name as the primary URL, as it is standard nowadays.

This change indicates to the hosting site that your temporary URL is not the primary URL anymore. Instead, your new domain name becomes the primary URL for this account. Once you've done that, it is time to point your domain name to these files.

WARNING

Once you make your primary URL your actual domain name, you will not be able to access the website until you point your domain name to these files (as you do in the next step). If you need to access your site after you change your primary URL, you can continue with the next step by pointing your A record to these files or you can change the primary URL back to your temporary URL.

Tell your nameserver where to find your files

Now it is time to point your domain to your new hosting service. In order to do this, you need to log into your nameserver. Your nameserver most likely is the registrar where you registered your domain name.

Log into your nameserver and find the area where you manage your DNS settings. You can access this screen by finding a link for Manage DNS, DNS Settings, or maybe Manage Zone Records — something like that. If you have trouble finding this screen, chat or call the support team at your nameserver (or search online).

WARNING

You will see a lot of records that look like Figure 13-3, which can be confusing. You won't make a ton of changes here, but you do want to be very careful during this process, because an incorrect change can cause disruptions in other services such as email. In addition, these records are not backed up. Once you make a change, you cannot go backwards. Document everything, double-check everything, and go very slowly. Don't multitask while you are changing your records!

	Type ⓘ	Name ⓘ	Data ⓘ	TTL ⓘ	Delete	Edit
☐	A	@	▬▬	600 seconds	🗑	✏
☐	NS	@	▬▬	1 Hour	Can't delete	Can't edit
☐	NS	@	▬▬	1 Hour	Can't delete	Can't edit
☐	CNAME	www	▬▬	1 Hour	🗑	✏
☐	CNAME	zb05569374	▬▬	1 Hour	🗑	✏
☐	CNAME	_domainconnect	▬▬	1 Hour	🗑	✏
☐	SOA	@	▬▬	1 Hour	🗑	✏
☐	MX	@	▬▬	1 Hour	🗑	✏
☐	MX	@	▬▬	1 Hour	🗑	✏
☐	MX	@	▬▬	1 Hour	🗑	✏

Type ▲	Name	Content	Proxy status	TTL	Actions
A	totoseo.com	▬▬	☁ DNS only	Auto	Edit ▶
CNAME	_domainconnect	▬▬	Proxied	Auto	Edit ▶
CNAME	www	▬▬	Proxied	Auto	Edit ▶
MX	totoseo.com	▬▬	DNS only	Auto	Edit ▶
MX	totoseo.com	▬▬	DNS only	Auto	Edit ▶
MX	totoseo.com	▬▬	DNS only	Auto	Edit ▶
TXT	mailjet._domainkey	▬▬	DNS only	Auto	Edit ▶
TXT	totoseo.com	▬▬	DNS only	Auto	Edit ▶
TXT	totoseo.com	▬▬	DNS only	Auto	Edit ▶
TXT	totoseo.com	▬▬	DNS only	Auto	Edit ▶

FIGURE 13-3: The screen where you change your DNS records looks something like these screens.

Follow these steps to point your domain name to your hosting files:

1. **In the DNS settings, find your A record for your root domain name.** Most likely it will be the first record in the list. In Figures 13-3a and 13-3b, the A record is the first entry. Your root domain is simply your domain name . com or .net or org, without www in the front. It's just your domain name with your extension (see Figure 13-3b). It may be referred to with an @ symbol (see Figure 13-3a).

Your A record will currently be assigned to an IP address (see Figure 13-3b). This A record might look like what you see in Figure 13-3b. It is the value under the Data/Content/Value/Record column (each nameserver calls each column a different thing).

If you registered your domain name but you never built a website before, you might see "Parked" or some other language as the value in the Data/Content/Value/Record column. This is shown in the A record in Figure 13-3a.

2. **Record the current entry first.** In order to see a live website when you visit your domain name, you must enter an IP address into the Data/Content/Value column. If you do see an IP address in the Data column next to the A record for your root domain or @ symbol, copy the information in the Content or Data column that appears.

TIP

Copy and paste this information into a new document in case you need to revert to this entry. This is in case something terrible happens and you have to revert to the old settings. These entries are not backed up and you have no way to revert to the entry if mistakes are made unless you record the current values.

3. **While you have your DNS records screen open, open a new browser window and log into your hosting account.** Somewhere in your hosting account you will be given an IP address. Record this number now.

I don't write this number down physically, instead I copy it with my mouse and I paste it into a document. You might want to paste it into a document that has all your other information, such as your registrar, your host, and your nameserver.

4. **After you have copied and pasted this new IP address into another document, point your domain name here.** Return to the browser window where you are logged into your nameserver. Edit the A record for your root domain by replacing the IP address or word Parked with the new IP address that was assigned by your new website host. Save this value.

5. **Now you have to wait until you can go to your domain name in a browser.** You'll either see your website or a certificate warning. Once that happens, your website is live!

You can tell when your site is live if you are able to open a web browser, type your domain name, and see a site or an error that there is a security issue. If you have GoDaddy or another very fast nameserver, your website might already be live by the time you switch screens. If you have a slower nameserver, it might take an hour or two files correctly. Once that happens, you can proceed to the next step.

>> If you see a security warning, that is usually a good sign that your site *is* live and you just need to go through the process in the later section titled "Setting Up Your SSL Certificate" to remove that warning.

>> If the site isn't coming up, you can use something like a DNS checker (https://dnschecker.org) to see if the change you made to the IP address is propagating throughout the Internet. If you wait an hour or two and still do not see that your new website is live or you still see the old IP address in dnschecker, contact your host and/or nameserver support for help.

When your new website comes up, that shows that you've pointed your A record to your hosting and everything is working as it should.

Cancel your old hosting

If you moved your hosting site from one host to another, it's time to cancel your old *hosting*. (You might have other services with your current host such as email, and if you do, do not cancel those services until you set up new email hosting elsewhere. Right now, just cancel the hosting.) Don't forget this step! You might be able to get some money back if you've prepaid for some time of hosting. Call your old hosting company to cancel the hosting. I've had clients that did not cancel their old hosting and went on to pay for it unnecessarily for many years! If you can't cancel the hosting right now, add an item to your calendar to remind yourself to cancel the hosting in the near future.

Going Live from a Staging Site

If you built your new website on a staging server, it's usually a fairly simply process to go live. Log into your hosting site, or wherever you set up the staging area. If that was MalCare, you'll need to log in there. Find the area where you manage your staging site. You are going to "push" the staging site live by clicking a button or link that says something like "Push Staging to Live" or "Launch Staging Changes." The program will take all the files that are in the staging area and move them over to the live area.

WARNING

Before you click that button, verify that no one in your organization has updated the live site recently. As soon as you push your staging site live, the live site that you see today right now is going to be overwritten. If you have good backup on the live site, you could do a restore to another temporary hosting and get the changes, but that's just a big mess. Before you click the button to go live, make sure no one has been updating the live site.

It will likely take about 5 to 10 minutes for this process to complete, depending on how large your site is. Go make some coffee or take your dogs for a walk and then come back. You should get a message in your inbox that the staging site has been moved to live, and when you browse to your domain name, you will see your brand new site!

TIP

Most likely if you had a website up and running, your SSL Certificate was installed and you had already pointed both versions of your website to this hosting site. Make sure that your SSL Certificate is still set up correctly and that you can browse to the www and non-www versions of your website and that the www version of your site sends you to the non-www version of your site.

Follow the steps for installing your SSL Certificate on the www and the non-www domains in the later section titled "Setting Up Your SSL Certificate."

Going Live When You've Been Building Live

If you are building on a live domain, there is not much that you need to do. Simply verify that you can type www.yourdomainname and yourdomainname into a browser and that both of those resolve to one or the other. Verify that you have the SSL Certificate set up and installed properly and follow the rest of the instructions in this chapter. If you can do that, you are good to go!

Setting Up Your SSL Certificate

Now that your website is live, the next thing to do is install an SSL certificate. You have to wait until all DNS servers see your new website prior to performing this step, so check dnschecker.org first.

An SSL Certificate is pretty much free with most hosting these days. It creates a secure connection between the computer visiting your website and the website itself. This is essential on today's Internet. Matter of fact, if you do not install an SSL certificate, search engines will not return your website when someone does a search.

EXAMPLE

I just experienced this. I searched online for the store where I purchased a moped for my daughter and their website did not come up, even though I knew that they did have a website. Their website was not protected with an SSL Certificate. I know this because when I went directly to their website, their URL began with http:// not https://, and I did not see the lock symbol in the browser bar, like you see in Figure 13-4. You might also see the words "Not Secure" on such a site.

FIGURE 13-4:
When a page is set up properly with an SSL Certificate, you will see a lock symbol in the browser bar.

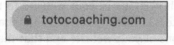
🔒 totocoaching.com

Follow these steps to install an SSL Certificate:

1. **Log into the area in your hosting where you found your IP address and where you assigned the primary URL.** There should be a place to install and configure an SSL certificate.

2. **Follow the prompts.** When you are asked on which domain to install this SSL certificate, verify that you are installing it on both the root domain (which is just your domain name) and the www domain. If you are asked if you would like to force https://, choose Yes for that option. You want everyone who visits your website to go the https:// version, not the http:// version. Let the server do its thing; this should take a few minutes.

3. **Once the SSL certificate is installed, you have another step to do.** Check every page on your website to make sure that you see the lock symbol in the browser bar. This lock symbol indicates that your entire web page — all of the assets on your web page, including the images, the videos, the PDFs, everything — is being delivered securely to visitors' browsers.

4. **If you do not see the lock symbol and you did install an SSL Certificate, some of your files might not be referenced with https://.** Check your code or check the area where you upload your images, PDFs, videos, and so on, to see if any items are loading over http://. If this is the case, edit your web page by adding an s to http:// so that the files are referenced with https://.

5. **After you follow these steps and save the page, you should see that lock in the browser.** If you still don't see the lock, look at more files referenced on this page and find the ones that are not being called with https://. Check each page on your website.

If you try to visit a page using http://, you are redirected to the https:// version of the website. When you see those two things (lock symbol and https:// pages), you know you have installed the SSL Certificate correctly.

TIP

You also might have a separate area in your hosting that will allow you to force all images and all your content over https. If you have that option, make sure that it is turned on.

Testing Your Design, Links, Forms, and More

Your website is live and that must feel amazing. However, don't send it out to your contacts just yet. You need to check some things before you send it, in order to ensure that everything is working as it should.

>> **First, check any social media links you placed on your website.** Click each link and make sure you are directed to the correct profile and that the site opens in a new tab. If they don't go to the correct profile or if they don't open in a new tab, fix that now.

» **Next, check the mobile responsiveness of your pages.** Spend about 30 minutes on your phone browsing through every page of your website. Make sure everything looks good. Sometimes words break in the middle, so you'll have one word on two lines. See Figure 13-5. If you can scroll left and right, that is not good, so figure out why that is. Check your platform or page builder to see what options you have to specify settings like font sizes in mobile only.

You do not want to be able to scroll left or right. Google will tell you this is a problem, so it's best to fix it now. Fix all the problems that you can. Do this step on an iPhone and an Android device, if possible.

» **Next, test your forms.** Fill out every form on your website. Make sure that the right people receive the forms. If you are not getting the forms, see if there's a configuration error or if you spelled the email address incorrectly. Even with all my experience, I've done that before. Matter of fact, I just did that a couple months ago! You might also need to set up an *SMTP server*, which is a special type of server that knows how to send emails. Some hosting companies do not provide this type of server. They are website hosting companies, after all, not email hosting companies. Contact your hosting company and let them know if your forms are not going out. They'll tell you the best way to receive the forms, because they may have a special SMTP server that they work with that they want you to set up.

FIGURE 13-5: You might see words breaking improperly in the mobile version. In this case, you need to decrease the font size of these words in the mobile version only.

FREQUE NTLY ASKED QUESTI ONS

WORDPRESS CLEANUP

If you have a WordPress website, do the following cleanup tasks:

- Resave the permalinks. Go to Settings --> Permalinks and choose the Page Name radio button, then click Save. Click Save even if Page Name is already chosen!

- Trash the sample post and sample page if you installed them.

- Trash any spam comments.

- Update all themes and plugins (keep only your child theme, your parent theme, and one extra default theme like 2023 and then delete the rest of the themes that are installed).

- Remove any unused plugins (you don't need old software hanging around, as they leave ways that bad actors can get in).

- Take a post-launch backup and download it, in case you need to reference it later.

Finally, Your Website Is Live!

Congrats — I hope you feel proud of yourself! Now it is time to use software to determine how this new tool is helping your business. The next chapter walks you through the process of securing your website against hackers.

IN THIS CHAPTER

» **Protecting your website with backups**

» **Finding a reliable backup system**

» **Protecting your website from hackers and malware**

» **Determining if your website has been hacked**

» **Fixing a hacked site**

Chapter **14**

Securing Your Website

Now that your website is up and running, you want to protect all of your work so you don't lose it to a problem. There are two main ways to protect your work: backups and malware protection. Most of the information in this chapter pertains to WordPress websites since those sites are self-managed, meaning you are in charge! Even if your website was built on a closed platform, you might want to skim this chapter so you understand some of the risks of being online and verify that you have the proper precautions in place.

Protecting Your Site with Backups

Your data is only as good as your backup. If you're using an all-in-one website builder platform or another closed platform, the platform usually does keep some kind of backup for you. Wix keeps different versions of your site and pages that you can revert to at any time, and Squarespace keeps backups of your website pages and blog posts for 30 days. You can't do much to change these backup policies, because they are closed platforms.

WARNING

Don't assume your website is being backed up! Be sure to verify these settings and plan for any loopholes.

WordPress backups

WordPress is a self-managed platform. That means you are in charge of doing some of the maintenance on your site. Quite often, people with WordPress websites skip the step of adding backups to their website because they assume that someone is doing this job. Well, I have worked with hundreds of clients over the past 20-plus years, many who come to me with a WordPress site. I can't tell you how many of these sites did not have any sort of backup running!

If you are using a Managed WordPress hosting program such as Flywheel, WP Engine, or Kinsta, you can rest assured that your website is backed up daily. These hosts keep many revisions for more than two weeks, their backups are reliable, and the restore process is easy. You can restore simply by logging into the hosting account, finding where the backups are stored, and clicking restore on that backup. Figure 14-1 shows a typical restore screen.

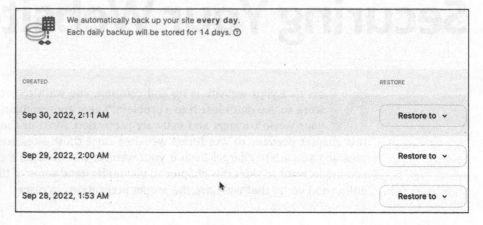

FIGURE 14-1:
Your hosting account might include the ability to easily restore your website from a previous backup.

If you are using a host that is not Managed WordPress, such as for example GoDaddy, BlueHost, HostGator, HostMonster, SiteGround, DreamHost, Liquid Web, and Green Geeks, or, if you're using a lower-cost (shared) hosting plan from one of these companies, you most likely need additional, paid backups discussed next. My go-to backup system for WordPress websites is BlogVault or MalCare, as they have all of the features covered next.

Essential features of a reliable backup system

Look for these features in a good backup system:

>> **Automatic, daily backups:** You don't want to have to rely on a person logging into your website each day and manually backing up your files. You might want this to happen daily, especially if you have a site that is updated frequently.

>> **Data retention:** How long does the system retain your data? Your hosting account may include backup, but most likely if your host is not a managed WordPress host, they will retain only one day of backups, and that backup may be from a week ago.

It's wise to keep backups for between 30-90 days (see Figure 14-2). Imagine that you have not looked at your website since you asked an intern to update something and then when you see it, the website is messed up! Or what if someone deleted an important page or post and you do not realize it for a few weeks. This happens, and frequently you have had to go back in time and find a backup that missing data. If you only have one day of backup, you may be out of luck. Remember, your website is the public, global front door of your company, so don't skimp on this.

94
BACKUPS

Last sync: 12 hours ago | Sync frequency: 1/day

Files Size : 404.06 MB

↻ Backup now   Restore Site

FIGURE 14-2:
The MalCare backup software shows the stats related to your backups.

>> **Storage location:** Many people using WordPress will install a "free" backup that will deposit the backup files on the same server as your hosting server. This is not a good idea, because if that server goes down you've lost your original files and the backups. Make sure those backups are stored in a separate location.

>> **Easy restore process:** Make sure the restore process is not cumbersome or difficult. One option for restoring your site is to call your hosting company and ask them to restore it from a backup that they created. But remember, most likely you will have only one backup to choose from. Some hosts are quick, some are slow. Some will also charge you and that can add up to hundreds of dollars. You should find out now from your hosting company how many days of backup they keep, how often they are backing up, and who does the restore.

>> **Database and files syncing:** It's also helpful to understand how WordPress works so you know what needs to get backed up. In WordPress, a website has files (pictures and documents) and databases (tables of information that the website needs to operate). You can log in and copy the files that make up your website to your own computer or to another place, but you cannot easily copy and paste the databases. You would have to use special software that knows how to read databases and copy them. If you only back up the files, you cannot restore your website. The database and the files need to match each other. They also need to be contemporaneous.

Protecting Your Website from Hackers

Malware, or malicious software, is a bad program or application. Malware is generally installed without your permission, and it may be used to steal personal information, send spam email, redirect visitors to other websites, or spread more malware, and more.

REMEMBER

If are building a WordPress website hosted on a non-managed WordPress host, you are most likely in charge of securing it. This is important information for you to be aware of, even if you are building on Squarespace, Wix, or another platform.

Wix, for example, claims that all of their sites are malware-free always, unless you add your own HTML code or use Velo by Wix. A notice on their website says: "If we detect that your site has malicious code, your site will be taken down immediately." Squarespace websites can also get hacked, although it is more difficult, as it is a closed system. If you are running a WordPress website, you want to choose malware protection that runs on your WordPress installation so that it can see all of your files.

WARNING

Do not choose a malware "protection" option such as an online scanner. The problem with online scanners is that they can scan only files that are publicly visible, and hackers can add malicious code to files and folders that are not viewable by the public, so these scanners will miss these files. You could get a "clean" result even when your site has been infected. Installing software on your website allows the malware scanner to take a deeper look into your files, therefore finding any and all malware on your site.

How your site can get infected

There are many ways that a hacker can add malware to your website. This section covers a few of the most popular ways hackers infect websites.

Outdated vulnerable software

Outdated software running on your website provides an easy way for hackers to add malware to your site. If you are running a WordPress website, you must update the software on a regular basis, either automatically or manually. This includes all the WordPress software, including the themes and plugins.

WordPress is constantly being updated, sometimes on a weekly basis! Good software developers update their software (sometimes called "patching their software") as they discover potential security holes in their code. If the program you use isn't supported anymore, hackers can easily discover vulnerabilities and use them to their advantage, because there is no one around plugging up those security holes.

AUTHOR SAYS

I recommend installing plugins and themes that are being supported and updated on a regular basis. Before installing a new plugin or theme, check when the software was updated last. Has it been over a year? If so, don't use that software on your website.

REMEMBER

You can update your version of WordPress, themes, and plugins manually or automatically. Manual updates are not ideal. You or someone on your team needs to log in to your website to perform these updates. You will see an alert under the Updates or Plugins section indicating that you have software that needs updating. Figure 14-3 shows an alert. You simply click the Update button to update the software. You can also set up plugin updates on many of the managed WordPress hosting platforms by paying a small monthly fee. This fee is worth it. You want to keep your software up-to-date.

It's better to set up automatic updates, so you don't have to depend on your memory to do this.

FIGURE 14-3:
When a plugin
has an update,
you might see a
notice in the
WordPress
dashboard telling
you to update the
plugin manually.

⟳ There is a new version of Yoast SEO available. View version 21.2 details or update now.

Automatic updates are ideal. You can set up updates to happen on a regular basis without your intervention. You can do this in WordPress, set this up with your host possibly if they offer this service, or use an external system.

WordPress also enables you to update the WordPress core software on a regular basis. If you are installing a new WordPress site, this functionality is most likely turned on by default. You might want to turn off the automatic updates to Word-Press if a huge update has just come out and it has not been tested on a lot of websites. However, this should be a rare occurrence.

TECHNICAL STUFF

To turn off the automatic updating of WordPress, you need to modify the wp-config file. You can find instructions online how to do that.

To update your plugins automatically in your WordPress installation, browse to the Plugin section. On the far right, you'll see an option to Enable Auto-Updates. See Figure 14-4.

FIGURE 14-4:
You can enable
automatic
updates in your
WordPress
installation for
most plugins.
When you click
this link, the
plugin will be
updated
automatically
when there is a
new release.

Enable auto-updates

You can turn this on or off yourself. A quick note here: Based on this setting alone, your site will not perform a backup until this plugin has been updated. However, if you have automatic daily backups running, you will have the most recent daily backup you can return to as well. You can also use an external system to back up your website, which will perform updates on a regular basis, such as once a week.

ManageWP, BlogVault, and MalCare can do this for you. Most of the time, these automatic systems perform backups before performing updates, which is a good practice. Managed WordPress hosts like WP Engine, Flywheel, or Kinsta also offer automatic updates of plugins, themes, and WordPress.

TECHNICAL STUFF

Sometimes to update some software, especially with themes, you have to go to the theme developer's website, download a new copy of the software, and update the software using a third-party program. This can be complicated and isn't recommended for anyone who is not super technical.

As far as updating your themes, you will likely have a child theme and a parent theme that need to be installed so your website works, and then you should have one additional theme installed in case you need to troubleshoot. Do not keep lots of themes installed on your websites — keep only one extra theme.

TIP

Always perform a backup before you manually update the software on your website! This is a good habit to get into, it takes just a minute, and it may save you hours of frustration if the software update breaks a part of your website.

Guessing IDs and passwords

The next way a hacker can hack into your website is by guessing your ID and password. Both of these pieces of information need to be unique and difficult to guess. For example, using *admin* as the username and *password* as the password is just asking for trouble.

WARNING

If you currently have a website and the account is called *admin*, you need to immediately create a new user with a unique username and then delete the admin user. If you are going to delete an account on WordPress, log in with another account with administrative privileges. Then, when you delete the admin account, you will be asked what to do with all of the data that the admin user uploaded. Make sure you attribute this data to another user during this procedure, otherwise the data will be gone!

A good rule of thumb for passwords is to make them long. The longer the password, the more difficult it is to guess. Of course, you should also use special characters, upper- and lowercase letters, and numbers, but the key to a good password is length. Make them as long as possible.

In WordPress, the usernames might also be visible to hackers. There are ways to hide this, such as setting the display name publicly as value to something other than the username. You can also have someone who's technical change the *user_ nicename* by editing the database table entries.

How can you tell if your website is infected?

Sometimes your website will get infected and you will have no idea. Sometimes you can tell because something seems off. Some clues that you might be hacked include these:

>> You try to visit your website and you end up on another website.

>> You see a message or text on your website that you did not put there.

>> You do a Google search and your listing looks terrible.

>> You notice that your website has slowed down and is almost unusable.

>> You try to visit your website and the virus protection software running on your own computer exclaims that the site is compromised.

>> You see links on your website that you did not put there.

However, if you can believe it, you might not notice anything! You might think your site is fine but in reality files have been deposited in a folder somewhere that are just waiting for someone to "run" or "activate" them!

If you suspect a breach, the best way to verify if your site has been hacked is to install malware scanner and remediation software, which is covered later in this chapter.

Dealing with a Hacked Website

There are three ways you can clean your website: You can hire someone like your web host, a security expert, or a developer, you can clean it manually, or you can clean it automatically.

Hire someone to clean your hacked website

If you are using Managed WordPress hosting such as WPengine, Kinsta, or Flywheel, you are in luck. These hosts guarantee that you will not get hacked and if you do they will clean it for free. Simply open a support ticket with the host and they will clean your site for you.

If you have a host that is not Managed WordPress, contact the hosting company to see if they will clean your site for you. Some hosts will clean sites for free, some hosts will charge you a hefty sum to clean the site, and some hosts will not clean the website at all. Do not wait until you are hacked to determine your options here. Find out now what will happen if you're hacked so you can prepare ahead of time.

You can also hire a security expert or website developer to clean your site. This can get very expensive very quickly and it's not my recommendation.

Manually clean your hacked website

Unless you are a very technically trained developer, you most likely will not be successful in cleaning your site manually. It is difficult to manually look at each file — the time stamps and code inside each file — and determine which line of code is malicious. I do not recommend manually cleaning a hacked website.

Automatically clean your hacked website

The best way to clean your website yourself is to install malware scanner and remediation software on your website *before* it is hacked so that it's automatically cleaned.

AUTHOR SAYS

There are many options for automatically scanning and cleaning websites, and they vary greatly in how effective they are. MalCare is my software of choice. MalCare has saved many of my client's sites numerous times! I have been working for decades with hacked sites on WordPress, and there is, bar none, no other software that works as well and as accurately as MalCare. MalCare is installed on your website and has permission to read all of your files. It logs each change to your website, which makes it easier to find the infection, and therefore, easier to get rid of it.

Once you install MalCare or another software package that runs on your WordPress installation, your files will be scanned on a regular basis. If an infection is found, you will be alerted to clean the site. MalCare walks through a few questions or cleans the site automatically. In either case, this is the best and easiest remedy, and it is well worth the time it takes to install the software and the money it costs to keep the license updated.

IN THIS CHAPTER

» **Setting up Google Analytics**

» **Using Google Analytics**

» **Setting up the Google Search Console**

» **Using heatmaps to interpret data**

» **Accessing reviews from your Google Business Profile**

» **Responding to reviews from your Google Business Profile**

Chapter **15**

Keeping Up with the Joneses: Measuring What You Built and Making It Better

T his chapter helps you set everything up so that you can measure your efforts. Measuring your website in different ways does many things for you going forward. Tracking metrics shows you how effective your website is at generating leads, driving sales, or sharing information. Without analytics, you are operating blindly. When you install tools to measure aspects of your website, you can pinpoint issues that are turning visitors away, and when you identify weak points, you can make changes to improve engagement. This also helps you identify new opportunities when you see how people navigate your site, where they linger, and what draws their interest.

In essence, analytics transforms guesswork into evidence-based business growth strategies. Rather than speculate what works, you can be more precise determining success based on your site's measurable performance. Analytics paints a picture of how people interact with your site so you can continually refine it to attract, engage, and convert more visitors.

There are many options to choose from when measuring your website, and in this chapter, I concentrate on Google Analytics, Google Search Console, using heatmaps, Google Business Profile, and getting reviews. First, you learn how to install Google Analytics on your website.

Setting Up Google Analytics

Tracking website traffic and performance is crucial for any small business owner or entrepreneur these days. You can track a lot of helpful data on your website, including how many visitors it attracts, how many of those visitors are returning and how many are new, the device the visitors are using, what country they are arriving from, what page they visit after another, and more.

That's where Google Analytics (GA) comes in (see Figure 15-1). It gives you data about visitors after they have arrived on your website. The data pertains to visitors viewing your pages or content. As a website owner, you should absolutely install GA. You want to install GA as soon as you go live so you can start capturing data as soon as possible. The sooner you start tracking analytics, the sooner you can start increasing growth.

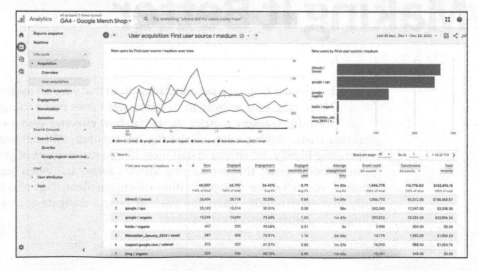

FIGURE 15-1:
A standard Google Analytics report.

Setting up GA involves three or four steps depending on your platform and the software you are using:

1. Set up an account at https://analytics.google.com.

2. Install GA on your website.

3. Connect the software on your website to your GA account.

4. Verify that GA is set up properly.

The following sections cover each of these steps.

Set up a Google Analytics account

If you had a website previously on this domain name, you might already have a Google Analytics account set up. If that is the case, use the same Google Analytics account for this new website so that you have historical data and new data. Don't set up another additional analytics account unless you are using a different domain name.

To see if you already have a GA account set up, browse to https://analytics.google.com with every Google account that you have access to (some people have multiple Google accounts). You will see your account in the upper-right corner (see Figure 15-2).

If this account exists, you can move to the next section.

If you don't have a Google Analytics account, set one up using the steps at https://support.google.com/analytics/answer/9304153. (If that link doesn't work for some reason, search for "How do I set up Google Analytics for my website.")

Install the software on your website

If you are using an online web builder platform such as Wix, Squarespace, or Shopify, the software to connect your website to GA is already installed on your website. If this is the case, you can move to the next section.

If you are using WordPress or another unmanaged platform, you have two options:

>> You can use software in the form of a plugin.

>> You can add a bit of code manually to your website to connect your site to your GA account.

I like to use a plugin to connect my WordPress websites to my GA account for a few reasons:

>> First, I know that once I connect my accounts using a plugin, the connection will be persistent. If I choose to connect the two with a bit of code that Google gives me, and I put that code in my theme file on my website, there is a chance that when the theme is updated, the code might be wiped out break my connection.

>> Second, I find it easier to use a plugin than to use code.

>> Third, some plugins will give you GA data right in your WordPress dashboard, which can be helpful.

AUTHOR SAYS

There are many plugins that allow you to connect your GA account to your website. These include MonsterInsights, ShareThis, GA Google Analytics by Jeff Starr, and more. My go-to plugin is Site Kit by Google. It is written and supported by Google, and you can connect multiple accounts to your website, including your Google Search Console! You can find Site Kit in the WordPress plugin repository by navigating to the dashboard of your website and then choosing Plugins ⇨ Add New. Then search for Site Kit. Install it, activate it, and then find the area where you configure the settings. Follow the prompts or use this link https://support.google.com/analytics/answer/11898619.

If you choose to add the code manually, you can find instructions on the following link. Scroll down this page and find the section titled "Add the Google tag directly to your web pages." See https://support.google.com/analytics/answer/10447272.

Connect your website to your Google Analytics account

Now you need to connect your website to your GA account so that the two can "talk" to each other. You find your specific Google Analytics ID and then you add it to your website. This way, Google Analytics knows which data to show you when you log in to view your data. Your GA ID begins with G-. Copy and paste the ID into the field that your platform provides on the backend of your website.

Follow the instructions on this link to find your ID and learn where to paste the ID depending on which platform you are using: https://support.google.com/analytics/answer/10447272.

Verify that GA is set up properly

When you set up your GA account, you will not have any data at first. You need to wait a while before data begins to populate in your account. This might take a week or two. Add a calendar reminder to go into your Google Analytics account in a week to verify that it's gathering data and that the account shows that somebody has visited your website.

If you don't see any data in your GA account after two weeks, something may be wrong. To troubleshoot this issue, first verify that you added the correct ID to your website in the correct spot. Then check that your GA account does not have any errors and that you entered the proper URL when you set it up. Don't wait until a year from now when you really need this data for some reason. Make sure you get this hooked up properly now.

If you decide to work with a new web developer, an ad agency, or an SEO agency, make sure that you give them access to your Google Analytics account. They should not set up a separate GA account. I have seen this sloppy and lazy mistake made time and time again. You want to keep your data in one spot. If the agency creates a new GA account, you will not have any of the previous historical data. In order to preserve your accounts, simply give the agency access to your account by adding them as a user to your account.

Do not give out your Google ID and password! Never do that. If you do, the other person will be able to see your photos, emails, documents, where you have been, your search history, and more. Instead, add other users to your Google accounts by giving them access via their email address. This way, they do not have access to all of your personal Google Account information and, as a bonus, you can always remove their email address from the access list if you do not want to engage with them anymore. Use these instructions on this link if you need to add a user to any of your Google Accounts: https://support.google.com/analytics/answer/9305788.

Using Google Analytics

There are a lot of things you can do with Google Analytics data, and here are a few ways that you might want to start using it:

» To understand your audience:

- **Demographics:** Find out the age, gender, and interests of your website visitors. This helps you tailor your content and marketing to better suit your audience.

- **Location:** See where your visitors are coming from, geographically. If you notice a lot of traffic from a particular city country, or region, you might consider targeted advertising or even offering specific services for that region.

» To analyze website traffic:

- **Source of traffic:** Discover how visitors are finding your website. Are they coming from search engines, social media, or other websites? This helps you determine which marketing efforts are working best.

- **Behavior flow:** Track the paths visitors take through your site. Identify the most commonly visited pages and the paths that lead to sales or inquiries.

» To evaluate performance:

- **Popular pages:** Identify which pages on your website are the most popular. This can guide you on what content resonates with your audience.

- **Bounce rate:** This shows you how many visitors leave your site after viewing only one page. A high bounce rate might indicate that your landing pages are not engaging or relevant to your visitors.

» To track conversions:

- **Goals:** Set up specific actions you want visitors to take on your site as Goals (such as signing up for a newsletter, making a purchase, or filling out a contact form). Google Analytics tracks how many visitors complete these actions.

- **E-commerce tracking:** If you're selling products or services, you can see detailed sales data. You can determine which products are popular and how the purchase process is working for your customers.

By determining where your traffic comes from and what demographics are most engaged, you can create more targeted and effective marketing campaigns. Analyzing visitor behavior helps you optimize your website layout, content, and navigation for a better user experience, potentially increasing sales or inquiries. Real data about your audience and their preferences can guide your decisions on product development, services offered, and content creation.

In summary, Google Analytics provides a wealth of data that can help you understand your audience, refine your marketing strategies, improve your website, and make informed decisions to grow your business effectively.

Setting Up Google Search Console

Next, set up Google Search Console (GSC). This used to be called the Google Webmaster Tools. I love Google Search Console and I think you will also!

Once you hook up GSC, you can see which search terms Google is returning your website for, what position you are returned in the SERP, how many times people clicked your listing in the SERP, and much more.

Setting up Google Search Console is similar to setting up Google Analytics, and you should do this as soon as possible after going live. Assuming you have set up a Google Account in the previous section, setting GSC involves a few steps:

1. **Set up a Google Search Console account.**
2. **Add your property.**
3. **Verify your account.**
4. **Submit your sitemap.**

People get to your website in one of a few ways. These include:

>> **From paid ads:** If you are running ads, people will come to your website from those ads.

>> **From referrals:** These are links on other websites or in emails that people click on to come to your website.

>> **Directly:** They type in your domain name because they know about it already.

>> **Organically:** The visitor has done a search in a search engine and they clicked on your listing in the SERP.

Google Search Console gives you information about how you are obtaining the last one in the list — the organic traffic to your website. This tool gives you a great indication of how Google understands your website and your offer, and how often Google is matching your website with an Internet searcher's "search intent." Keep checking this account and make changes to your website so that Google understands your offer in a very clear way and returns your website in the SERP when people are searching for what you offer.

You can also run special activities from GSC, such as submitting your sitemap to Google so they can find all of your pages, seeing pages that Google is having trouble returning in the SERP, and disavowing toxic backlinks you may have obtained to your domain. It is a valuable tool!

Set up a Google Search Console account

Head over to `https://search.google.com/search-console`. If you see your domain name in the dropdown list in the upper-left corner and you see some data in your account, GSC is set up already; you can skip to the "Using the Google Search Console" section.

If you see your domain name but it contains no data, or if you do not see your domain name listed in the dropdown, you need to set up your property.

Add a property to the Google Search Console

Just like you told Google Analytics what domain to start tracking, you need to tell Google Search Console what domain to start tracking. When you do this in Google Search Console, Google refers to this as "adding a property."

You may already have this set up if you had a website up and running at this domain name. Just like with Google Analytics, you want to log into Google Search Console with all of the Google IDs that you know of and see if you have access to your account. If this is a new domain name or you have never had a website set up on this domain name before, you need to set this up by first adding a property to GSC.

To add a property to your GSC account, follow the instructions at this URL: `https://support.google.com/webmasters/answer/34592`.

You will see in the instructions that you can set up a new GSC property in one of three ways:

» Using a URL-prefix property

» Using a domain property

» Using a Google-hosted property

I like to add my website as a domain property. Most likely you will want to add a domain property because this method will track all the ways of getting to your website, including http://, https://, www, and the root domain.

Verify your Google Search Console account

Just as you needed to verify your account when setting up Google Analytics, you also need to verify your GSC account. You can do this in a few ways. Visit the following URL for instructions on different ways to verify your property: `https://support.google.com/webmasters/answer/9008080`.

Once you have verified your website property, you should start seeing data in your GSC account within a few days. Create a calendar reminder to log back into this account in a few days or a week to verify that the account is set up.

TIP

If your domain and website are new, you might log into Google Search Console and see very little data. I remember when I set up my `totocoaching.com` website and logged in. I saw only two entries: "toto coaching" and "coaching center." I was discouraged. Most likely when your website is new, it will not be returned by Google very often. As long as you continue to check this account and make the changes that Google is looking for, your site will be returned for more search terms and will move up in the SERP.

Submit your sitemap

You want to make sure you submit your sitemap to Google in an `xml` format. Recall that a sitemap is a listing of all of the pages, posts, products, events, and other links on your website that someone can visit. When Google has all this information, it can more easily index all of the content on your website, and that is a good thing! Make sure that Google visits all of your content and puts all of it in their database.

A `sitemap.xml` file is made for you automatically using a tool. If you are building on a platform such as Wix or Squarespace, search online for "submit XML sitemap Google Search Console" and then add your platform. Each platform creates an XML sitemap differently.

TECHNICAL STUFF

If you are using WordPress, you can install a plugin that will generate an XML sitemap for you, or you can use Yoast SEO. Simply navigate in your dashboard to Plugins ⇨ Add New and search for an XML sitemap generator. Or install Yoast SEO and then find your XML sitemap under General ⇨ Site features. Copy the path to your XML sitemap and then visit your Google Search Console account. On the left menu, find Sitemaps under the Indexing section and paste the URL there.

No matter which way you submit your XML sitemap, under the Status column, you want to see the word *Success* in green! If you do not see this, you should resubmit your sitemap and verify that you have a tool on your website that is generating your XML sitemap.

Using Google Search Console

Once you log in to GSC, head over to the Performance section, which you can find on the top-left side of the screen. You will see two boxes that are in color: Total Clicks and Total Impressions. Click the other two boxes so that they light up in color: Average CTR and Average Position. See Figure 15-3.

FIGURE 15-3:
Click the headings of Google Search Console so that all of the boxes light up with a color.

☑ Total clicks	☑ Total impressions	☑ Average CTR	☑ Average position
2.03K	278K	0.7%	26.5

Above those boxes you will see that GSC is returning data from the last three months by default. You can change the time period by clicking Date: Last 3 Months if you like.

Below these boxes, you will find a table of all of the search terms (keyword phrases) that were used when Google returned your website in the SERP. You can sort this table of information by clicking any column heading. You will see an up or down arrow next to the column heading; this is the column you are sorting your data by. You can click this column heading again to reverse the order. This information tells you how Google understands your website.

To get more leads, look at the search term that you want to get traffic for and use the table in Figure 15-4 to determine what you should do to reach your goals.

FIGURE 15-4:
To achieve your website goals, use this table in conjunction with Google Search Console to determine the steps you should take.

Clicks	Impressions	CTR	Position	Goal	Strategy
Low	High	Low	High	Get more clicks	Juicy Title and Meta Descriptions
High	High	High	High	Stay on top	Encourage Exploration of website, Determine Page with Traffic, Add CTA/Links/Video/Learn More/Lead Magnet on this page
Low	High	Low	Low	Move up in search	Get noticed for keyword phrase, Optimize your pages for phrase, Write more content using phrase, Work on backlink profile
High	Low	High	High	Corner the market, Stay on top	Write more content around this phrase, Keyword research: What other phrases are searchers using that are similar & create content around other phrases
Low	Low	Low	High	Expand on this keyword phrase	Keyword research: What other phrases are searchers using that are similar & create content around other phrases
Low	Low	Low	Low	Refine Keywords	Keyword research, Optimize pages for new phrases, Create content around new phrases
Low	Low	High	Low	Move up in search	Write more content, Refine keywords, Keep visitors on page/site
NA	NA	NA		Get noticed for keyword phrase	Optimize your pages for phrase, Write more content using phrase, Work on backlink profile

You will find a wealth of information in GSC. The information you find here is kind of like a "report card" for your website and your efforts. Review this data from time to time and take steps to improve your website.

Using Heatmaps to See How People Behave on Your Website

Heatmaps come in many forms and give you a ton of information. They can be used in a variety of applications and you probably are familiar with some of these. For example, a heatmap can be used when looking at brain activity: Areas with more brain activity show more color. You may have seen heatmaps that show where flooding has occurred on a satellite map of a geological area. A heatmap is simply a graphical representation of data, where different values are represented by different colors.

While hard data is great, it can be difficult to interpret. It is easier when you have a graphical interpretation of data, and that is where heatmaps come in.

Heatmaps are used to visualize user activity on websites, like clicks, taps, scrolling, and mouse movements. Once you install the heatmap software on your website, it will track what users are doing on the pages. A heatmap will show the frequency of interactions. You will see a picture of the web page, and overlaid on the picture of that page, areas where visitors spent the most time have more intense colors. When you view these heatmaps, you will understand where most visitors are clicking, how far they are scrolling down the page, and more. Figure 15-5 shows an example.

FIGURE 15-5:
Once you install
heat-mapping
software on your
website, you can
see where people
click as those
areas light up red.

Heatmaps help you identify parts of pages that get lots of attention and engagement as well as areas that are being ignored. With this insight, you can optimize site content, navigation, CTAs, page layouts, and more, all to improve conversion rates.

EXAMPLE

As an example of how heatmaps can help you, years ago I was working with a client on his e-commerce website. Their menu is shown in Figure 15-6.

FIGURE 15-6:
One of my clients
had this menu on
their website
years ago.

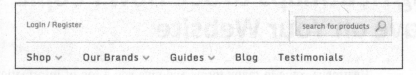

This menu structure is not the best for an e-commerce website. For one, the products are hidden under the Shop menu. Right above the main menu is a search box.

When I installed heat-mapping software on the website, I saw that the main menu had hardly and clicks — the menu was not very colorful. But the search box was lit up in red.

From the heat-mapping software, I learned that visitors to the website could not find what they were looking for. That's because the product categories were hidden behind the Shop dropdown menu. Instead, visitors were using the search box. This website was created in a WordPress website and the native search functionality in WordPress is not good. Visitors were having a difficult time finding what they were looking for and their experience using this website was probably frustrating.

We took this information to heart; we moved the menu items and removed the search box. The new menu is shown in Figure 15-7.

FIGURE 15-7:
After using heat-mapping software on this website, we changed the structure of the header row and put all the categories as dropdown menu items on the main menu.

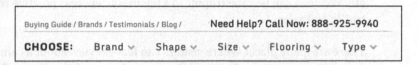

Buying Guide / Brands / Testimonials / Blog /   **Need Help? Call Now: 888-925-9940**

CHOOSE: Brand ⌄   Shape ⌄   Size ⌄   Flooring ⌄   Type ⌄

After this small change, my client saw an increase in sales!

For this reason alone, I recommend implementing heatmaps if you have an existing site and want to improve user experience and conversion performance. Heatmaps are also very useful on new pages you might build to quickly see what works well and what doesn't.

Implementing heatmaps is actually quite easy these days. You simply add a few lines of tracking code provided by the heat-mapping service to your site.

As visitors interact with your pages, the tool records all the activity and visualizes the aggregated interactions through a heatmap dashboard that you can log into and analyze. Popular heat-mapping tools include Hotjar, Mouseflow, Crazy Egg, and Clicktale. Most have free plans for basic functionality or on a trial basis.

AUTHOR SAYS

You can usually choose which pages to track. In terms of where on your site to use heatmaps, I recommend setting them up on your highest traffic pages first. This likely includes your homepage, service pages, and key category/landing pages. This gives you user insights where it matters most right away. Once you get value from these implementations, you can add heatmaps across more areas of your site over time.

The more time goes by and the more data you gather, the better decisions you can make about what is working and what is not working on your website. Use the data about where users are dropping off or not clicking to either rearrange content, change headlines, add more whitespace, swap out fonts or colors, or more.

Getting Reviews

We live in a review-driven world. Have you booked a vacation lately? Most likely you looked up reviews of different hotels, restaurants, or excursions before you booked anything. Have you gone out to eat at a new restaurant lately? Most likely you looked up reviews of different restaurants before you made reservations. Negative reviews can be catastrophic to a business, whereas positive reviews can drive traffic and sales.

There are many places where visitors can leave review about a company, including Google Reviews, Yelp, Facebook Reviews, Anji, and the Better Business Bureau. After your website is up and running, it's time to focus some of your marketing efforts on getting more reviews, especially Google Reviews if you have a local business.

REMEMBER

Local businesses who service customers at a central location or within a two-hour driving distance are eligible to set up a Google Business Profile. If your business isn't eligible for a Google Business Profile, you can focus on getting reviews on other platforms. The important concept to keep in mind is that getting reviews for your business helps you.

Google Business Profiles can be set up in the same way as Google Analytics or Google Search Console, which is by creating a Google account to manage the business profile and then verifying that you are the owner. Instructions can be found here: https://support.google.com/business/answer/10514137?hl=en.

For reviews left on Google Business Profiles, Google uses the number of reviews, combined with the overall review score, to determine how likely the site should be returned in a local search. It is in your best interest to get as many reviews, especially Google Reviews, as possible.

Why you should request reviews

Google reviews are great for several reasons:

>> **First, Google Reviews level the playing field.** A business that does not have as much to spend on marketing campaigns can compete nicely in this space. Any business with multiple customers can ask for, and receive, Google reviews. They are free to get and free to leave. The only barriers to entry are having a Google profile, asking for the reviews, and having customers leave a review. This all costs nothing, and therefore, it levels the playing field for businesses.

>> **Second, Google reviews create transparency because there is a real feedback loop.** A company cannot claim that they are the best without data backing this claim up. Visitors add their thoughts and impressions and those thoughts and impressions may reinforce the marketing messaging from a business or may refute those messages. Show, don't tell. Showing illustrates, while telling merely claims. Reviews help you "show" the world how great you are instead of just "telling" the world. A potential customer reading your reviews can deduce the same positive information they'd get from the business who is "telling" the world how great they are, but in a much more compelling and believable way.

>> **Third, Google reviews also serve as what is called *social proof*, meaning that this is word-of-mouth proof.** Social proof is a psychological concept that states that people are more likely to engage in an action when other people are doing it.

>> **Fourth, solid Google reviews can help develop your business as a *trusted authority*.** Trusted means that people consider this business reliable and authority means that the company knows a lot about this subject and is an expert in this field. Wouldn't you like to be considered the trusted authority in your field? Google Reviews are one avenue to get there.

Reviews are pretty easy to leave. Visitors can post a review without downloading an app or any special software — they simply need a Gmail account or an email associated with a Google account. If they are logged into their Google account, they can leave a review.

Visitors without Google accounts leave reviews on other sites, such as Facebook, Yelp, Angi, and Houzz. Google might pull those reviews into your Google Business Profile. These are displayed in a section entitled Reviews From the Web. Figure 15-8 shows an example. You can't control where Google pulls these reviews from. Focus on trying to get more reviews, both on Google and on other review websites.

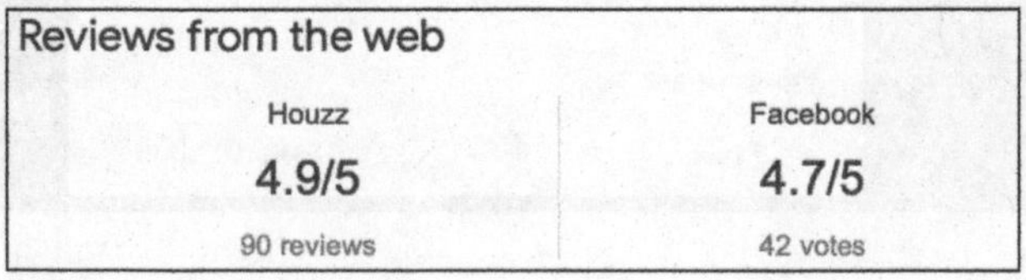

FIGURE 15-8:
Google sometimes pulls in "Reviews from the Web" to a Google Business Profile, and they may do this on your Google Business Profile.

Reviews from the web	
Houzz	Facebook
4.9/5	**4.7/5**
90 reviews	42 votes

Are you nervous about getting reviews? Are you nervous that you may get some negative reviews? If you are skilled at what you do and truly care about your customers, you can and will get positive reviews. But you do need to ask for them. How do you do this?

Obtain your Google Review link

The first step it to get your Google Review link. An example link is shown in Figure 15-9. This link goes directly to the page where people leave reviews. You do not want to ask your customers to search for your company online. Make it easy for visitors to leave reviews and send them the link directly to the review window. They can write comments and choose stars. The link opens up to the screen shown in Figure 15-10.

FIGURE 15-9:
Your personalized Google review link will look something like this image.

Review link
https://g.page/r/Ccy-lAwOIlPvEB0/review

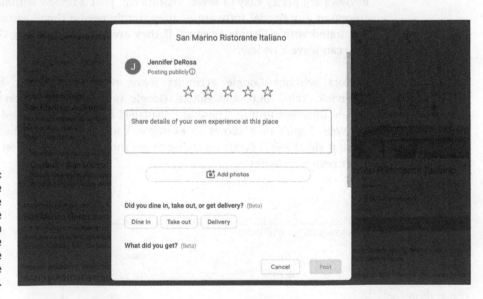

FIGURE 15-10:
Once someone clicks your Google Review link, the screen will open directly to the place where they can leave a review.

There are a few ways to get your Google Review link. Probably the easiest is to pull up your Google Business Profile by typing "my business" into Google. If you are logged in to Google with the same email you set up your Google Business Profile, scroll down, and you will see the profiles you manage with a link to View Profile (see Figure 15-11). Once you see your Google Business Profile on the right side of the screen, you will see a link called "Get More Reviews." Figure 15-12 shows that link.

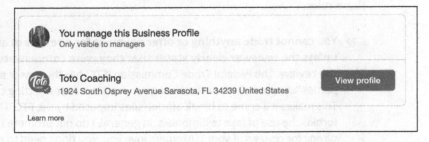

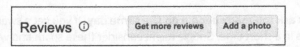

There is another tool I love to use by BrightLocal. You search for your company and can copy the link to get more Google Reviews. You can find that tool at www. brightlocal.com/free-local-seo-tools/google-id-and-review-link-generator/.

Ask for Google reviews

Once you have this link, the next step is to ask your best customers, the ones who love you, to leave you a quick review. How you ask your customers depends on the type of business you have.

>> If you run a restaurant or a car wash or another type of busy storefront, you can hang a sign in your place of business that asks for reviews. You can also include a QR code on your receipts that links directly to your Google Review entry page.

>> **If your company deals more one-on-one with customers or online sales, you might want to ask personally for reviews.** Consider writing a quick email that is personal to each customer. Thank them for being a customer and tell them you value their opinion. Be sure to include your Google Review link. Keep this email as a template, so that you can simply copy and paste this request to other customers as needed.

You can get creative with how you ask for reviews. Just make sure that you follow these rules:

>> **You cannot trade anything or offer payment for a review in any way, unless the reviewer clearly states that they were compensated to leave the review.** The Federal Trade Commission (FTC) has the power to penalize parties "using unfair or deceptive acts or practices in or affecting commerce." This makes it a crime to break official rules imposed by the FTC. The FTC forbids the use of fake testimonials. In general, I do not promote the idea of paying for reviews. If your customers love you, you don't need to pay them to leave you a glowing recommendation.

>> **Always supply the link to the review screen.** Make it as easy as possible for visitors to leave reviews.

>> **Do not ask too many people on the same day.** If you get a swarm of reviews in a short time, Google might consider these spam and will not post all of them.

>> **Make sure you respond to every review.**

Respond to all reviews

Every review that you receive deserves a public response, especially the negative ones. Sometimes you may get negative reviews. This is a good thing. See the sidebar in this section for more about negative reviews.

You should also respond to all positive reviews as well. Thank the reviewers for taking the time to leave you this review. You may want to mention something that you love about working with them, to make it more personal. Your personality can come across in the responses. The public will see how responsive you are and the strong relationship you have with your customers, and they will want to be part of your business. This is social proof in action!

WHAT ABOUT NEGATIVE REVIEWS?

If the content of a negative review has some truth to it, this is a good time to turn the criticism into constructive feedback. Did a customer complain that the rest rooms were dirty? Maybe they are! Maybe you need to have a new process for cleaning them. Did a customer complain that a salesperson was rude or slow? Maybe this is true, and maybe you need to work with your staff on a few things. If there is truth to a negative review, acknowledge this publicly, apologize, and tell the world how you are making changes. This shows that you listen to your customers. When visitors see logical, thankful responses to negative reviews, they may have a whole new level of respect for your company.

If the content of the negative review is out of line or isn't real, this gives you an opportunity to address the real issue in a calm, level-headed way. Internet users will read your response and intuit that the review isn't for real. For example, one of my clients was a pediatrician. A parent wrote a horrible Google Review about how terrible the front desk staff was. What the customer did not know was that, at that time, there was a medical emergency in a patient room. The front desk was not a priority. The office responded to the customer; they explained the situation and invited the patient back. When the public read the negative review and the response, most would "throw out" the negative review in their minds.

6

The Part of Tens

IN THIS CHAPTER

» Planning your website

» Appealing to your audience

» Optimizing your website for search engines

» Optimizing your assets

» Making your website as appealing and as simple as possible

» Focusing on lead generation

Chapter **16**

The Ten Commandments of Building a Successful Website

This chapter gives you the "Cliff Notes" to building a highly effective website. Think of this as your website 101 starter course — a digestible introduction to the methodology behind winning web design. This easy-to-implement advice gives you a foundation to grow your online home. Paired with a platform like WordPress, Wix, or Squarespace, you have all the know-how needed to build a website that achieves your goals while impressing your visitors.

Plan for Success

We all know the old adage — failing to plan means planning to fail. This is especially true when it comes to building a business website, which is one of the most important investments you'll make. However, many people dive in without proper planning. They click a few buttons, throw up a generic template, and wonder why their site fails to attract customers or drive business goals.

Proper planning is crucial to website success. Before starting on development, think through these key areas:

>> **Secure your domain name and build strategy:** Have you purchased and registered the domain name you want to use? This will dictate your web address that you use for promotion. Where will you develop your new website: on a live URL, temporary URL, or on a staging area? See Chapter 2 for help and advice.

>> **Messaging and keywords:** Understand your ideal customers and their pain points and strategize how you address their needs. At the same time, think about how to attract you ideal visitors, get found by search engines, and convert visitors to customers. Research the terms that people search for related to your business. After you do these things, you'll have a better understanding of what to put on your website and how it should be arranged. Chapter 5 covers lots more about keywords.

>> **Site organization and architecture:** Map out your site navigation and the key pages based on your messaging and offerings. Remember, the structure impacts the visitor experience. Chapter 6 covers this process.

>> **Develop relevant, scannable, optimized content:** Write useful content around targeted keywords so visitors quickly see how you can meet their needs. Add this content to your website and ensure that the images, videos, and assets properly support your content and *are optimized*. See Chapter 4 for more.

>> **Finally, design the visuals:** Now make your content look gorgeous by styling it. This is the final step to making your website usable, friendly, and stylish. See Chapter 10 for everything related to design.

Think through these key elements upfront, before you ever type a single word or select a template. It's not the tech that creates success — it's having a strategy and purpose behind what you build, which is based on your business goals and customers. With a plan as your foundation, your website will better position you to achieve your goals.

Understand Your Audience

Want to create a site that truly connects with who will use it? Then first, get to know your audience!

Understanding your target audience is key to crafting messages that resonate with their needs and motivations. This book walks you through some exercises to recognizing your target customers' pain points. These include creating a buyer persona and a table of pain points, benefits of your offer, and features of your offer. Through these exercises and your research, you gain insight into customers' pain points and desires.

With this knowledge, you can create content and messaging that speaks directly to their hearts. You want to talk to the heart of your customer. You want to pull on their heartstrings. You want to let them know that you understand their problems, and you have the solution.

REMEMBER

Audience insight also enables you to optimize your website for search engines. When you comprehend which words and phrases your potential customers are using in web searches, you can incorporate these into your website. When you place these keywords strategically on your website in places where search engines are looking, search engines will then match people's search intent to your offerings and recommend your website.

The effort to know your audience always results in big returns. You forge strong bonds and boost discoverability. And that means more conversions and growth for your business! Let the visitors' needs guide your messaging and content creation. Meeting your audience where they are drives conversions and grows your business.

Crystalize Your Message (Show Don't Tell)

Ever visit a website that feels a bit. . .sales–y? You know, the ones that tell you how amazing they are without much proof? They claim to have the best hair salon in town but only use stock photos. Or they say they're tennis pros yet show stock photos or people barely playing tennis.

This "tell not show" approach can feel disingenuous. Telling visitors how they should feel can be a turn off. Rather than just claiming you offer the best services, prove it! Show visitors how great your services are with real photos or videos of your services in action. Share genuine customer testimonials that detail specific ways you've solved problems. Provide case studies telling stories of how you've impacted lives.

Showcasing your experience and expertise, rather than stating it, builds authority and trust. When potential customers see actual evidence and proof, it feels real. Skip the generic stock imagery and cut the blatant horn-tooting! Demonstrate how you live up to the hype through helpful content that shows rather than tells. It's an infinitely more convincing way for your website to display expertise.

Implement SEO Best Practices

Your goal is to help search engines understand your site. What good is an amazing site if people can't find it? Make sure search engines like Google can interpret and recommend your content. Search engines "figure out" what a website is all about by using programs to crawl billions of sites, looking for specific pieces of information in specific places on websites. If you do not give search engines very specific clues in very specific places, they simply won't grasp what you offer.

Doing SEO well means both crafting descriptive messaging *and* structuring your site to clearly showcase relevancy. It's about helping algorithms understand the value you provide to searchers. High-quality SEO starts with the customer in mind and understanding what truly motivates them to purchase from you. After you understand their motivations, create language that speaks to the heart of your customers.

Next, figure out what keywords and phrases they are searching for, which involves keyword research. Keyword research is subjective. Finding those words that have the right competition level for your website and industry can be tricky, but well worth the time spent. Add those keywords to those specific places where search engines are looking. Ongoing, you need to continue to create new, fresh, original, and complete content around those keywords and phrases.

Carefully crafted sites that clearly telegraph your offer to algorithms lead to higher rankings and visibility. Then you reap the rewards of a site built to connect with both customers and search engines. Chapter 4 is devoted to all things SEO.

Create Amazing and Unique Content

There are billions of websites on the Internet. Most of these pages are filled with information that is incomplete, copied, or the same regurgitated information. When the same information appears on multiple websites, search engines do not return all of those websites in position one. They pick the best one and return it in position one and all the rest fall below that. In other words, search engines spot duplications and only showcase the single best version in the top results.

REMEMBER

If your content blends into the crowd like clowns at a convention, why expect preferential treatment in rankings? Generic information doesn't grab attention.

To get found and be helpful, you must publish unique, high-value content. This means writing an article that goes deep into a subject. Other ways to provide unique information include:

>> Include a "what happens next" section in your articles.

>> Include your own personal experiences or expertise opinion.

>> Provide more thorough analysis.

>> Include concrete examples other sites lack.

>> Craft visually engaging graphics and videos.

>> Share more insightful analogies and actionable takeaways.

>> Add testimonials from others to back up your claims. Sometimes it is helpful to research what's out there on your topics and deliberately take it up a notch.

The goal is to create resources so superior that search engines take notice and recommend them to searchers. This captivating content earns the prime real estate of prominent rankings.

Outdoing others requires more effort upfront. But you'll reap rewards for years through higher conversions and loyalty. So, while playing copycat may be easier, only breakthrough content gets you noticed. Don't settle for more of the same — create signature resources and watch your site traffic soar!

TIP

To understand this more, read about the HCU (Helpful Content Update) in Chapter 4, where you learn to think like a search engine.

Optimize Your Assets

Optimizing your assets is vital. From images to videos to PDFs and text, every element impacts enjoyment and search rankings.

Let's start with images — size matters! Before you upload images, send them through an optimizer so they are sized as small as possible. If you do not optimize your images, your website will likely slow down. No one wants to visit a slow website. Visitors love fast websites, and search engines love them too! Make sure you optimize your images, as described in Chapter 8.

In addition to compressing your images, name files descriptively so search engines understand the content and can show them in image results. There are a few rules for naming your images and other files properly, so make sure you employ the rules listed in Chapter 8.

Your videos can be optimized as well. For the most part, you want to host your videos at a video hosting service. Although it's not recommended, if you do decide to host a video on your own website, make sure it's the smallest size possible.

PDFs can be massive space hogs, especially those with lots of images. Be sure to save them down as small as possible so your pages don't lag when loading them. Remember to name your PDF something that is descriptive and always include the name of your company in the filename!

Even text warrants optimization. Break content into scannable sections with descriptive headers so visitors can quickly digest key points. Use heading tags properly. Search engines also rely on properly marked up, semantic content to comprehend meaning. Optimizing text helps human readers and search bots!

While you may not think of images or docs as crucial optimization areas, every asset plays a role in the user experience and search visibility. So beyond creating great content, carefully enhance and optimize all website elements for happiness all around! By ensuring top-notch quality and performance, you delight visitors while rising in rankings — achieving both marketing goals.

Simplify, Simplify, Simplify (or Write a Short Letter)

When visitors land on pages flooded with dense text, many diverse font styles and weights, too many colors, or tons of elements like buttons and images all over the place, their eyes will glaze over. These competing elements are all virtually screaming "Look at me!!!" There is so much going on, that visitors can't concentrate on anything.

REMEMBER

When you have a cluttered website with large walls of content that are not broken up with whitespace and headings, this is more work for your visitors. They can't find what they are looking for quickly. You are giving your visitors a job to do. No one wants more work.

Instead, simplify across the board:

>> Streamline the writing.

>> Pare down the design elements.

>> Declutter your page layouts.

>> Use whitespace.

>> Break up content with headings.

>> Use the same design elements.

>> Use color to attract attention to important items.

These practices remove distractions and focus the attention on what truly matters. Take the time upfront to refine your messaging and design for simplicity. By guiding visitors seamlessly and clearly to next steps, they will become customers faster!

Follow the Big Guys

Rather than reinventing the wheel, you can learn from organizations that devote huge budgets to web design research. Study what works for major players in your industry and beyond — their publicly available sites offer you a free education!

Find sites that you like and think work well and ask yourself these questions:

>> How did they arrange their content?

>> What design elements do they employ?

>> What does their sitemap look like?

>> What fonts do they use? What colors do they use?

>> How much whitespace do they use?

>> What it is that you like about a particular website?

Identify the specific qualities that catch your eye and consider how you might adapt those to your own content and brand. The big companies invest a ton of money effort and time into research. They drop serious coin figuring out optimal user engagement and conversions.

WARNING

While slavishly copying rarely pays off, smart borrowing of design aesthetics, layouts, and organizational schemes can absolutely shortcut your process. The website blueprint for success has been mapped for you — there is no need to reinvent the wheel.

Energize Lead Generation

There are many reasons that people build websites. One of the reasons is to generate leads. A website is a great tool to help companies do this. First of all, they can spend a minimal amount of money to have their information out for the entire world to see. No expensive print ads or TV spots.

To leverage your site to gather more leads, first nail the fundamentals like understanding your audience, writing good messaging, employing search engine optimization with strategic keywords, and creating unique, value-driven content. Ensure simplicity in site navigation and readability too — remove visitor friction.

Once you've built web traffic, actively guide visitors toward your lead generation sources:

>> Offer free downloadable resources (eguide, videos, webinars, etc.) in exchange for an email signup. Send follow-up emails nurturing these warmer leads over time.

>> Prominently display phone/email contact info for quick inquiries. Respond swiftly to demonstrate reliability.

>> Implement chatbots or live chat for instant website Q&A. Continual engagement builds relationships and trust.

>> Feature client testimonials prominently, especially videos. Nothing inspires action like hearing first-hand stories.

>> Blog regularly with practical, relevant advice that offers snippets of your expertise.

Think of your website as an always-open shop to welcome newcomers daily. Continually enhance the site and focus on meaningful engagement. Guide visitors seamlessly toward lead generation opportunities. Done right, this virtual real estate can become your most powerful salesperson!

Iterate and Improve

Completing your website build brings sweet relief! Sure, take a break to celebrate, but don't neglect nourishing this vital marketing asset — your site needs care and feeding to stay robust.

Anything that you build needs to be maintained to keep it fresh and relevant. Untended websites wither in relevance. Traffic and leads dwindle when content goes stale. Don't let your hard work go to waste! In order to keep it working for you, you should keep it fresh and updated.

REMEMBER

Google tracks when each page was last updated and ranks frequently refreshed sites higher. Websites that are updated on a regular basis are returned higher up in the SERP.

After you launch your site, establish an editorial schedule to regularly add new blog posts, case studies, videos, and statistics — anything that keeps visitors engaged. Sprinkle in some larger revamps too — update your service pages and swap old images for new photos showcasing improvements.

TIP

Be sure to install web analytics to see what works and what doesn't. Watch for low-traffic pages that need a reboot. Check where visitors lose interest and consider layout changes. Updating shows customers that you offer modern solutions, and conveys an energized, thriving business they'll be excited to engage. Updating shows search engines that your business is alive and offering new material and information for the world to see, and they like that.

Chapter **17**

Ten Rookie Mistakes to Avoid

This chapter provides some quick tips that help you avoid some beginner mistakes. If you read through only this chapter and follow this advice, you will be off to a great start building a website that attracts visitors, ranks well, and converts leads! I compiled this list from years and years of working with clients. I hope that these tips help you out as well.

Choosing Cheap Hosting

The first biggest mistake you can easily make when deciding to build a website is to choose cheap hosting. This applies to anyone building on an open source platform, such as WordPress. (If you are going to build on an all-in-one software platform such as Wix or Squarespace, your hosting is included with the platform so this does not pertain to you.)

Although there are inexpensive options out there, you typically get what you pay for. You don't want to choose a very inexpensive hosting option because most likely your website will be hosted on a shared web server. A shared web server means you are sharing the server and its resources with many other websites. The server's resources include the disk space, the memory, and the bandwidth in and out of the server, among other things.

If another website on the same shared server gets a lot of traffic for some reason, it will be difficult for anyone who wants to visit your website to do so, because your site will slow way down.

So don't fall for tempting intro rates and shared plans. The small added cost of quality hosting pays for itself exponentially in site performance, security, and customer satisfaction. Chapter 2 covers the different options for hosting and explains why they matter.

Not Installing Protection

You have spent all this time and effort building your website, and you want to protect what you have built! There are a few key types of protection I strongly recommend installing on your website:

>> **Security plugins:** For WordPress websites, installing a quality security plugin like MalCare is crucial to implementing firewall blocking, malware scanning, and other measures that protect you from hack attempts or exploits. Without security layers, your site is incredibly vulnerable.

>> **Backups:** Many people think that their website is backed up "automatically" or "magically." Do not make this assumption! If you are using cheap hosting, you may only have one or no backups running on your website! Regular automated backups via a service like BlogVault or automatic, daily backups through your hosting save you from losing your site due to hacks, corruption, or hosting issues. You retain the ability to restore intact site files and databases if disaster occurs. Also make sure that whatever backup you choose is easy to restore.

>> **SSL certificate:** Activating SSL forces HTTPS connections and encrypts data transmitted between visitors and your site. This prevents snooping of sensitive user data like logins. If you choose good, reliable hosting, a free SSL certificate should be included with your package. Install and configure it!

>> **Spam protection:** Services like Akismet filter out spammy user signups, registrations, contact form submissions, comments, and more. Otherwise, you'll be overwhelmed by garbage data and possibly abuse.

Robust all-in-one secure hosting solutions like WordPress.com, Wix, and Squarespace bundle protection, and at minimum handle these first three bullets on self-managed sites (especially WordPress sites)!

WARNING

Hackers target big and small sites for takeover, so don't skip these safeguards. The consequences of compromises, data loss, and downtime make security essential and not "nice-to-have!" Install core protective measures ASAP!

Not Including a Powerful Hero Message

This is the biggest mistake. I see on almost every DIY website.

If I had a nickel for every DIY website that buried its central offer, I'd be lounging on a tropical beach right now! I meet with many small business owners to give them advice or help them with their websites. I often pull up the website prior to meeting with them and I will have absolutely no idea what they do. Talk about frustrating for visitors.

EXAMPLE

I recently looked at a website and thought the small business owner was selling shoes. After I met with her, I found out that she was selling an accessory that you could add do flip-flops that would cover up bunions and other issues with your feet. This is a completely different market and a completely different customer and a completely different message. If visitors to her website did not understand that this was an accessory that could help them solve a problem, they wouldn't have any interest in continuing to look at her website and they would leave.

The first row of your homepage should clearly explain your offer. Crystallizing your core value proposition is key. Reserve this hero section exclusively to communicate your purpose in four to ten straightforward words. Name the common problem you fix and state your solution. Doing this simply yet powerfully is easier said than done. It may take experimenting with different phrases to encapsulate that "Aha!" moment, but once you nail it, banner that baby prominently!

There are many ways to crystallize your message, and there are many tools that you can use to do this, but the best way is to create a table of problems that people have and describe how your solution addresses them. You do this in Chapter 5. If you completed that exercise, you are in a great position to distill your offer into a couple words.

Don't get discouraged if this is a difficult process. It may take some time. Write a message and ask others if they understand your offer. You can also run a five-second test using an online tool like the ones at usertesting.com or lyssna.com. This test shows your website to strangers for five seconds; it's a great way to judge whether people understand your offer immediately.

Remember, when someone comes to your website, you have anywhere from three to eight seconds to let visitors know that they're in the right place and they should stick around.

Uploading Huge Images and Unoptimized Assets

Here's an easy website speed win — optimize those assets!

Prior to reading this book, you might have never thought about reducing the sizes of the images you're adding to your website. You should now understand how vitally important it is and what a huge difference this makes. You want to upload images to your website that are crystal clear, but as small as possible. While great photos attract visitors, giant uncompressed files painfully slow the download process. Sluggish sites drive folks away almost instantly.

One of the easier ways to ensure your site has a good response time is to optimize the size of the images on it. Stock photography and photos taken on phones or cameras are large, because many people use them in printed material, even on billboards. Websites, though, are best with images that are optimized for speed.

Many people use WiFi or cell phone data to look at websites, which can be slower. They can only download so much information so fast. Every visual is transmitted to the browsers before it's displayed. If you have giant photos on your website, they will download more slowly. This will deter visitors and search engines, which measure how long it takes for your website to download.

Always run your downloads through an optimizer before uploading them. This strips unneeded background data, allowing visually lossless compression.

Two quick ways to optimize:

>> **First, shrink the image dimensions.** A background photo might only need 2500 pixel width instead of 8000. Similarly, an accompanying article image could be 600 pixels rather than 4000. Smaller canvases reduce file size.

>> **Next, use a metadata removal utility such as** `tinypng.com`. This deletes invisible excess camera data from files that browsers ignore anyway. Protection without bloat!

Follow this two-step dance of resizing and optimizing. Visitors will appreciate faster browsing and search engines will award swift performance with better rankings.

Forgetting about Title and Meta Descriptions

You spend all this time building your website, learning the software, getting your messaging spot on, and gathering, optimizing, and adding your content. Pop some bubbly — your website is complete! But before officially launching it, make sure you haven't overlooked search engine result page (SERP) presence.

In all the excitement of beautifying site pages and posts, it's easy to forget that search engines present only title tags and meta descriptions in the SERP. If your site is poorly optimized, stellar internal content is ignored.

REMEMBER

You need to write great titles and descriptions for each page. These titles and descriptions appear in search results. If you do not write a title and description for each page of your website, search engines will do whatever they want. They may grab a portion of the page, or they may grab the first lines of code, or something else.

To write amazing titles and meta descriptions, you need to understand the intent behind relevant keyword searches and address those needs. What will convince someone comparison shopping your products to visit your website listing that very moment?

Doing this additional SERP-focused optimization amplifies all your earlier efforts. Don't leave visibility to chance — guide perception with customer-centric listings so searchers eagerly investigate further.

Using Unhelpful Content

Unhelpful content is information that doesn't give your visitors any specific information about your solution to their problem. It doesn't answer their questions. It doesn't go deeper so that visitors feel satisfied after they read it. It probably is the same information that appears on other websites.

Search engines are in the business of returning the best websites possible. If you're doing all this work, and you decide to spend some time writing articles, why not make them specific and tailored? If you need a refresher, Chapter 4 explains how search engines operate.

AUTHOR SAYS

Here's my friendly suggestion — approach content creation from an abundance mentality of how you can blow visitors' minds with high-octane guidance. Explore your topics and become known as the definitive teaching resource in your niche. Establish unmatched authority!

Hosting Videos from Your Own Website

As a new website owner, you might want to use video on your website. This is a great idea! Not only does it allow visitors to understand your offer or learn a little bit more about you or your customers, it is also an engaging way to interact with viewers. Search engines measure these engagements as well. Video can also keep visitors on your website for longer, which search engines love.

If you plan on adding video to your website, do not upload the video to the hosting platform where you host your website. These standard web hosting servers are not optimized to deliver video smoothly and quickly to browser devices on demand. Visitors expect playback to start instantly, without delays from extended buffering or downloads. In addition, search engines measure the time it takes for a page to download completely. Delays will derail your efforts on both accounts.

Instead, leverage dedicated video streaming platforms like YouTube, Vimeo, or Wistia. These services are purpose-built to send video data the moment someone starts viewing, with the rest continuing to load invisibly in the background. There are no lags or interruptions. The video will download and buffer as needed, so that visitors can click the Play button and begin watching the video immediately, while the rest is downloading in the background.

Additionally, streaming services can be easily embedded or linked from many locations while centrally hosting content in one place. This allows you to show videos across your website, social channels, and so on, without duplicating any files. They also have many other features, such as end or title screens, captions, and security features.

Some of these video hosting services are paid and others are free. There are different pros and cons of using each, and you should explore those before deciding where to host your videos. Chapter 8 covers these issues in detail.

Cramming Everything Together

Have you ever landed on a website that was crammed top-to-bottom with words and images and links — no margins or breathing room whatsoever? How quickly did you become overwhelmed and click away?

Whitespace, whitespace, whitespace! Throughout this book I talk about whitespace. Whitespace buffers your content. It can be around text, images, videos, and more.

Effective web design requires plenty of whitespace, allowing elements like text, headlines, and graphics to "breathe." When it is used properly, visitors can easily digest your content. Whitespace makes sites scannable. Without it, pages become visually inaccessible walls of stimuli that no one can digest.

REMEMBER

Proper whitespace allows visitors to rapidly absorb messaging as they scroll while avoiding fatigue. It guides the eyes between logical content groupings.

Look at the big guys — any high-authority site — and you'll notice ample whitespace. The whitespace isn't wasting real estate but is instead helping to optimize comprehension. Breathing room pays dividends for UI and UX! So use it liberally on your website.

Using Headings Improperly

On most any quality website, skim the content and you'll immediately spot differences between textual elements. You have body copy, or text, and then you have headings that break up the content and allow you to skim the page.

A website that is built properly will employ heading tags, and you want to use them as well on your website. Headings break up your content so that visitors can skim the page and understand your message.

REMEMBER

In addition to structuring content for visitors, heading tags are very important for SEO. Search engines use headings to better categorize pages and their content.

Using headings properly does not mean changing the weight and size of text so that it is larger and heavier. You need to define the heading tags when you are laying out your content. Most regular text on your website is called "body," "normal," "paragraph," or something similar. If you want some text to be a heading, you need to change this field to a heading style.

There are six heading levels in HTML. The largest, most prominently placed headlines use the H1 tag. For most of the other subheadings, you will use H2 tags. If you have subheadings under a heading 2 or H2 tag, use H3 tags, and so on, all the way to H6. I rarely use H5 and H6 tags, but they are there if you need them.

Without a technical hierarchy, pages become monolithic walls of equally weighted text, lacking hooks for emphasis. For sight impaired users, screen readers vocalize these heading tags first to outline the structure.

In many ways, deliberately styled headings create content structure. The power of headings (visibly and beneath the surface) can truly make or break your website conversions and connectivity. Don't underestimate their value!

Choosing Fonts Improperly

Choosing the right fonts is one of those small steps that has a huge impact on the look and feel of your website. Pick a font that matches your brand identity. Is your company formal? Then you want to use a more formal font. Is your company technical? Then you probably want to use a more technical font.

If something seems off, try simply changing the fonts. You will be amazed at the impact a different font can make. Most website platforms take advantage of Google fonts. Visit fonts.google,com and spend some time looking at different options that you have. Make a list of the ones you like and then try them on your website.

As Chapter 10 explains, you can use one font on your website for your headings, navigation, and text, or you can pair one display or headline font with a complementary body style for optimal harmony.

If fonts on a site feel visually discordant, outdated, or sloppy, visitors will make negative assumptions about your business. The typography feel reflects directly on overall credibility and competence. There are a set of fonts you should never use, and those are the original fonts that were available to early web designers. Make sure you do not use those fonts and instead choose some that match your brand, give the impression and feel you are going for, and that look amazing on your website.

REMEMBER

Be sure to change the fonts in the central settings of your website. Define your fonts for the body copy and the headings, as well as the menu fonts. Do not define the font choice in every module, as this is way more work.

Using different font formatting helps highlight key website areas. For example, making calls to action bold or eye-catching through color/size changes makes visitors more likely to notice them, like emphasizing important words in speech through changes in volume or tone.

Flipping between a few complementary fonts also helps break up dense sections of copy into more scannable portions for readers. Walls of single-font text can easily lose visitor attention. Subtle font variations regain interest.

Overall, fonts that appear simple, inviting, and well-formatted improve perceptions of professionalism for a site. Sloppy, chaotic typography feels untrustworthy, because on some level fonts represent the "voice" of the site.

Index

About the Author

Jennifer DeRosa is the visionary behind Toto SEO and Toto Coaching. As the founder of Toto SEO, she specializes in offering SEO solutions tailored for small businesses. Through Toto Coaching, she provides interactive online courses, complete with weekly coaching sessions, empowering small businesses and entrepreneurs to create websites that not only presell their offerings but also foster trust among their clientele.

Before her current ventures, Jennifer was the driving force behind TechCare, a web development agency she founded and led from 2001 to 2021, when she had a successful exit.

Dedication

To my husband Dave, for his complete support, belief, and love.

Author's Acknowledgments

I would like to thank my husband for going on this adventure with me! I would also like to thank Mark Howell and Leslie Topor, who both planted the seed that I should write this book. They are both amazing, smart, supportive friends who I cherish. I would like to thank my children, grandchildren, family, and friends for encouraging me through the process, and Roy Jeffrey and Penny Allen for supporting me by purchasing the first copies! My web building career has been filled with so many wonderful people who have taught me new things and worked alongside me, including Josh Libatique, Greg Volpe, Clint Warren, Kristin Hawley, Julio Andrade, Akshat Choudhary, as well as Dianna Shivvers and Jen Buzza from the UGURUS team.

Thanks, everyone!

Publisher's Acknowledgments

Senior Acquisitions Editor: Steve Hayes

Project Editor: Kezia Endsley

Technical Editor: Greg Volpe

Production Editor: Pradesh Kumar

Cover Image: © Varijanta/Getty Images